MW01202090

Wisdom and Beauty
in Plato's *Charmides*

Foro di Studi Avanzati Series

The *Foro di Studi Avanzati/Roma Series in Ancient, Medieval, Renaissance and Modern Texts and Contexts (FSA/AMRMTC)* publishes studies in philosophy, theology, religion, aesthetics, and politics. Each volume of this series contains works arising out of FSA research projects commissioned by FSA Fellows. The aim of the series is to offer diachronic and synchronic studies on concepts and problems shared by thinkers and their traditions.

FSA Editoral Committee

Robert M. Berchman, FSA/Roma, Italia
Claudia D'Amico, Universidad de Buenos Aires, Argentina
Salvatore Lavecchia, Universita degli Studi di Udine, Italia
José Maria Zamora, Universidad Autonoma de Madrid, España

Wisdom and Beauty in Plato's *Charmides*

Inbal Cohen-Taber

PICKWICK *Publications* · Eugene, Oregon

WISDOM AND BEAUTY IN PLATO'S *CHARMIDES*

Foro di Studi Avanzati Series 2

Pickwick Publications
An Imprint of Wipf and Stock Publishers
199 W. 8th Ave., Suite 3
Eugene, OR 97401

www.wipfandstock.com

PAPERBACK ISBN: 978-1-6667-0177-7
HARDCOVER ISBN: 978-1-6667-0178-4
EBOOK ISBN: 978-1-6667-0179-1

Cataloguing-in-Publication data:

Names: Cohen-Taber, Inbal, author.

Title: Wisdom and beauty in Plato's *Charmides* / Inbal Cohen-Taber.

Description: Eugene, OR: Pickwick Publications, 2022. | Foro di Studi Avanzati Series 2. | Includes bibliographical references and index.

Identifiers: ISBN 978-1-6667-0177-7 (paperback). | ISBN 978-1-6667-0178-4 (hardcover). | ISBN 978-1-6667-0179-1 (ebook).

Subjects: LSCH: Plato. Charmides. | Wisdom. | Beauty. | Sophrosyne (The Greek word).

Classification: B366 C68 2022 (print). | B366 (ebook).

VERSION NUMBER 102722

This book is dedicated to those who do not feel
beautiful enough to be considered
or wise enough to be heard

"Most of the world says that telling stories puts people to sleep, I say telling stories can wake people up from their slumber!"

—Rabbi Nachman of Breslov

"When you just say the ideas they sound foolish, whereas if they're dramatized one feels it."

— Stanley Kubrick, film director

Contents

Tables

Acknowledgments

I BEGAN MY WORK on the dialogue *Charmides* fifteen years ago, in the Department of Philosophy at the University of Haifa. There I learned from Ivor Ludlam about the benefits of reading Plato's dialogues as philosophical dramas, and under his supervision I devoted my M.A. thesis to the *Charmides*. For this I will always be grateful. In the following years I continued working independently, developing my approach to this dialogue with a view to refining and extending my work into a monograph.

I would like to thank Menahem Luz who influenced my scholarly path in various ways, including introducing me to the *Foro di Studi Avanzati, Roma* (FSA), of which I have been a fellow since 2017. My intention to publish my research in book form was reinforced by the fruitful and collegial environment of the forum. I am indebted to Robert Berchman, the General Director of the FSA, for encouraging me to complete my project so that it could appear in the FSA book series, and grateful for his true friendship. I also would like to thank the anonymous reviewer for helpful comments that improved this book.

I am grateful for the financial support I received from the FSA for attending even conferences outside the FSA's own conference, as well as for the support from the Technion — Israel Institute of Technology, where I was appointed as an adjunct lecturer while working with Ron Fuchs. With this help I presented my work in *The International Association of Greek Philosophy* (IAGP), and benefited from valuable feedback.

Of all possible times, it was when the world shut down due to the Covid-19 pandemic that I had the opportunity to invest in writing and revising this book. Merely days before the lockdown, unaware of it coming, I moved from Israel to Maryland, USA. I was fortunate to be appointed as a Scholar-in-Residence at St. Mary's College of Maryland, and later on as an adjunct instructor, in The Department of Philosophy and Religious Studies. This allowed me to dedicate myself to finishing this manuscript. I thank the members of the department who welcomed me warmly to Margaret Brent Hall. The office, the college's facilities, the wonderful library resources and the devoted library staff, especially Brenda Rodgers the Interlibrary Loan Technician who can find any needed material, all contributed to the completion of this book.

My deepest appreciation is for my parents, Shoshana and Yair, and for my husband Michael Taber. Whichever path I take in life my parents' inculcation that the most important thing is being a good person accompanies me. And in my chosen path with Michael Taber, who is always my first reader and critic, everything in my life always falls into its right place, and the Jewish saying "everything is for the best" (*Hakol Letova/Gam Zu Letova*, said by Nachum Ish Gamzu) is in evidence.

Inbal Cohen-Taber
St. Mary's College of Maryland, USA

Introduction: Why Wisdom and Beauty?

PEOPLE OFTEN USE THE traits wisdom and beauty as swords against each other. The perfectly featured may be projected as being foolish, and the unsightly as compensated with having wisdom or a good heart. Absurdly, the desirability of such highly valued traits opens a door for ranking people's worth. To excel in both wisdom and beauty seems rare and a cause for admiration, or even envy. To have one but not the other never feels fair to the individual involved. And what seems more tragic than nature depriving someone of both? Every generation and culture, therefore, inevitably questions whether some people are superior because of their inherited and nurtured appearance and intellect. In Athens of the fifth century BCE, the social elite of aristocrats claimed to be the exclusive possessors of both natural beauty and intellectual capacities (*kalokagathia*). I believe that Plato saw such claims to superiority as continuously threatening to the stability of his *polis*, and therefore decided to write the dialogue *Charmides*.[1]

Plato's *Charmides* is a fictional conversation among historical figures concerning *sōphrosunē*, one of the four Greek cardinal virtues. The word *sōphrosunē* is often translated as "moderation," "temperance," or literally as

---

1. For my speculation on the approximate date of the dialogue's composition, see discussion in the final section "The Status of Being Wise and Beautiful," and n. 297. See other speculations about the date of the dialogue and its position in Plato's corpus by e.g.: Moore and Raymond, *Charmides*, xvi–xx; Lamb, *Plato VIII*, xii–xiv; Joosse, "*Sōphrosunē* and the Poets," 586; Kahn, "*Charmides* and the Proleptic Reading," 541; Brandwood, *Chronology of Plato's Dialogues*; Thesleff, *Studies in Platonic Chronology*, and "Platonic Chronology"; Howland, "Re-Reading Plato"; Barker, "Problems in the *Charmides*"; Luz, "Knowledge of Knowledge." On ordering the dialogues according to their fictive dramatic chronology, see e.g.: Griswold, "*E Pluribus Unum?*"; Zuckert, *Plato's Philosophers*; Lampert, *How Philosophy Became Socratic*; Altman, "*Laches* Before *Charmides*."

1

"sound-mindedness," in addition to other proposals.[2] None of these translations, however, is entirely adequate, because the ancient Greeks used the word
sōphrosunē with a wide variety of meanings and contexts.[3] Even the dialogue
Charmides, we will see, reflects a cultural and social ambiguity concerning
its meaning. I therefore will use the transliteration of the word (and of the
singular and plural adjectives *sōphrōn* and *sōphrones*), but my analysis will
lead to a proposal as to what Plato wished to convey through his dialogue
about this virtue.

There is a dizzying array of approaches for interpreting Plato's dialogues,[4]
which might cause one to doubt the possibility of ever making sense of his

2. Scholars translate the concept *sōphrosunē* variously. North, *Sōphrosynē*, 3–4 n.
10, discusses the literary meaning of the term, which is a compound of the words *sōs*
(healthy, safe, sound) and *phrēn* (mind). Moore and Raymond, *Charmides*, xxxiv–xxxvii,
discuss the limitations in various translations offered for *sōphrosunē*, including sound-
mindedness, moderation, self-control, and temperance. They argue that in the *Charmides*
the word denotes "discipline." Press, "*Charmides*," 41, translates *sōphrosunē* as temperance
or moderation. McCoy, "Philosophy, *Elenchus*, and Charmides," translates it as sound-
mindedness. Tuckey, *Plato's Charmides*, 5–6, indicates the difficulty in translating the
word, but during his work translates it as self-control. Schmid, *Plato's Charmides*, and
"Socratic Moderation and Self-Knowledge," 339, translates *sōphrosunē* as moderation, but
mentions the various meanings associated with it and their appearance in the dialogue
Charmides, such as temperance in the sexual context, self-control, and modesty demonstrated by shame.

3. The virtue *sōphrosunē* became increasingly significant in Greek literature around
Plato's time, during the fifth and fourth centuries BCE. On the various meanings attributed to it, see: North, *Sōphrosynē*; Rademaker, *Sōphrosynē and Rhetoric*; Tuozzo, *Plato's
Charmides*, 90–96; and Tuckey, *Plato's Charmides*, 5–9. On the appearances of the virtue in
other Platonic dialogues as the *Protagoras*, *Gorgias*, and *Republic*, see: North, *Sōphrosynē*,
176–230; Rademaker, *Sōphrosynē and Rhetoric*, 293–356; and Tuozzo, *Plato's Charmides*,
96–98.

4. Scholars divide the approaches to interpreting Plato's dialogues by various catego-
ries. See for example the taxonomy presented by Corlett, *Interpreting Plato's Dialogues*,
dividing the approaches to mouthpiece and anti-mouthpiece. As Corlett explains, mouthpiece approaches hold that Plato conveys his opinions through one or several characters
in his dialogues. These approaches may be further subdivided, for example, into those
claiming for unity of thought in Plato's dialogues (e.g., Kahn, *Plato and the Socratic
Dialogue*, 40), and those claiming a developmental approach and attempting thereby to
explain inconsistencies between the various dialogues (e.g., Vlastos, *Socrates, and Socratic
Studies*). According to Corlett, anti-mouthpiece approaches emphasize the dialogic and
dialectic form of Plato's works. These approaches can be also further subdivided. Dramatic interpretations (e.g., Press, *Who Speaks for Plato*, and *Plato's Dialogues. New Studies*)
claim that the dialogues do not convey doctrines as in treatises, but similarly to dramatic
plays they convey broad dramatic lessons. See also discussion by Byrd, "Summoner Approach," 372–4. Another subdivision is of Socratic interpretations, which assume that the
method of Plato's dialogues are influenced by his mentor Socrates, though the character of
Socrates does not serve as Plato's mouthpiece (e.g., Corlett, *Interpreting Plato's Dialogues*,
14–17, 67–94, and "Interpreting Plato's Dialogues"). Further anti-mouthpiece approaches

works. Recent decades have seen increasing attention to the dramatic form of these dialogues, proposing that this can reward us with a better understanding of Plato's intentions. Because Plato himself is not one of the speakers in his dialogues, it makes sense to assume that what he wished to convey lies in the dramatic interaction among the characters he presents. Yet how to conduct a dramatic analysis of a Platonic dialogue is still debated.[5]

With regard to the *Charmides* in particular, some progress has been made in understanding the philosophical significance of the dialogue's unfolding drama. Although only few books have been devoted to this dialogue,[6] some of the most recent ones attempt to address its dramatic aspects. Additionally, several articles focus on specific dramatic aspects.[7] These interpretations share some similarities with each other concerning various points, as will the

are the Esoteric theories, such as the Tübingen school and the Straussians, which are discussed critically by Byrd, "Summoner Approach," 369–72. As Byrd explains, the Tübingen school claims that Plato does not convey his doctrines through the dialogues; the dialogues are protreptic works intended for beginners in philosophy, presenting an ideal practice in dialectic discourse. The Straussians claim that Plato's doctrines are concealed in his dialogues and only the fitting reader may extract them. See also e.g.: Findlay, *Written and Unwritten Doctrines*; Ludlam, *Plato's Republic*, 4–8, who distinguishes "Plato says" from "Plato dramatizes" approaches and develops his own dramatic approach. Ludlam, "Paradigm Shift," 88–9, argues that in each dialogue Plato's characters represent particular examples (deigmata) of abstract forms (paradeigmata) which are aspects of an idea; Brumbaugh, "Four Types," 239–48; Rutherford, *Art of Plato*, 1–38; Gonzalez, *Third Way*, 1–22; Nails, "Mouthpiece Shmouthpiece"; Hyland, "Why Plato Wrote Dialogues"; Thesleff, "The Philosopher Conducting Dialectic," and "Looking for Clues"; Tarrant, "Where Plato Speaks"; Clay, "Origins of the Socratic Dialogue"; Ford, "Beginnings of Dialogue." More on dramatic approaches see below n. 5.

5. On the Esoteric, dramatic, and Socratic, anti-mouthpiece approaches, and on Ludlam's dramatic approach of the characters as deigmata of paradeigmata, see previous n. 4. See also: Desjardins, "Why Dialogues," 110–25; Arieti, *Interpreting Plato*, 1–17, and "How to Read a Platonic Dialogue"; Cain, *Socratic Method*; Press, "Plato's Dialogues as Enactments" and "Logic of Attributing Characters' Views to Plato"; McKim, "Socratic Self-Knowledge." Despite the growing attention to the dramatic form of the dialogue, relatively few attempts at dramatic analyses of complete dialogues have been published, for example: Miller, *Plato's Parmenides*; Ludlam's two books, *Hippias Major*, and *Plato's Republic*, as well as his article "Hippias Minor"; Burger, *Phaedo*. See also below, nn. 7 and 8.

6. Those written in English are: Tuckey, *Plato's Charmides*; van der Ben, *Charmides of Plato*; Hyland, *Virtue of Philosophy*; Schmid, *Plato's Charmides*; Tuozzo, *Plato's Charmides: Positive Elenchus*; Levine, *Profound Ignorance*; Moore and Raymond, *Charmides*. Worth noting are also Lampert, *How Philosophy Became Socratic*, who devotes a large section of his book to the *Charmides*, and the dissertations of Brown, "Plato's *Charmides*," and Vielkind, "Philosophy, Finitude, and Wholeness."

7. E.g.: Press, "*Elenchos* in the *Charmides*"; Notomi, "Origin of Plato's Political Philosophy"; Brann, *Music of the Republic*, 66–87, chapter 4, "The Tyrants' Temperance: *Charmides*"; Burger, "Socrates' Odyssean Return"; Joosse, "*Sōphrosunē* and the Poets"; McAvoy, "Carnal Knowledge in the *Charmides*."

present analysis.[8] These similarities should be observed as a point of progress in uncovering Plato's intentions in this dialogue. My analysis, nonetheless, differs from that of others in attending more systematically to the characters.I suggest that Plato, using well-known historical figures and their moral failures, carefully built consistent dramatic characters. These characters are presented as foils against each other as they differ in their consideration or lack of consideration for two related aspects of human conduct, the internal thought and the external practice. This approach leads to a more coherent understanding of the philosophical content that Plato wished to convey concerning what *sōphrosunē* is and is not. Attention to the similarities and differences between my interpretation and those of others is given in footnotes. The body of my work is devoted to the philosophical analysis of the dramatic dialogue. All translations from the Greek are mine unless otherwise indicated.

So what did Plato intend to accomplish by writing his dialogue the way he did? This book is my answer to this question. My analysis begins with addressing the narrative structure of the dialogue. Plato has Socrates narrate to a silent, unnamed listener the details of a conversation that he previously had held with Chaerephon, Charmides, and Critias in the palaestra of Taureus, a place the Greeks used for training their bodies and for socializing.[9] Why Socrates addresses his narration to an opaquely passive listener may be explained only through analysis of the content that Socrates narrates. Socrates' narrative consists of his conversation with more interactive figures than the silent listener of the narrative. However, I will show that they also demonstrate

8. My analysis shares similarities especially with Levine, *Profound Ignorance*. Levine, 327, argues that the dialogue is a "dramatic argument" and indicates the importance of taking into account the dramatic aspects. He presents a sensitive interpretation of the characters and the dramatic interaction between them. Throughout my account, I will indicate the many similarities my analysis shares with his work, as well as where we diverge. My analysis also shares similarities with points made by Press, "*Elenchos* in the *Charmides*," and by Notomi, "Origin of Plato's Political Philosophy." Other scholars, although taking into consideration the dramatic aspects of the dialogue, propose interpretations that greatly differ from mine on some points. For example, Schmid, *Plato's Charmides*, vii, states that his book is an attempt at understanding the characters' arguments in their dramatic context. Schmid suggests that there is "an intimate relationship between the drama and argument, the *logos* and *ergon* of the dialogue," as he follows the approach of Desjardins, "Why Dialogues." Tuozzo, *Plato's Charmides*, 5–6, says that his approach to the dialogue is one that recognizes the importance of the drama (*ergon*) in interpreting the elenctic arguments (*logos*).

9. Little is known of the palaestra of Taureus. It was located in front of the sanctuary of the kings Kodros and Neleus, and of another character named Basile (153a1–5). See: Lawton, *Attic Document Reliefs*, A.4, IG.I.3.84; Moore and Raymond, *Charmides*, xxi–xxii; Shapiro, "Attic Deity Basile"; and n. 294.

passive tendencies, whether with regard to their internal thoughts, their external actions, or both.

In order to understand Plato's full message, I will explain the dramatic role of each of the four characters that he presents in his dialogue. I will argue that the opening question that Plato has Socrates ask his interlocutors in the palaestra is significant for understanding the four characters participating in the conversation. Socrates asks whether, during his recent military absence, any of the youth has come to excel in wisdom or in beauty or in both. This question is not intended merely to lead to two conversations, one with the beautiful Charmides and the other with his guardian Critias. Plato presents all the four characters of the dialogue through the prism of this question, using them as foils against each other to emphasize their different traits. The characters deliberately exemplify the passive attitude towards, or focus on, their own wisdom or beauty or both. While Charmides appears to excel in beauty, his cousin Critias appears to excel in wisdom; and while both Chaerephon and Socrates appear to be neither beautiful nor wise, one is oblivious to his own manner of speaking and appearance and thus is described as crazy and the other, we will see, represents a virtuous *sōphrōn* man.

Most of the dialogue involves Socrates' conversations with the cousins Charmides and Critias. The two were also Plato's relatives,[10] and were well-known to his contemporary readers as cruel tyrants who lived and died violently. Plato, however, portrays the cousins as yet young, attractive in the eyes of others, and politically uninvolved. We will see that Plato gradually reveals that the life errors that led the cousins to their eventual notorious conduct are rooted in their aristocratic, traditional views and education. This he does in order to present his own, better, philosophical interpretation of *sōphrosunē*, and to warn his contemporaries from the recurrence of history lest they would learn his universal lesson. His message will turn out to be a life lesson for us today as well.

We will see that by the two traits, wisdom and beauty, Plato calls to mind the socially charged epithet "beautiful and good" (*kalos kagathos*), that aristocrats attributed to themselves. Plato thus allows his reader to gather that Charmides and Critias, who each appears to excel in only one of these traits, do not satisfy even their own noble ideal. However, Plato is not interested in questioning their noble birth, but in revealing their contorted aristocratic world-view and education in order to explain why they misunderstand the morally "beautiful and good."

---

10. According to Nails, *People of Plato*, 244, Plato was related to Charmides and Critias. His mother, Perictione, was a cousin of Critias and a sister of Charmides.

While the dialogue opens with a question about wisdom and beauty, the focus quickly turns to the virtue *sōphrosunē*. One may ask why the apparent change of subject. I will argue that Plato uses the traits wisdom and beauty to reflect two aspects, the internal and the external, of the whole of a human being and his conduct, and therefore also to represent two aspects in which the virtue *sōphrosunē* manifests. Plato demonstrates through the interaction between the characters that the traits wisdom and beauty in their true, moral sense cannot be manifested without *sōphrosunē*. The only character in the dialogue who understands this is Socrates. He therefore consistently encourages his silent listener and his interlocutors in the palaestra to take into account both the internal and the external aspects of human conduct. However, Socrates inevitably fails. His silent listener remains entirely unresponsive, Charmides and Critias obstinately continue to neglect one of the two aspects, and Chaerephon neglects both and therefore is described as crazy.

The fact that Socrates' interlocutors in the palaestra are more interactive than his silent listener is not enough to lead a successful conversation about *sōphrosunē*. Charmides and Critias attempt to answer what *sōphrosunē* is, and fail, because they neglect to take into account both the internal and the external aspects of human conduct together. The dialogue inevitably ends with the impasse of *aporia*, a lack of means to answer in this discussion what *sōphrosunē* is. By the time of the dialogue's composition, the gloomy end of the tyrants Charmides and Critias was already a matter of historical record, which explains why Charmides and Critias do not progress in the dialogue. However, we will see that Plato allows his reader to learn more than they do about the meaning of *sōphrosunē* and about its importance for individual happiness as well as for a thriving community.

Some scholars assume that Socrates' conversation with Critias is more significant philosophically than other sections of the dialogue, as it includes an intriguing discussion concerning the possibility of "knowledge of knowledge."[11] I will argue, however, that all the parts of the dialogue are equally significant for understanding the philosophical content that Plato wished to convey. The opening directs Socrates' interlocutors and Plato's reader, to take

11. Many scholars focus almost exclusively on Socrates' conversation with Critias, assuming that it contains the key philosophical ideas that Plato wished to convey. Tuckey, *Plato's Charmides*, 18–23, discusses the first half of the dialogue in only few pages, and devotes the rest of his book to Socrates' conversation with Critias. He regards the opening section as a dramatic and historical background, and (91–93) extrapolates what he thinks Plato meant to convey from Socrates' conversation with Critias as "doing what is good with the knowledge that it is good." Other scholars who focus on this section of the dialogue are: McKim, "Socratic Self-Knowledge"; Dyson, "Some Problems Concerning Knowledge"; Morris, "Knowledge of Knowledge"; Politis, "Place of *Aporia*," and "*Aporia* in the *Charmides*."

into account two aspects, the internal and the external, of human conduct. Plato then uses Socrates' following two conversations to present Charmides and Critias as foils against each other. Charmides focuses on the opinion of his fellow aristocrats concerning his external appearance but neglects his soul by not thinking for himself about the meaning of *sōphrosunē*. Critias, on the other hand, focuses on his soul by nurturing his literary, sophistic, skills but his arguments do not apply to anything practical. Thus, the two cousins fail to explain what *sōphrosunē* is and what benefit it produces. The dialogue, therefore, ends with an *aporia*. My analysis will point out the danger in getting caught up in the discussion of "knowledge of knowledge" at the expense of losing sight of Plato's larger point. I will show that Plato uses the discussion of "knowledge of knowledge" as part of his plan to reveal the problematic nature of the aristocratic view of social hierarchy. How the failings of Charmides and Critias result from their aristocratic education and world-view will be expounded in my analysis. For this I will use the works of scholars from a variety of disciplines in order to provide the twenty-first-century reader with the cultural history required to understand what Plato's readers would have been easily immersed in.

Plato's drama demonstrates unmistakably that ideas do not create history by themselves. It is people with virtues or vices, with the way they form their opinions and the way they act upon them, who influence the course of events in history. Plato takes his reader on a journey beyond the superficial myth of social superiority. His dialogue shows that true beauty is not a mere external physical trait, and true wisdom is not a mere internal intellectual capacity. We can all acquire both true wisdom and true beauty, as they are manifestations of a moral way of life that benefits society as a whole.[12]

12. Beauty has been associated with morality throughout history. See discussions for example by Harris, "Beauty and the Good"; Gadamer, *Relevance of the Beautiful*, 13–53; Doran, "Moral Beauty, Inside and Out"; and the contemporary scholarly field of aesthetic-ethics.

1

Wisdom and Beauty as Reflections of the Virtue *Sōphrosunē*

... I asked them about the situation here, about philosophy, how things are now, about the youth, if anyone of them had come to excel in wisdom or in beauty or in both.[13]

—PLATO, *CHARMIDES*, 153D2–5

An Opening Question about Wisdom and Beauty

THE LENGTHY OPENING SECTION of the *Charmides* takes a quarter of the dialogue (153a1–159a5), and makes immediately apparent that the dialogue is narrated. Socrates tells a silent, unnamed listener the details of a conversation he previously had in the palaestra of Taureas. The listener peculiarly never responds throughout the whole narration. We therefore begin with asking why Plato has Socrates narrate a story to a listener who never responds. The answer will be revealed through analysis of the content of Socrates' narrative, which is intentionally directed to this opaquely passive listener.

In the opening section we meet the four characters who participate in a conversation in the palaestra: Socrates, Chaerephon, Charmides and Critias.

13 As I note in the Introduction, all translations from the Greek are mine unless otherwise indicated.

Plato motivates his reader to learn about their different traits and personalities through the prism of the first question that he has Socrates ask those present in the palaestra: whether anyone of the youth, in his absence on military duty, has come to excel in wisdom or in beauty or in both (153d1–5). This question assumes that as youth mature, they ideally should come to excel in these traits. We are thus encouraged to examine whether also the adults present in the palaestra excel in wisdom and beauty. Furthermore, Socrates' question intentionally leads to a conversation with two related characters, the aristocratic cousins Charmides and Critias.

Critias answers Socrates that his younger cousin and ward Charmides is considered to be the most beautiful (153d5–154b2).[14] He conspicuously does not describe him as wise, and everyone else in the palaestra also focuses merely on Charmides' extraordinary attractive appearance. Socrates, therefore, suggests examining whether in addition to his appearance Charmides has "a good nature" in his soul (154e1). The description of Charmides' external beauty received a lot of attention by scholars since it is very rich and vivid as dramatic descriptions of the visual world naturally tend to be. We will gradually see, however, that all the characters participating in the dialogue are driven either by passive attitude towards, or by focus on, their own wisdom or beauty or both. Socrates' opening question will therefore help us understand the way the plot, driven by the characters and the differences among them, develops over the course of the whole drama. It also will help to account for the extreme passivity of the silent unnamed listener who serves as a foil against the continuously active narrator Socrates.[15]

Given his question, we would have expected Socrates to examine whether Charmides possesses the virtue wisdom (*sophia*) in addition to his beauty (*kallos*). Instead, he turns to examine whether Charmides possesses the virtue *sōphrosunē* (157a6) by investigating whether he can explain what it is. Later on Socrates also examines whether Charmides' guardian, Critias, knows what this virtue is and therefore possesses it (162d7–e6). In order to understand properly what Plato intended to convey through this dialogue, we must

14. Critias is slightly older than his cousin Charmides (154b1–2, 162d7–e6), and is Charmides' guardian (155a5–7). On Plato's use of historical characters, see next section.

15. Lampert, *How Philosophy Became Socratic*, 235–6, suggests a vastly different interpretation concerning the identity of Socrates' silent listener. He argues that Socrates attempts to convey his philosophy to his listener, Plato, by telling him about his own failure to educate Critias and that this led to Critias' corruption. Brann, *Music of the Republic*, 72, also speculates that the listener is Plato. My analysis suggests that it is unlikely that this passive listener is Plato. Bruell, "Socratic Politics," 142, suggests that the listener is a foreigner to Athens. See also discussion concerning the identity of the listener by Schultz, *Plato's Socrates as Narrator*, 40–41.

explain why he has Socrates open with a question about wisdom in the same context as beauty—and why he introduces contrasting characters that seem to exemplify the presence or absence of wisdom or beauty or both—but then changes the focus of the discussion to the virtue *sōphrosunē*.[16] The analysis of the opening section of the dialogue will suggest that the division between wisdom and beauty is merely a use of a convention, made to facilitate the conveying of philosophical content concerning the nature of *sōphrosunē*. Wisdom and beauty represent two aspects, the internal and the external, of the whole of a human being and his conduct, and therefore also represent two aspects in which the virtue *sōphrosunē* manifests. Since everyone focuses on Charmides' external appearance, Socrates attempts to direct the attention to his soul and then to the virtue *sōphrosunē*. This process requires a quarter of the dialogue. While some mistakenly focus on external beauty, others, like Critias, focus on the internal thought. In the opening, Socrates attempts to indicate that the virtue *sōphrosunē*, however, concerns not only the soul, but the soul and the body together, because having it entails a good relation between the internal thought and the external conduct.

Four Answers in Four Characters

Plato as writer chooses a quiet, solitary listener for Socrates' narrative. We will begin with asking who this listener is and why he is silent. In this narrative, Plato uses four historical figures as his characters. As we will see, he deliberately emphasizes certain traits that they had in reality. In the dialogue, these traits make the characters appear beautiful, wise, or neither. Plato thus allows Socrates' listener to infer four possible answers to Socrates' opening question, whether anyone present excels in wisdom or in beauty or in both.

That Socrates relates the story to his silent listener is apparent throughout the dialogue since Socrates occasionally addresses him directly or indirectly. On three occasions he uses the vocative voice to address his listener directly: (1) "o companion" (*ō hetaire*, 154b8); (2) "o friend" (*ō phile*, 155c5); (3) "o nobleman" (*ō gennada*, 155d3).[17] We do not receive any information

---

16. While the two virtues are generally distinguished, in some cases *sōphrosunē* is used in the sense of wisdom in contrast to "foolishness." See for example discussions in Donlan, *Aristocratic Ideal*, 90. As indicated by North, *Sōphrosynē*, 31, a connection between wisdom and *sōphrosunē* already appears in Heraclitus, fr. 116 (Diels and Kranz).

17. Tuozzo, *Plato's Charmides*, 105–6, suggests that by the three direct addresses Socrates intends to evoke in his listener a similar emotional reaction as he and the others have for Charmides' beauty. In this chapter I will suggest differently, that Socrates directs his narrative to the passive listener, including the description of the crowd's reaction to Charmides' beauty, in order to attract him into the conversation and encourage him to

about where, when or why Socrates narrates the story to his companion, or who exactly he is. However, he may very well be an aristocrat, as Socrates' third address to him, "o noble," may likely indicate that he is of elite standing.[18]

The literary structure of the dialogue as a narration has two main purposes. First, it allows Plato to provide the reader with more than simply the transcript of the conversation in the palaestra. A dramatized work clearly requires the reader to learn also about the appearance as well as the behavioral and emotional attitudes of the characters. Plato therefore gives his reader direct access to Socrates' inner world, to his appreciation of his interlocutors and of what happened during his conversation with them. The second purpose of the narration method is directly related to the issues that Plato addresses in the dialogue. The interaction between Socrates and his listener is peculiarly uneven. As if Socrates gives a very long speech, the listener never responds. Thus Plato uses Socrates and his listener as contrasts, demonstrating the substantial difference between them. We cannot regard this listener as a participating character due to his passivity. However, his being a passive nobleman would explain why Socrates tells him about his previous conversation in the palaestra, where he conversed with two other aristocrats, Charmides and Critais, who, we will see, also exemplify passive attitudes, each in his own way. This means that we should take into consideration that the narration is intentionally directed to an extremely passive, noble man.

While we do not receive information about when Socrates narrates his story to his listener, early in his narration he gives indications for when it was that he had the conversation in the palaestra (153a1–b2). On some indefinite evening, Socrates returns to Athens after being away for a long time on a military duty near the *polis* of Potidaea. A few lines later, we learn that shortly before his return Socrates participated in a fierce battle (153b4–8). Scholars debate over which battle is being referred to here, and when exactly Socrates returned from it. This is an attempt at explaining the long time that Socrates was away from Athens on the one hand, and on the other hand how his return could have been so soon after this battle. Because of the chronological difficulties of these issues, many scholars suggest that Plato uses a fictional date.[19] In any case, Plato sets the conversation at an important historical point,

---

become an active participant in both thought and conduct.

18. The Greek words *gennadas* and *gennaios* were used to refer men of noble birth. See for example discussions by: Donlan, *Aristocratic Ideal*, 49–50, 127, 136, 163, and 203 n. 22; Andrewes, *Greek Tyrants*, 11–14.

19. Scholars disagree on the exact historical date of the conversation in the dialogue, which seems to be fictional. It is possible that it is set either closely after the battle of Potidaea or with the return of the troops in 429 at the end of the whole campaign, which took three years (432–429 BCE). See discussions by: Nails, *People of Plato*, 311; Moore and

the opening years of the long Peloponnesian War that swept the whole Greek world, fought between Athens and Sparta and their respective allies (431–404 BCE), possibly after the battle of Potidaea, which was a catalyst for this war.[20] Thus, Plato would be writing around fifty years later about a nostalgic setting of Athens' greatness and before its submission to Sparta, leading to the tyranny of Charmides and Critias. We thus look back in hindsight to the old, strong Athens.

During the first two pages we are introduced to all four characters participating in the dialogue and their characterizations. Socrates begins with a description of his own entrance to the palaestra. On the morning following his return to Athens, Socrates goes straight to the palaestra, a place where he used to spend time before his long absence. There he sees many familiar people. As they see him enter unexpectedly, they greet him, but only from afar.[21] The only man who approaches Socrates is Chaerephon, but Socrates says that this is because he is crazy (*hate kai manikos ōn*, 153b2). Chaerephon crazily jumps out of the crowd and runs towards Socrates. When he reaches Socrates he grabs his hand, and at first asks how he was saved from the battle (153b4), but only later whether he was in the battle at all (153c3). Scholars seem to overlook that these questions are asked in the reverse of the logical order. Both the fact that Chaerephon crazily jumps out of the crowd and runs towards Socrates and that his questions are asked in an illogical order imply that he behaves in a socially unexpected way. The Greeks occasionally used the word "madness" (*mania*) in opposition to the virtue *sōphrosunē*.[22] This should

Raymond, *Charmides*, xx–xxi; Luckhurst, "Note on Plato *Charmides*." Planeaux, "Does the *Charmides* Have an Historical Setting," suggests that the dialogue refers to a different fierce battle that took place in the area. See also discussion by Lampert, *How Philosophy Became Socratic*, 337–40.

20. The battle of Potidaea was a catalyst for the long Peloponnesian War according to Thucydides, *Histories*, 1.2.

21. Some scholars suggest that by the description of Socrates' return to Athens Plato calls upon Homer's model of Odysseus' return to Ithaca. For example, Burger, "Socrates' Odyssean Return," 221–24, 226, 232, suggests that Socrates disguising himself as a Thracian medical doctor is akin to Odysseus disguising himself as a beggar. The theme of "recognition" is thus introduced, as well as the problem that both characters face in establishing the regime each sees as best. More on Burger's interpretation in light of the *Odyssey* see below n. 225. Lampert, *How Philosophy Became Socratic*, 151–4, also compares Socrates' return to Athens with Odysseus' return to Ithaca. He argues that the opening correspondence between Socrates and Chaerephon is comparable to formulations found in Homer's *Odyssey*. Lampert, draws comparisons between the *Charmides* and the *Odyssey* throughout his work. See also: Raymond, "*Aidōs* in Plato's *Charmides*," 24. On Raymond's comparison between Charmides and Telemachus, the son of Odysseus, see below n. 116.

22. On the contrast between *sōphrosunē* and *mania* see for example North, *Sōphrosynē*, 24, 47, 91, 206. Bruell, "Socratic Politics," 142, also remarks that madness and moderation

already make us suspect that Plato uses the crazy Charephon not simply as a marginal character, but to convey aspects of his ideas about *sōphrosunē*.

Chaerephon grabs Socrates' hand, and literally makes him sit next to Critias on a bench, as told by Socrates to his silent listener (*me kathizei*, 153c6). Socrates then answers all the questions that people nearby ask him about the camp of Potidaea (153b2–d1). After they have had enough he immediately asks about his own concerns, about the situation inside Athens, particularly with regard to philosophy and the youth (153d2–5). His concerns, together with the earlier description of his return from servicing his homeland in the army, indicate his civic-minded personality.[23]

Socrates then asks his first question in the dialogue, whether anyone of the youth has come to excel in wisdom or in beauty or in both. This question directs the conversation to two related characters, the cousins Critias and Charmides. Critias, who is caught by Socrates' distinction between wisdom and beauty, says that Charmides is considered to be the most beautiful, and indicates that he is about to enter the palaestra (154a3–6). Critias guesses rightly that Charmides is about to enter because he sees at the door a group of young suitors (*erastai*) desiring his beauty running ahead before his arrival (154a3–6).

We are informed about Charmides' extraordinarily attractive beauty through various other statements of the characters and through the reaction of the crowd in the palaestra to his visual appearance. For example, Socrates tells his silent listener that even when Charmides was younger he seemed amazing with regard to his size and beauty; that all the others in the palaestra seemed to desire him as they were amazed and excited; and that many more desirers came after him (154c2–5). Socrates adds that not only were the adults in this situation, but even the smallest child looked nowhere but at him, and that in general everyone gazed as if he were a statue (c5–8). We are to understand from this that he had perfect features. The description indicates that Charmides is an attractive and courted adolescent, not a child anymore but just before adulthood (154b4–5). This means that he reached a suitable age to be courted by suitors. In ancient Greece homosexual activity took different

---

are opposites, and refers to Plato's *Protagoras*, 323b4–5, where *sōphrosunē* is contrasted with madness with regard to speaking the truth and justice. Bruell claims that Chaerephon's madness is due to his excessive joy and his unrestrained behavior. See also discussion by Schultz, *Plato's Socrates as Narrator*, 44–6, on Chaerephon's intemperance, and McAvoy, "Carnal Knowledge in the *Charmides*," 81–82, on his unrestrained desire for knowledge. See also below, nn. 38 and 39.

23. Schmid, *Plato's Charmides*, 3–4, argues differently, that as opposed to the excitement of those in the palaestra about information from the war, Socrates is not concerned with the values of politics and war but of peace, philosophy and education of the youth.

forms and with culturally different aims. In Athens it was culturally accepted among the elite that a youth would be engaged by an adult admirer as part of his introduction into society. This relationship between the youth (*erōmenos*) and the adult (*erastēs*) was not always romantic, and a youth would be stigmatized if he conducted himself immoderately.[24] More about Charmides' beauty and its effect on others in the palaestra will be discussed in the next section.[25]

Within merely the first two pages, we have thus been introduced to the four characters participating in the dialogue: the civic-minded Socrates, the crazy Chaerephon, the physically attractive Charmides, and Critias, whose characterization is only gradually revealed to the reader. Critias conspicuously does not describe Charmides, or anyone else, as wise. However, in the middle of the dialogue Socrates and Charmides each say on different occasions that Critias is considered to be wise (161b8–c1, 162b1–3). We are gradually given to infer, as others do, that Critias ascribes wisdom to himself because of his eloquence. Critias increasingly demonstrates his verbal self-assurance. In the opening of the dialogue he dominates the conversation with Socrates, while the others sitting next to them on the bench become silent listeners. In the middle of the dialogue we learn that Critias waited as Socrates conversed with Charmides for the opportunity to show his better literary skills (162c1–4). Also, Socrates explicitly mentions Critias' care for philosophical conversations (*heneka kai epimeleias*, 162e2). Finally, Critias displays his literary gymnastics as he replaces Charmides in the discussion regarding what *sōphrosunē* is (discussed in Chapter three).[26] This alleged unplanned conversation takes a considerable portion—a half—of the dialogue.

---

24. Moore and Raymond, *Charmides*, 40, claim rightly that the description of Charmides surrounded by desirers casts him as an ideal beloved (*erōmenos*). Schmid, *Plato's Charmides*, 7–8, indicates that in Greek culture *sōphrosunē* and moderation were expected from the desired youth as opposed to the courting adult. See Ormand, *Controlling Desires*, 55–72, on sexual roles and pederasty in Greece, 112–13 about the description of Charmides' beauty in the dialogue *Charmides* as an example for the Greeks' value of beauty of young boys, and 111–29 on sexuality in Plato's writings. According to Percy, "Reconsiderations about Greek Homosexualities," 14–17, pederastic relationships between adults and youths were incorporated into Greek pedagogy in order to lead youths to manhood. See also Percy, *Pederasty and Pedagogy*, and Dover, *Greek Homosexuality*, 9–16, 44, 81–109, 136. Fisher, "Athletics and Sexuality," 257–61, discusses pederasty in the setting of the palaestrae and gymnasia. Skinner, *Sexuality in Greek Culture*, 10–16, especially 11–12, on Charmides, and 118–124 on pederasty and social class. Lear, "Ancient Pederasty. An Introduction."

25. In the next sections I discuss Chaerephon's description of Charmides as "beautiful altogether" (154d), and Socrates' description of the power of Charmides' beauty over him (155c–e).

26. In Chapter three I present an analysis of Critias' conversation with Socrates, which reveals that Critias' verbal skills do not reflect wisdom or *sōphrosunē*.

Plato uses historical figures as his characters, and the traits that he emphasizes in his dramatic characters were traits historically exemplified by these four figures. To begin with Charmides (ca. 446–403 BCE),[27] he was a regular participant in athletic training and competitions.[28] In the dialogue he is a youth of about seventeen years old,[29] with an attractive physical appearance. It is fitting that the crowd anticipates his arrival to the palaestra, a place the Greeks used for training their bodies and for socializing. His cousin Critias (ca. 460–403 BCE) was slightly older and at some point became his guardian.[30] Critias was known as a writer of poems and tragedies,[31] and the remainder of his works ever. include a reference to *sōphrosunē*.[32] In the dialogue he is about thirty years old,[33] very likely prior to his literary apex, but his attractive eloquence is already apparent.

Plato sets the fictional conversation between the characters at an important point in history, after the famous battle of Potidaea (432 BCE). He thus allows his reader to imagine Charmides and Critias as they may have appeared before the war, young and attractive men. This is significant, because, after the war, in their maturity, the two cousins took part in the notorious regime of the Thirty Tyrants, a pro-Spartan oligarchy installed to govern Athens following its defeat by Sparta (404–403 BCE).[34] Critias was one of the main leaders and conducted mass executions and wide property confiscations, attempting to

27. On the historical figure of Charmides see: Nails, *People of Plato*, 90–91; Moore and Raymond, *Charmides*, xxv–xxvii; Krentz, *Thirty at Athens*, 59, 92; Tuozzo, *Plato's Charmides*, 86–90.

28. Plato's *Theages*, 128d8–129a1, Xenophon's *Memorabilia* III.7. See also discussion by Moore and Raymond, *Charmides*, xxvi–xxvii.

29. According to Nails, *People of Plato*, 90–91, Charmides' age in the dialogue is probably no more than seventeen, which would explain why he still requires a guardian.

30. See: Nails, *People of Plato*, 108–11; Moore and Raymond, *Charmides*, xxiv–xxv; Krentz, *Thirty at Athens*, 45–6; Pownall, "Critias in Xenophon."

31. On Critias' writings, see for example Gerber, *Greek Elegiac Poetry*, 456–471; Moore and Raymond, *Charmides*, xxv, and n. 41; Pownall, "Critias in Xenophon," 11–12; Tuozzo, *Plato's Charmides*, 53–54, 70–85; Philostratus, *Lives of the Sophists* 1.16.

32. Critias wrote an elegiac poem praising the *sōphrosunē* and moderation of Spartan youth with regard to drinking. See Freeman, *Pre-Socratic Philosophers*, 154–5, fr. 6, and Diels and Kranz, *Die Fragmente der Vorsokratiker*, fr. B 6. The fragment is discussed by Pownall, "Critias in Xenophon," 12.

33. See Nails, *People of Plato*, 108–9, on Critias' age in the dialogue.

34. Cf. McAvoy, "Carnal Knowledge in the *Charmides*," 80, for his argument that Plato deliberately sets the drama "as far as possible from" Charmides' and Critias' "ignominious end." On the rule of the Thirty Tyrants see, e.g.: Wolpert, "Violence of the Thirty"; Krentz, *Thirty at Athens*; Nails, *People of Plato*, 111–13; Pownall, "Critias in Xenophon," 4; Xenophon, *Hellenica* 2.3.11–2.4.43, and *Memorabilia* 1.2.12–18; Tuozzo, *Plato's Charmides*, 53–66.

allow only the Thirty and their friends whom they considered "the best" to live inside the city of Athens.[35] Charmides was one of ten men appointed by the Thirty to govern Piraeus, the port of Athens.[36] The regime did not survive for long, and neither did Critias nor Charmides, who both died in 403 BCE during a battle with a large group of exiled Athenians and democratic supporters led by Thrasybulus on the hill of Munychia in Piraeus.[37] This led to the reestablishment of the Athenian democracy.

Turning to Chaerephon, his characterization as crazy corresponds with other ancient sources, where he is depicted as odd or comic.[38] Chaerephon was exiled together with the democratic supporters by the Thirty Tyrants at the beginning of their reign. He returned after the fall of the regime, and died in 399 BCE. Although Chaerephon is a representative of the democrats, Plato describes him unfavorably as crazy, and has him socializing with the two cousins, unaware of their capacity for future brutality. While in the dialogue Charmides seems to excel in beauty and Critias in wisdom, Chaerephon lacks both. The visual appearance of his impulsive behavior is described as crazy, and he does not seem to be wise because the manner of his speaking is illogical.[39] We will gradually see that this unfavorable description of Chaerephon deliberately insinuates that the contemporary Athenian democrats were not much better than the oligarchs.[40]

Plato also emphasizes the historical misunderstanding of Socrates' personality, which eventually led to his execution in the year 399 BCE under the reestablished democracy. One accusation against Socrates was that he corrupted the youth, for example in associating with Critias, who grew up to

35. Krentz, *Thirty at Athens*, 64–5; Nails, *People of Plato*, 110. See also below n. 76.

36. Krentz, *Thirty at Athens*, 59; Nails, *People of Plato*, 92.

37. Krentz, *Thirty at Athens*, 91–92, 152.

38. Chaerephon is described as "intense" in Plato's *Apology*, 21a3, as indicated by Moore and Raymond, *Charmides*, xxiii–xxiv, and by Moore, "Chaerephon the Socratic," 285. On his comic character see Nails, *People of Plato*, 86–87, and Aristophanes' *Clouds*, 143 and forwards.

39. I explain Chaerephon's peculiar dramatic character in the dialogue through the prism of Socrates' opening question about wisdom and beauty. Other scholars have suggested different interpretations. For example, Hyland, *Virtue of Philosophy*, 21–22, argues that Chaerephon represents an uncritical discipleship to Socrates' teachings. Moore, "Chaerephon the Socratic," 289–90, claims that Chaerephon does not conform to the contemporary social norms. Schmid, *Plato's Charmides*, 3, 165, argues that Chaerephon's reaction to Socrates' entrance is immoderate as opposed to the moderate behavior of the majority in the palaestra who greet him from afar.

40. Cf. Press, "*Charmides*," 43. See also my discussion below in the concluding chapter, section "'The Status of Being Wise and Beautiful."

inflict terrible evils on the city.[41] In the dialogue Plato demonstrates how the crowd does not appreciate Socrates' civic-mindedness and his concern for the youth. This is because he simply does not appear to them to be either beautiful or wise, though for two completely different reasons than for Chaerephon.

First, Socrates' entrance is unexpected (*ex aprosdokētou*, 153b1). Upon seeing him the people there greet him only mildly from afar, each one from his place (a5–b2). The only one who reacts enthusiastically to his entrance is Chaerephon, but he is described as crazy. In contrast, Charmides' entrance is so exciting that the silent listener, and with him the reader, might forget that it was preceded by the earlier entrance of Socrates. Since Socrates' entrance does not provoke such enthusiasm, the reader may gather that, as opposed to Charmides, he is not a young, beautiful, or desired man. Plato opened the dialogue with the description of not one but two entrances to the palaestra because he intended his reader to compare them. The comparison sharpens the distinction between the characters, and contributes to revealing their characterization.[42]

Secondly, despite being civic-minded and leading the conversation in the palaestra, Socrates may not appear to be wise in the eyes of the crowd if the crowd does not properly understand what he is up to by his exasperating investigations of his interlocutors. This is especially because the conversation does not seem to progress, and in the final stage Socrates even publicly blames himself for the poor results of the inquiry concerning *sōphrosunē*, claiming that he is a bad inquirer (175e6). Later on we will see that in fact it is not Socrates who should be blamed for these results.[43]

The historical Charmides and Critias had gloomy ends. The dialogue implies that even as young men they were heading in the wrong direction, as their discussion concerning the nature of *sōphrosunē* does not culminate with a favorable conclusion. The reader, however, has the opportunity to learn more than they do through Socrates' informative narration. Socrates tells not only the transcript of what each of them said in the palaestra, but also gives his impression about their external appearance and internal world. The reader

---

41. See Xenophon, *Memorabilia* 1.2.12–18, and discussion by Pownall, "Critias in Xenophon," 13.

42. Cf. Byrd, "Summoner Approach," 376–7, who argues that through presenting contradictions and the need for comparisons Plato attempts to summon his readers to move from relying on the perception of the senses to dialectic thinking. Byrd discusses in this context Socrates' example in Plato's *Republic*, 7.522e–25b, of comparing between the three fingers of one's hand. See also Ludlam, "Paradigm Shift," 82, who argues that Plato's Socrates intends to cause puzzlement over inconsistencies that he sets, and thus encourage his interlocutors to dialectic thinking.

43. See discussion above, Chapter 4, section "'The Force Opposing *Sōphrosunē*."

may thus learn about the main traits of the characters, which are summarized below, in Table 1. These traits give the impression that the characters have wisdom or beauty or neither. However, we may gradually learn that their appearances are deceiving. As we will see, true wisdom and true beauty manifest together, and only in the presence of the virtue *sōphrosunē*. My analysis in the next sections will therefore unravel which of the characters possesses this virtue, which does not, and why. It will also explain why Socrates narrates his story to a listener who is a consistently passive nobleman.

	Charmides	Critias	Chaerephon	Socrates
Characterization	The physically attractive	The eloquent	The crazy	The civic-minded
Apparent trait	Beauty	Wisdom	Neither beauty nor wisdom	Neither beauty nor wisdom

Table 1: Apparent Characterizations

The Whole and Its Parts

Socrates' first question in the dialogue allows the possibility of exceling in both wisdom and beauty. However, the crowd in the palaestra focuses only on Charmides' beautiful body. In reaction, we will see, Socrates suggests examining Charmides' soul as well. This would have been easier to do if only Critias had not called Charmides over with the false claim that Socrates is a doctor for his headache. His lie draws the attention back to Charmides' body—his head. Socrates' response is a four-stage fictitious story about the remedy for Charmides' headache. Through this story, I argue, Socrates intends to turn the attention back to Charmides' soul, and ultimately to encourage everyone in the palaestra to consider two aspects of the whole of a human being, the internal and the external, in which the virtue *sōphrosunē* manifests.

As Charmides enters the palaestra everyone gazes at him. Chaerephon says that Charmides has a beautiful face, but that if he wanted to get undressed he would seem faceless, since he is "beautiful altogether" (*pagkalos*, 154d4–5). Everyone around agrees (d6), except Socrates. Although accepting that Charmides has a beautiful face (*euprosōpos*, 154d1–3), Socrates does not agree that his having a beautiful body as well entails that he is "beautiful altogether." Socrates says that they seem to claim that Charmides is *amachos* (154d7), a term which may be translated as "impossible to fight against," "invincible," or "irresistible." Socrates claims, however, that Charmides is *amachos* only if he has another little thing, if he happens to have a good nature (*eu pephukōs*, 154d7–e1) in his soul. In this way he extends the meaning of being "beautiful altogether" to include both the body and the soul of a person. Once he does this, we should speculate likewise about whether wisdom should also be extended to include both the soul to the body. We will gradually see that this is only one of many ways by which Socrates emphasizes the need to consider the whole of a person, rather than just the physical body.

From Chaerephon's words we may understand that Charmides has already been seen naked in the palaestra, as was customary for the Greeks during physical training.[44] Clearly, the crowd anticipates that Charmides will get undressed again. Since everyone focuses on Charmides' body, Socrates suggests inviting him to the conversation to examine his soul (154e5–7). He presents his plan in an erotic way, using terminology which emulates the immediate physical attraction to his appearance. He suggests "undressing" Charmides' soul before his body in order to cause anticipation. His formulation "before his appearance" (*proteron tou eidous*, 154e6) allows the possibility that after examining Charmides' soul the young man will physically get undressed as well.

Socrates' plan does not proceed without complications. Critias who agrees to his suggestion sends a slave to call Charmides with the false claim that he has found a doctor for his headache (155b1–3). He compels Socrates to collaborate with his lie by saying "what prevents you from pretending to him that you know the remedy for the head?" (155b5–6). Socrates surprisingly answers that nothing prevents, "only let him come" (155b7).[45] Socrates and the crowd do not uncover Critias' lie when Charmides joins them, probably because they do not want to endanger the opportunity to converse and spend time with him. In the next section we will get back to why Critias lies,[46] and only in Chapter 3 to why he thinks nothing prevents one from pretending to be a doctor.[47] At this stage, it is important to observe that Critias' lie directs

44. See Fisher, "Athletics and Sexuality," 257–61, and above n. 24, on pederasty.

45. ἀλλὰ τί σε κωλύει προσποιήσασθαι πρὸς αὐτὸν ἐπίστασθαί τι κεφαλῆς φάρμακον; Οὐδέν, ἦν δ᾽ ἐγώ· μόνον ἐλθέτω (155b5–7).

46. This is not the sole lie by Critias. Later on he lies that Charmides did not hear from him the phrase "to do your own things," which is discussed below, in Chapter 2, section "Thinking for Yourself." Critias also does not admit that he is unable to provide a satisfying answer as to what *sōphrosunē* is, which is discussed in Chapter 3, section "The Practicality of *Sōphrosunē*," and Chapter 4, section "To Be or Not to Be in *Aporia*." Later in this section, and in Chapter 4, we will see that Socrates also uses lies as a tool to motivate actions and events.

47. Chapter 3, section "Discerning the Morally Good."

the conversation back to Charmides' physical body, his headache, instead of his soul. It was previously suggested that Charmides' headache is a hangover because of immoderate drinking.[48] If this is true, it would already imply that Charmides is not *sōphrōn*, since the Greeks considered excessive drinking as an indication for immoderation and lack of *sōphrosunē*.[49] Another suggestion, offered by Levine, is that Charmides' "head weakness" represents his underlying cognitive inabilities,[50] about which we will learn in the next chapter. Whatever the reason for his headache, Socrates' fictitious story gradually suggests in its own unique way why Charmides' headache indicates that he lacks *sōphrosunē*.

Although Critias' lie clearly impedes Socrates' plan to speak openly with Charmides, Socrates tells his silent listener that it was because of Charmides' beauty that he experienced a difficulty in conversing with the youth. At first he describes the effect that Charmides' beauty had on the crowd in the palaestra as he approached the bench. Each of those sitting on the bench next to them pushed the person besides him in order to make space for Charmides, resulting in a few at the ends of the bench falling off (155c1–4). Picturing it to ourselves, the comic nature of this scene is obvious. Next, Socrates describes his own internal reaction when Charmides sat on the bench in between him and Critias (155c5–e2). He says that he was caught with *aporia* (c5), a lack of means to answer or respond. He lost his boldness (*thrasutēs*, c6) thinking he could speak with him easily. Charmides looked into his eyes in an irresistible way as if asking for the remedy (155c7–d1). At that point everyone in the palaestra flows around in a circle (d2–3), clearly to gaze at Charmides. Then, Socrates says, when he looked into Charmides' cloak he got enflamed (*ephlegomēn*, 155d4) and was not himself anymore.

Socrates further emphasizes to his silent listener the power of Charmides' attractive beauty over him through a line from a poem by Cydias,[51] which he claims to have recalled upon seeing Charmides (155d4–e1). In this line, advice is given to someone about his attraction to a beautiful youth, to be careful not to go like a fawn in front of a lion and to be taken as meat. This

---

48. Hyland, *Virtue of Philosophy*, 41–42; McPherran, "Socrates and Zalmoxis," 14–15.

49. On the connection made by the Greeks between excessive drinking and lack of *sōphrosunē*, see for example Rademaker, *Sōphrosynē and Rhetoric*, 93–95. See also the remains of a poem by the historical Critias which praises Spartan moderation and *sōphrosunē* in drinking, above n. 32.

50. Levine, *Profound Ignorance*, 146.

51. Cydias was a poet of whom only this line remains, as quoted in the dialogue: εὐλαβεῖσθαι μὴ κατέναντα λέοντος νεβρὸν ἐλθόντα μοῖραν αἱρεῖσθαι κρεῶν· (155d6–e1). The line appears apparently with slight changes in the dialogue. Page, *Poetae Melici Graeci*, 370, has reconstructed its original metric structure.

line turns around the relation between the desire and the desired. In the aristocratic Athenian culture where adults desire the young and beautiful,[52] it is expected that the adult who desires would be described as the lion that preys on the young desired fawn. But in Cydias' line the desired youth is represented by the dangerous lion while the adult who desires him is represented by the innocent fawn. This line is a simile for the dangerous power that the desired has over the desirer The meat is a simile to the desire and attraction, and being taken as meat is the result of losing control of the desire. Socrates uses this simile to make his listener think of Charmides as a powerful young man simply because of his beauty. Through his beauty he controls all the adults and supposedly even Socrates, who says that he seemed to himself to be taken by this kind of creature (155e1–2).[53]

While Socrates tells his silent listener that the *aporia* he experienced was caused by Charmides' beauty, the rest of his description suggests otherwise. When Charmides asks Socrates if he knows the remedy for his headache, Socrates answers with difficulty (*mogis*), clearly caused by his *aporia*, that he does (155e1–3). It is then revealed that, as others of his age, Charmides knows Socrates' name. He also adds that at a younger age he had seen Critias spending time with Socrates (156a4–8). At this point Socrates admits to Charmides that a moment ago he experienced *aporia* about how he would explain to him the cure for his headache (156b2). This confession of *aporia* differs from the earlier one that Socrates gave to his listener, claiming that Charmides' beauty affected him (155c5). A connection seems to be made here between Charmides' awareness of who Socrates is and Socrates' recovery from his *aporia*. This should make us suspect that Socrates' earlier description of Charmides' appearance as the cause for his *aporia* is merely intended for his silent listener. The listener, who we are given to understand is a noble aristocrat (155d3), is probably interested in the beautiful youth, as pederastic relationships were common among aristocrats, and the beautiful Charmides has reached a suitable age to become a beloved.[54] Socrates probably uses his listener's interest in order to attract him to continue following his narration, and Plato, the writer

52. On Charmides being at the suitable age to be engaged in a pederastic relationship see above n. 24.

53. Other scholars have suggested different interpretations for this passage. Vielkind, "Philosophy, Finitude, and Wholeness," 70–72, argues that the reference to the wisdom of Cydias in love matters by the sentence from his poem is Socratic irony. McCabe, "Looking Inside Charmides' Cloak," 184–5, sees Socrates' dramatic struggle as he looks into Charmides' cloak in context of "assimilation of knowledge and self-knowledge to perception and self-perception." See also below n. 55, on scholars' suggestion that Socrates struggles with his attraction to Charmides' beauty, but then demonstrates self-restraint.

54. See above n. 24.

of the dialogue, uses the same method to attract his reader.[55] We may gather that Charmides' beauty is not the genuine cause for Socrates' *aporia*, but Critias' lie is. Socrates recovers from his *aporia* because he is relieved that he does not need to play along and pretend to be a doctor.

There are further reasons to doubt that Socrates is experiencing *aporia* due to the effect of Charmides' beauty over him. Although Socrates occasionally asserts that Charmides is beautiful with regard to his external appearance, he does not seem to gaze at Charmides as others do. He is able to describe to his silent listener how everyone behaves, both adults and young, right down to the youngest (154c5–8).[56] Moreover, he immediately diverts the conversation from Charmides' external appearance to his soul (154e1). Finally, as we will now see, Socrates is able to craft a complex, fictitious story about a cure for Charmides' headache. This story indicates that Socrates does not pursue a conversation with Charmides for sexual interest as would one who desires a beautiful youth. A courted youth was expected to learn about virtue and *sōphrosunē* from his lover and through the need to refrain from unsuitable lovers.[57] Socrates' upcoming story, however, indicates that Charmides could acquire virtue without engaging in a pederastic relationship.

We now come to Socrates' fictitious story about the cure for Charmides' headache. Socrates seems to be a more polished liar than Critias, by crafting a masterly lie where he pretends to possess a remedy for Charmides' headache. He seems to avoid presenting himself as a doctor, probably because Charmides knows that he is not. However, Socrates does not want to endanger the continuation of the conversation, and adapts to Critias' lie. He refers to the authority of various doctors. His story may be divided into four stages, and is intended, we will see, for two purposes. The first is to return the focus of the conversation back to Charmides' soul after being diverted to Charmides' body

---

55. Brown, *"Plato's Charmides,"* 48–54, also sees that Socrates' two confessions of *aporia*, one to the silent listener and one to Charmides, slightly differ from each other. He rightly indicates that Socrates' description of his attraction to Charmides' beauty does not seem genuine, but is intended for the sake of the silent listener. Brown argues that although Socrates claims to have been attracted to Charmides, it does not seem to affect him as he is able at the moment to judge the situation and think of the wise sentence from Cydias. Thus, there seems to be a contradiction between what Socrates tells the listener and the description of his actions in the palaestra. Tuozzo, *Plato's Charmides,* 108–10, also claims that Socrates' description is meant for the listener, but provides a different interpretation. Most scholars, however, understand Socrates to describe a genuine attraction which he subsequently controls, e.g.: Schmid, *Plato's Charmides,* 8–9; Gonzales, *Dialectic and Dialogue,* 42; Tuckey, *Plato's Charmides,* 18; Stalley, *"Sōphrosunē* in the *Charmides,"* 266; Reece, "Drama, Narrative," 67–68.

56. This is observed also by Tuozzo, *Plato's Charmides,* 107.

57. Ormand, *Controlling Desires,* 62–65; Skinner, *Sexuality in Greek Culture,* 15–16.

by Critias' lie. This is because of the tendency of everyone to ignore his soul while focusing on his body. The other purpose of the story, we will see, is to encourage everyone to realize the need to take into account both the internal and the external aspects of a human being, of human conduct, and therefore also of *sōphrosunē*.

In the first stage of his story, Socrates tells Charmides that the remedy for his headache is both a leaf (*phullon*) and a charm (*epōdē*), but that without the charm there is no use for the leaf (155e5–8). Clearly, the leaf has to do with the physical aspect and the charm with the internal soul. This recalls Socrates' initial distinction made between beauty and wisdom, beauty relating to the bodily aspect while wisdom to the internal soul. Socrates is not satisfied with a concise explanation concerning this remedy since Charmides wants to write it down (156a1–2), as if simply reading it will magically cure him. This leads to the second stage of the story where he adds a more complex explanation regarding the abilities of this charm (156b1–157c6).

In the second stage of his story, Socrates mentions good doctors in general (156b4–6). We may gather later on that he refers to Greek doctors (156d6–7). He tells Charmides that according to them a part cannot be treated without the whole. Just as the eyes cannot be treated without the head, so the head cannot be treated without the body (156b4–c7). Socrates emphasizes the need to examine the whole as opposed to some people's habit to focus on a certain part while ignoring its connection with the whole. This seems to be the tendency of the crowd, as we understand from Chaerephon, who says that if Charmides wanted to get undressed he would seem to be faceless (*aprosōpos*, 154d4–5)—his beautiful face would be forgotten because all would be concentrating on his even more beautiful body.

The third stage of Socrates' story is directed to the general tendency of the crowd to pay attention to Charmides' body but not to his soul. Socrates adds another claim which he attributes to a second medical authority, Zalmoxis, who is a god and the king of the Thracians.[58] One of Zalmoxis' immortal (*apathanatizein*) Thracian doctors (156d5–6),[59] told Socrates that as it is impossible to treat the eyes without the head and the head without the body, it is impossible to treat the parts of the body and the body as a whole without treating the soul as well (156d3–e2). This claim extends the meaning of "the whole" to include the soul in addition to the body. There seems to be a

58. On Zalmoxis the god of the Getae and the Thracians see Herodotus, *Histories* 4.93–96. According to his description, Zalmoxis was a slave of Pythagoras who was freed and later taught about immortality. See discussion by Eliade, *Zalmoxis, the Vanishing God*, 21–75, and Burger, "Socrates' Odyssean Return," 220.

59. For further discussion on the meaning of the word *apathanatizō* see Murphy, *Doctors of Zalmoxis*, 290–91, and Tuozzo, *Plato's Charmides*, 115–18.

parallel made by Socrates between "the whole" (*to holon*, 156c4, e4) and Chaerephon's earlier description of Charmides as "beautiful altogether" (154d5). Thus, Socrates extends the meaning of being "beautiful altogether," as used by Chaerephon, to include the soul. Beauty is now used as a trait of both the physical body and the soul.[60]

The fourth and last stage of Socrates' story finally returns the focus to Charmides' soul. Although the Thracian doctor is claimed to have initially said that the soul and the body need to be treated simultaneously, he is then claimed to have given priority to the soul (156e6–157a1). All the bad and good things come to the body and to people from the soul, and from the soul they flow up to the surface, although seeming to come from the head to the eyes. The soul, therefore, needs to be treated first and foremost (*prōton kai malista*, 157a1).

As we have seen, in his story Socrates mentions the Greek doctors and Zalmoxis' doctors. Later on he also mentions the charms of Abaris the Hyperborean (158b7–8).[61] Why does he refer to three medical authorities? The mention of the various authorities together with the earlier description of Socrates' participation in the military expedition, which took place in the area of Thrace, contribute to the credibility of the story in the eyes of the crowd, the silent listener, and even the reader. Socrates moves freely from reality to myth, which was easy to do in the ancient world. The Greeks represent reality; the Thracians neighbored Greek settlements in the north but were sufficiently distant to allow Zalmoxis to be considered a god; and Abaris was an intriguing mythical figure. Socrates extends and embellishes Critias' lie to the point that it is credible that he lately acquired the knowledge of a special remedy in the area of Thrace.[62]

Many scholars seem to read too much into Socrates' fictitious story, as they attempt to understand what Plato intended to convey concerning the

---

60. This clearly has moral implications for the meaning of beauty. See Luz, "Erlangen Papyrus 4," 164–5, 167–70, on the similarity between the description of Charmides' beautiful face and body and a passage in P. Erlangen 4 (45–61). The papyrus is the remains of a Socratic dialogue by unknown authorship and deals with cures for desiring the physical beauty of a person, mentioning the interlocutors' beautiful face and body. The papyrus is dated to the second or third century CE, and written perhaps in the fifth or forth centuries BCE.

61. See Kingsley, *Story Waiting to Pierce You*, on the possible origin of the myth about Abaris.

62. See McPherran, "Socrates and Zalmoxis," 16–17, on Plato's use of the beliefs of his Greek audience in Socrates' fictitious story. See also Rutherford, *Art of Plato*, 89–90; Faraone, "Socratic Leaf Charm for Headache"; McAvoy, "Carnal Knowledge in the *Charmides*," 85.

connection between the soul and the body.[63] I contend that Plato has Socrates invent a story for several other reasons. Firstly, instead of calling on Critias' lie that presented him as a doctor for Charmides' headache, thus endangering the continuation of the conversation, Socrates manipulates the lie for his own philosophical purposes.[64] Secondly, Socrates uses the story to attract Charmides, who is merely a teenager, into a philosophical conversation. Only in the next chapter we will see that Charmides is reluctant to engage in such conversations. The intriguing story should be attractive to Charmides if he wants to preserve his powerful youthful beauty. He might learn how to become immortal (*apathanatizein*) like Zalmoxis' Thracian doctors, or how to acquire eternal youth and health as the Hyperboreans.[65] Thirdly, the story is intended to appeal to the crowd in the palaestra who listen to the conversation. The crowd tends to ignore "the whole" of Charmides while focusing on his parts, but the story gradually directs the crowd's attention from focusing on parts of Charmides' body (his face or the rest of his body) to his whole body, and then from focusing on his whole body to his soul as well.

We end up with descriptions of three kinds of beauty in the opening of the dialogue. The first is Charmides' extraordinary physical appearance. The second is "the whole" (*to holon*) and its parts, which need to be "in a beautiful/ fine condition" (156e4–6), that is, not only the body and its parts but rather the body together with the soul. Socrates seems to switch deliberately between the terms "is in a beautiful condition" (*kalōs echei*, 156e5) and "is in good condition" (*eu echei*, e6) when he says that if the whole is not in a beautiful condition then the part will not be in a good condition.[66] As he had done with Chaerephon's description of Charmides as "beautiful altogether," Socrates now extends the meaning of beauty to include both the body and the soul. Socrates challenges the convention that beauty is a trait of only the body, and

---

63. See for example Tuozzo, *Plato's Charmides*, 118–23, who discusses various interpretations to Socrates' story about Zalmoxis' holistic treatment, about the connection between "the whole" and the parts, and about the connection between the soul and the body. Tuozzo, "What's Wrong with These Cities," 328, argues that Socrates presents the health of the body as a conditional good, depending on the health of the soul that comes from possessing *sōphrosunē*. See also other interpretations by, e.g.: McPherran, "Socrates and Zalmoxis"; Vielkind, "Philosophy, Finitude, and Wholeness," 93–100; Guthrie, *Greeks and their Gods*, 174–6; Rutherford, *Art of Plato*, 89–90; Schmid, *Plato's Charmides*, 14–18.

64. See Tuozzo, *Plato's Charmides*, 130, who also indicates that Socrates' story is a result of Critias' lie, but interprets Socrates' intentions differently.

65. According to Pindar the poet, *Pythian*, 10.41–2, the Hyperboreans were blessed with eternal youth and health.

66. The terms also appear in 156c1 (*eu echei*) and 157a3 (*kalōs echei*).

this should lead us to speculate likewise about whether wisdom should also be extended, but in the direction of the soul to the body.[67]

The third description of beauty has to do with *sōphrosunē*. Socrates says that according to the Thracian doctor the soul must be treated through charms which are *kaloi logoi*, "beautiful discourses" as I translate it,[68] from which *sōphrosunē* comes to be in the soul (157a3–5). Once it is present it is easy to bring health to the body and its parts (157a6–b1). The mistake of many doctors, however, is that they do not address *sōphrosunē* and health together (157b5–7), and all the good things come to the body from the soul. This description clearly directs the focus once again to the soul through the topic of the virtue *sōphrosunē*.

While it may seem that *sōphrosunē* is a good state of the soul and health is a good state of the body, a close attention allows the reader to infer that *sōphrosunē* has to do with both the soul and the body. The first question that Socrates asks in the dialogue, whether anyone excels in wisdom or in beauty or in both, suggests the possibility of exceling in both aspects. The need to take into consideration two aspects of the whole of a person continues also in Socrates' four-stage story. The reader should draw the conclusion that all the divisions in groups of two presented in the opening (beauty and wisdom; body and soul; leaf and charm; health and virtue) reflect in different ways two essential aspects: one relating to the external (beauty, body, leaf, health) and another relating to the internal (wisdom, soul, charm, virtue). When Socrates extends the meaning of being beautiful to include both the body and the soul, we are implicitly invited to think that wisdom should also include both the body and the soul. Thus, the division of the external and internal is merely a use of a convention, made to facilitate the conveying of the philosophical content concerning the nature of *sōphrosunē*. The crowd and the participating characters are encouraged to consider two aspects of the whole of a person, as well as two aspects of *sōphrosunē*. The reader may gradually appreciate that the virtue *sōphrosunē* involves both body and soul; and in its presence true wisdom and beauty manifest together. Later on we will see that not only the

---

67. Tuozzo, *Plato's Charmides*, 103–4, proposes a different interpretation, that Socrates opens with a question about wisdom and beauty in order to begin with a preliminary discussion about the beauty of the body and the control of appetite, but then moves to the more essential philosophical discussion about the beauty of the soul.

68. The word *logos* can be translated in various ways, as speech, argument, reason, word, etc. I have chosen to translate it as "discourse," since Socrates is trying to attract Charmides into conversing. Vielkind, "Philosophy, Finitude, and Wholeness," 102, also translates the phrase *kaloi logoi* as "beautiful discourses." The phrase is translated as "beautiful speeches" by: Schmid, *Plato's Charmides*, 15; Tuozzo, *Plato's Charmides*, 123–24; and McPherran, "Socrates and Zalmoxis," 11.

patient needs *sōphrosunē*, but also the doctor (Chapter 3, section "Discerning the Morally Good").

As we see, the first time that the term *sōphrosunē* appears in the dialogue is in Socrates' fictitious story about the remedy for Charmides' headache. Socrates' story is intended, among other things, to tempt Charmides intos focusing on his soul and into conversing by motifs of beauty, which would attract and interest him. Socrates then emphasizes that the Thracian doctor commanded him not to be persuaded to give the cure to anyone who did not first present his soul for treatment, not even to the most wealthy, noble or beautiful man (157b7–c6). Clearly this implies that Socrates is aware of Charmides' tendency to use his powerful beauty and social status in order to obtain whatever he wishes. Socrates tells Charmides that if he does not obey the command of the Thracian doctor and first present his soul for treatment, he will not be able to help him (c3–6). He thus reveals the only way in which Charmides could get the remedy, by conversing with him.

Does It All Stay in the Family?

Socrates' opening question about wisdom in the same context as beauty leads the conversation to focus on two related characters, the aristocratic cousins Charmides and Critias. In the final section of this chapter, we will see how Plato uses the family dynamics between the cousins as symbolic of the unappreciated relationship between two essential aspects of human conduct, the internal, which is represented by wisdom, and the external, which is represented by beauty. Plato, however, needed a cast of four characters to convey fully his philosophical ideas concerning the concept *sōphrosunē*. His ideas are, therefore, presented by the dramatic interaction among these characters and their contrasting traits that reflect different attitudes concerning the internal and the external aspects of human conduct.

Plato has Socrates initiate a discussion about wisdom and beauty. This deliberately leads the conversation to focus on the cousins Critias and Charmides. Critias says that Charmides is considered to be the most beautiful, but he conspicuously does not describe him as wise. As we will see, Socrates is aware that Critias' answer indicates a competitive dynamic between the two cousins. He thus provokes this competitiveness for his own philosophical purpose. When everyone else also praises Charmides' mere beauty, Socrates says that they seem to claim that Charmides is *amachos*, impossible to fight against, but that he is *amachos* only if in addition to his beauty he has another small thing, a good nature in his soul (154d7–e1). Socrates' choice of the word *amachos* to describe Charmides is not accidental. It anticipates a possible battle. This is suitable to the location in which the dialogue occurs, as training of athletic competitors took place in the palaestra. If Charmides lacks the additional good nature in his soul, it means that someone else could prevail over him in wisdom, if not with youthful beauty. That in this way Socrates provokes Critias to compete with Charmides gradually becomes apparent.

After questioning whether Charmides has a good nature in his soul, Socrates immediately adds that it is appropriate that Charmides does, because he is from Critias' family (154e1–3). He thus highlights that the two cousins belong to an aristocratic, noble family. Critias clearly confirms this, as he replies that in these aspects Charmides is also quite *kalos kai agathos* (154e3). The epithet *kalos kai agathos*, or its shorter version *kalos kagathos*, literally means "beautiful and good." It was a socially charged epithet, used by the aristocratic class during the fifth century BCE to identify its supposed inherent superiority over the lower classes, the common people (*dēmos*).[69] The epithet "beautiful" (*kalos*) referred both to physically inherited traits and to physical appearance resulting from aristocratic education, cultural manners and life-style.[70] The epithet "good" (*agathos*) referred to inherited intellectual traits and virtues, including *sōphrosunē* and wisdom.[71] The aristocrats described common men using opposing pejoratives, for example "base" (*kakoi*) and "knaves" (*ponēroi*).[72]

By means of the compound epithet "beautiful and good," the aristocrats attempted to cling to their historically superior status even as it weakened

69. On the aristocratic use of the epithet *kalos kagathos* see, e.g., Donlan, "Origin of *Kalos kagaqos*," and *Aristocratic Ideal*, 78, 100, 129–34. In the fourth century BCE the epithet came to refer any good citizen regardless of social class according to Donlan, "Origin of *Kalos kagaqos*," 373–4, and Andrewes, *Greek Tyrants*, 11–14. See also: Ober, *Mass and Elite*, 248–92; Gomme, "Interpretation of *Kaloi Kagathoi*," 65–68; Wankel, "*Kalos kai Agathos*"; Nikityuk, "*Kalokagathia*: A Question on Formation." On the epithet *kalos kagathos* as a characteristic of Spartan aristocracy see: Bourriot, *Kalos Kagathos. Kalokagathia*; Cairns, "Review of *Kalos Kagathos. Kalokagathia*"; Davies, "*Kalos Kagathos*, Scholarly Receptions."

70. See: Donlan, *Aristocratic Ideal*, 106–7, 129, and "Origin of *Kalos kagaqos*," 369–71; Ober, *Mass and Elite*, 251–52.

71. Wisdom and *sōphrosunē* were considered by the aristocrats as exclusively hereditary aristocratic traits, see Donlan, *Aristocratic Ideal*, 90–95, 104–8, 138. In some cases *sōphrosunē* is used similarly to wisdom in contrast to "foolishness," see above n. 16. On the relation between "virtue," "good"(*agathos*) and *sōphrosunē* in Athenian inscriptions, see North, *Sōphrosynē*, 15–16. North, 88, also indicates that the question whether the virtue *sōphrosunē* is heredity or learned, belongs to the debate concerning nature-convention (*nomos-physis*).

72. On the usage that the aristocrats employed to refer to the lower classes see for example Donlan, *Aristocratic Ideal*, 113–53, and "Origin of *Kalos kagaqos*," 365–74 and n. 26.

following the gradual democratization of Athens that began with Solon the lawgiver[73] in the sixth century BCE.[74] The aristocrats claimed that these inherited traits led to their exclusive economic and political competence.[75] Even the Thirty Tyrants, of which regime Charmides and Critias were leaders, used this epithet to refer to themselves despite the evils that they perpetrated.[76] We will gradually see, however, that Plato indicates through his dialogue that true wisdom and true beauty are neither hereditary nor exclusively aristocratic traits.

Critias indicates that Charmides, as all aristocrats, is *kalos kai agathos*. However, we gradually see that he denies that Charmides is the best among aristocrats. We have already seen that Critias admits that Charmides is considered to be the most beautiful (154a3–b1) but noticeably does not describe him as wise. We will now see that Critias denies Charmides two further crucial qualities, poetic skills and *sōphrosunē* in a mature sense.

Before Charmides joins the conversation, Critias denies that Charmides is poetic. Socrates suggests inviting Charmides to the conversation to examine his soul "before his appearance." Socrates says that at his age, Charmides probably would already like to converse (154e6–7). That Charmides actually does not want to participate in the conversation will be shown in the next chapter. Critias, however, says in response that Charmides is quite philosophical, and seems to others and to Charmides himself to be quite poetic (154e6–155a1). Critias is willing to describe Charmides as philosophical but notably refrains from describing him as genuinely poetic. He emphasizes that Charmides is considered to be poetic by others and by Charmides himself, but he does not reveal his own opinion.[77]

Socrates then once again emphasizes that Charmides' excellence comes from the family to which he and Critias belong. He says that this beautiful trait, being philosophical and poetic, comes to them from as far away as

73. See Nails, *People of Plato*, 269, on Solon, a poet and lawgiver.

74. Donlan, *Aristocratic Ideal*, 122–9; Kagan, *Fall of the Athenian Empire*, 106–7.

75. Kagan, *Fall of the Athenian Empire*, 106–9; Donlan, *Aristocratic Ideal*, 129, 140–6, 153; Ober, *Mass and Elite*, 248–92; Andrewes, *Greek Tyrants*, 11–14.

76. The oligarchic groups used the epithet *kalos kagathos*, as well as the phrase "the best" (*hoi beltistoi*), to refer to the members of their government, see Xenophon, *Hellenica* 2.3.18–19, Aristotle, *Athenian constitution*, 36.3–4, and discussion by Krentz, *Thirty at Athens*, 64–5 n. 39. See also discussions in: Woodruff, *Thucydides. Justice, Power and Human Nature*, 157; Gomme, "Interpretation of *Kaloi Kagathoi*," 66; Davies, "*Kalos Kagathos*, Scholarly Perceptions," 272. On Critias' oligarchic perception, see for example Pownall, "Critias in Xenophon," 11. That the oligarchs used pejoratives against the lower classes see above n. 72.

77. That Critias qualifies his praise is indicated also by Moore and Raymond, *Charmides*, xxv–xxvi.

their kinship with Solon (155a2–3), the lawgiver and poet. The relation of the cousins' family to Solon is not completely clear. As far as the evidence shows, Solon was a contemporary and probably merely a friend of Dropides II, the ancestor of the two cousins who is mentioned a few lines later alongside another mention of Solon.[78] Interestingly, Dropides was probably an archon immediately succeeding Solon.[79] In the concluding chapter we will also see that Plato makes several allusions to Solon and his tradition, and that Solon's tradition, therefore, is significant for understanding the ideas that Plato conveys through his dialogue.

After Charmides joins the conversation, it is revealed that Critias also deprives him of *sōphrosunē* in a mature sense. Following his fictitious story about the remedy for Charmides' headache, Socrates says that if Charmides does not present his soul to treatment by the Thracian charm he will not be able to help him (157c2–6). We expect Charmides to respond, but instead Critias reacts and praises Charmides once again, but this time in his presence. He says that he is gifted more than anyone of his age, not only in appearance, but also in *sōphrosunē* (157c7–d4) and other such things (d6–8). A close reading reveals that Critias praises Charmides only with respect to his young age: "of those at this age" (*tōn hēlikiōtōn*, 157d2); "as much as he is in age" (*eis hoson hēlikias hēkei*, 157d7). Critias, therefore, refrains from describing Charmides as having *sōphrosunē* in a mature sense. We may gather that someone who is older than Charmides could certainly prevail over him in *sōphrosunē*, if not by youthful external beauty. This would thus prove that Charmides is not *amachos*, that is, impossible to fight against or irresistible.

Only in the middle of the dialogue it is revealed that Critias competes with Charmides. Socrates says explicitly that for a long time in this conversation Critias wanted to compete and receive respect from Charmides and everyone present (162c1–4), clearly by demonstrating his better literary skills.[80] Thus, we are to understand, Critias denies that Charmides has wisdom, poetic nature, and mature *sōphrosunē*—since, he ascribes these qualities to himself.

---

78. Nails, *People of Plato*, 106–8, 244, indicates that Solon was most probably merely a friend of the family, although later sources present him as a brother of Dropides, e.g., Diogenes Laertius, *Vitae Philosophorum* 3.1. In both cases, however, there is no direct lineal connection between Solon and the cousins Critias and Charmides.

79. See Philostratus, *Lives of the Sophists* 1.16, and Nails, *People of Plato*, 244, Plato's stemma.

80. Καὶ ὁ Κριτίας δῆλος μὲν ἦν καὶ πάλαι ἀγωνιῶν καὶ φιλοτίμως πρός τε τὸν Χαρμίδην καὶ πρὸς τοὺς παρόντας ἔχων, μόγις δ᾽ ἑαυτὸν ἐν τῷ πρόσθεν κατέχων τότε οὐχ οἷός τε ἐγένετο· (162c1–4). See further discussion on this passage in Chapter 2, section "Thinking for Yourself," and on Critias' literary skills in Chapter 3.

Socrates continues to provoke the existing competitiveness between the cousins through a manipulative description of their joint family. In response to Critias' praise of Charmides in appearance and *sōphrosunē* among those of his age (157c7–d4), Socrates says that it is appropriate that Charmides will excel in such things as he is a descendant of two excellent families. Socrates thus begins a lengthy praise of Charmides with respect to his families that takes about a page (157d9–158b4).

Socrates elaborates on the good aspects of each of the two families that gave birth to Charmides. At first, he describes the paternal side of the family from which Critias descends as well. He strangely mentions relatives who lived six generations before Charmides and Critias, as well as an earlier figure named Critias the son of Dropides, whose name our Critias IV clearly inherited. He most likely refers to Critias II, son of Dropides II, who both were active during the sixth century BCE.[81] This older Critias II, Socrates says, was praised by many poets (*pollōn poiētōn*, 157e6), including Anacreon[82] and Solon, for his excellence in beauty and virtue (*aretē*, 158a1),[83] and in many other things that are considered to be related to happiness.

Socrates' emphasis on the traits beauty and *aretē* recalls Critias' indication that Charmides is "beautiful and good" (*kalos kai agathos*, 154e3). It also recalls Socrates' opening question about beauty and wisdom. Wisdom, as we have seen, is one of the virtues and intellectual traits that the aristocrats ascribed to themselves by the epithet "good" in the compound "beautiful and good."[84] Socrates' opening question is clearly deliberately intended for the two aristocratic cousins, who, we may gather, assume that their noble birth implied that they should naturally grow up to be beautiful and wise.

It sounds like no better family exists, but then Socrates turns to describe the maternal side of Charmides' family, which Critias does not share. Socrates praises Charmides' maternal uncle Pyrilampes, than whom no one was more beautiful or bigger (*kalliōn kai meizōn*, 158a3), and who was an ambassador

---

81. See Nails, *People of Plato*, 244, Plato's stemma; 106–7 on Critias II son of Dropides II; and 108–11 on Critias IV which is the character participating in the dialogue *Charmides*. See also the above, nn. 78, 79 on Dropides II.

82. See Nails, *People of Plato*, 107, 332, on the poet Anacreon who became a lover of either Critias II or more probably of his grandchild Critias III. For a reference to Anacreon in the remains of Critias' (IV) writings, see Tuozzo, *Plato's Charmides*, 75–76. See also Campbell, *Greek Lyric*, vol. II.

83. The word *aretē* appears only once in the dialogue (158a1), although the topic of the work is *sōphrosunē*, one of the four cardinal virtues. I discuss the reasons for the appearance of the word at this stage of the conversation in the conclusion chapter, section "The Status of Being Wise and Beautiful."

84. See above n. 71.

who spent time with the Great King (i.e. the king of Persia).[85] The description of Pyrilampes' beauty and size recalls Socrates' earlier description of Charmides, that even when he was younger he seemed wonderful with regard to size and beauty (*megethos kai to kallos*, 154c1–2).

Socrates says that the maternal side of Charmides' family does not fall below the paternal side in anything (158a5–6). We are thus left with two equally excellent families instead of one family which is the best in all of Athens. It is my contention that Socrates deliberately uses the description of the two families to provoke the competitiveness between the cousins. At first, he falsely implies that Charmides and Critias excel in the same fields as descendants of the same good family. The paternal family allows Socrates to imply that Charmides and Critias are equally good. Whenever Socrates mentions their common family he stresses their familial connection by addressing them both in plural. When praising Charmides' father's side he addresses both Charmides and Critias by the second person plural of the dative pronoun "to you" (*humin*, 157e5).

Even before Critias invites Charmides to the conversation, Socrates praises Charmides twice through his paternal family. Socrates says that Charmides is impossible to fight against (*amachos*) only if he happens to have a good nature in his soul in addition to his beautiful appearance (154d7–e1). He then immediately adds, as he addresses Critias, that it is appropriate that Charmides would have a good soul because he is from "your" family (*humeteras*, 154e1–3). Following that, Critias says that Charmides is also philosophical, and that he is considered to be poetic by others and by Charmides himself (144e8–155a1). Socrates then says that they have this beautiful thing from their being related to Solon (155a2–3). Whatever their relation was to Solon, in this way Socrates once more stresses the familial connection between Charmides and Critias, and implies that they should excel in the same fields.

Through the description of the paternal family Socrates implies that every good quality which is appropriate that Charmides would naturally have as its descendant is appropriate for Critias to have as well. Socrates even says that Charmides is inferior to no one born to these families before him (158a7–b2), and therefore not even to Critias, who is probably half a generation older than Charmides. The reader may infer, nonetheless, that Charmides is a descendent of two good families, while Critias is a descendent of only one. While praising Charmides' mother's side and his uncle Pyrilampes, Socrates directly addresses Charmides using the singular second person possessive pronoun "your" (*sou*,

---

85. See Nails, *People of Plato*, 257–59, on Pyrilampes.

158a2). Socrates thus implies that Charmides might inherit and enjoy traits of two good families, and could therefore be superior to Critias after all.

Socrates' flattery implies that beauty, *aretē*, and other such traits are inherited. This would appeal to the cousins who, as aristocrats, ascribed these traits exclusively to those of noble birth.[86] However, the reader may gather that Charmides is not passive with regard to his external appearance, but nurtures it. He regularly comes to the palaestra and has been seen there training, which explains why the crowd eagerly waits for him to undress again (154d4–5, e5–6). Critias, on the other hand, nurtures his literary skills. Charmides had previously seen him spend time with Socrates (156a7–8), probably experiencing Socratic conversations; and Socrates will later on indicate that Critias takes care of his literary skills as opposed to Charmides (162e1–2). Plato, through Socrates, encourages us to distinguish between two members of the same family, each nurturing a different aspect for which they may have a tendency: Charmides nurtures his external appearance, and Critias his literary poetic skills.

We may thus see that each of the cousins represents one of two aspects that aristocrats attributed to themselves by the epithet "beautiful and good" (*kalos kai agathos*), and which attracts the attention of the crowd. Charmides and Critias do not usually invade each other's field of expertise. Critias does not compete with Charmides' youthful external beauty, and Charmides does not compete with Critias' mature literary skills. However, Socrates provokes them to invade each other's domain, and exposes their competitiveness over the attention of the crowd. Socrates implies that Charmides should excel in literary skills (155a2–3, 157e5), and Critias should be as beautiful as Charmides, if not more; while praising Charmides' family he says that he does not fall below anyone who was born to his family before him in his appearance (158b1–2), making him at least the equal of Critias. The reaction of the crowd, however, indicates that he appears to be superior to Critias in beauty, as no one is described as desiring or gazing upon Critias.

We may now appreciate the symbolism applied by Plato. Critias and Charmides belong to the same noble family, but unfortunately, they compete with each other, either through wisdom or beauty, for the attention of the crowd. The division between wisdom and beauty, however, is merely a convention, recalling the aristocratic two-part epithet *kalos kai agathos*. Plato intends to convey that the two traits are not competing traits, but related, as the cousins are. They belong to the same family tree of virtue, which involves both the soul and body. The opening of the dialogue allows the reader to conclude that *sōphrosunē* has to do with the connection between the internal and

86. See above, nn 69–76.

the external of a human being and therefore of human conduct.[87] This is why true wisdom and true beauty manifest only together and only in the presence of the virtue *sōphrosunē*. While Charmides and Critias were to become cruel oligarchs who exemplify the conventional class-related interpretation of the epithet "beautiful and good" (*kalos kagathos*), Plato promotes a moral interpretation as the drama about *sōphrosunē* unfolds.

Already during the opening of the dialogue Plato gives his reader reasons to suspect that the two cousins do not possess *sōphrosunē*. Critias lies to Charmides that Socrates is a doctor for his headache. This seems completely contradictory to his duty as his guardian.[88] Charmides, on the other hand, suffers from headaches. According to Socrates' fictitious story, when *sōphrosunē* is present in the soul it is easy to bring health to the head and the other parts of the body (157a5–b1). Thus, we may infer, Charmides would not have suffered from headaches if he had *sōphrosunē*. Throughout the dialogue, however, we will gradually learn why Charmides and Critias do not possess *sōphrosunē*: each of them focuses only on one aspect of *sōphrosunē*, either on the internal or on the external of human conduct, aspects which are represented in the dialogue by the traits wisdom and beauty.

Plato the dramatist uses Charmides and Critias as foils against each other, thus emphasizing their contrasting traits. Charmides appears to excel at and focus on the external, and Critias appears to excel at and focus on the internal. We may now infer that Plato also uses Chaerephon and Socrates as foils against each other. We may recall that Socrates describes Chaerephon as crazy. Clearly, Chaerephon is not considered to be either wise or beautiful, in his erratic and even irrational behavior (discussed above, in section "Four Answers in Four Characters"). We may already suspect that although Socrates also does not seem to the crowd to be beautiful or wise, he exemplifies a virtuous *sōphrōn* man. He attempts to encourage his interlocutors and the crowd in the palaestra to take into account both the internal and the external aspects of a human being. Thus, Chaerephon the crazy and Socrates the *sōphrōn* are used as contrasts. As summarized below in Table 2, Charmides, Critias and Chaerephon, all lack *sōphrosunē*, although for different reasons, while Socrates is the only one in the dialogue who represents a *sōphrōn* man, as I will argue later.

87. Cf. North, *Sōphrosynē*, 180, who also observes contrasts used in the dialogue between the internal and the external aspects, soul and body, etc.

88. See also McPherran, "Socrates and Zalmoxis," 14–15, who claims similarly that Critias is a plotter, as he deceives Charmides, and fails to care for Charmides' health.

	Charmides	Critias	Chaerephon	Socrates
Characterization	The physically attractive	The eloquent	The crazy	The civic-minded
Apparent trait	Beauty	Wisdom	Neither beauty nor wisdom	Neither beauty nor wisdom
Focuses on	The external	The internal	Neither the external nor the internal	Both the external and the internal
Sōphrosunē	Not *sōphrōn*	Not *sōphrōn*	Not *sōphrōn*	The *sōphrōn*

Table 2: The Internal and the External Foci

In the next two chapters, we will continue to see that the active approach of Charmides and Critias to only one aspect of *sōphrosunē*, the internal or the external, is accompanied to the exclusion of the other aspect. Therefore, their coming attempts to answer what *sōphrosunē* is will necessarily fail to satisfy. This in itself will be a demonstration of their lack of *sōphrosunē*, and would thus explain the aporetic nature of the dialogue. In a broader sense, we will see, the internal aspect refers to the soul, theory, and speech, while the external aspect refers to the physical, manual, and practical actions.[89] Finally, this would explain that Socrates as an extremely active narrator is contrasted with his silent listener who exemplifies complete passivity towards both speech and practice. The narrative is therefore directed to this listener as an implicit attempt to encourage him to become a more active participant in life.

89. Tsouna, "Socrates' Attack on Intellectualism," 66–69, and "Subject of Plato's *Char-mides*," 43–45, interprets the qualities of Charmides and Critias as ambiguous, and not meant to be either good or bad. Tsouna, "Subject of Plato's *Charmides*," 45, argues that Plato attempts to make us feel "a sense of lost opportunity and frustrated hope for Plato's relatives as well as for Athens." Danzig, "The Use and Abuse of Critias," proposes his own explanation for why Plato's portrayal of Critias seems more positive than that of Xenophon. I contend that the positivity of Charmides and Critias is merely apparent, and Plato intends his reader to learn why. See also discussion on Critias' character below in n. 150.

2

Being Active on the Inside

"And he at first hesitated and altogether did not want to answer."

—Plato, *Charmides*, 159B1–2

An Unengaged Beauty

Charmides is praised by Critias regarding his *sōphrosunē* with respect to his age (157d2), and by Socrates for being a descendant of good families (157e–158b). Nevertheless, Socrates does not take these praises as settling the matter of whether Charmides has a good soul, and so he turns to examine him. The second quarter of the dialogue (158c1–162b11) reveals why Charmides is in fact deficient in *sōphrosunē*. Socrates' conversation with Charmides about *sōphrosunē* has the form of a joint inquiry. It thereby seems on the face of it to have a more formal philosophical structure than the preceding opening section. However, we must keep in mind that Socrates is conversing with a teenager and not with an experienced philosopher. Thus, Charmides' answers should be understood as spontaneous attempts and not as scholarly definitions. Even Socrates, we will see, does not present formal arguments, although he is an experienced philosopher.

Socrates asks Charmides directly whether he agrees with Critias' praise, and does he have enough *sōphrosunē* (158b5–c4). Charmides blushes and does not share his own opinion about himself, saying that it is difficult for him to answer. If he says that he has *sōphrosunē* he would seem annoying (*epachthes*) to some people; yet if he says that he does not have *sōphrosunē*, he would imply that Critias and others who say that he does are liars (158c5–d6). His blush and answer clearly show that he cares for the opinion of the crowd about him and that he values what others would think of whatever he says or does.[90] In these lines (158c5–d6), we will see, Charmides is already performing a kind of interpretation of *sōphrosunē*, which is also embodied in the proposals that he will later raise for what *sōphrosunē* is (158e6–162b7).

Socrates suggests that in order that Charmides would not need to say what he does not want to say, they could examine the matter in a different way, if he is willing. Charmides agrees and tells Socrates to examine in whatever way he deems best (158d7–e5). Socrates then says that if Charmides has *sōphrosunē*, it probably creates in him some kind of a feeling, from which he may draw an opinion as to what *sōphrosunē* is and what sort of a thing it is (158e6–159a4). This question does not seem to be a genuinely novel way to examine the matter, for this question would have appeared one way or another. Regardless of whether or not Charmides says that he has *sōphrosunē*, Socrates would have asked him to explain what it is. The point of these lines, however, is to dramatize Charmides' consideration of the opinion of the crowd through his reluctance to answer openly whether he has *sōphrosunē*.

We soon learn that Charmides does not even address the question what *sōphrosunē* is without considering the opinion of the crowd about him. At first he fails to take the initiative to provide an answer as to what *sōphrosunē* is (159a5). Socrates therefore attempts to motivate him into speaking. He says that since Charmides understands Greek he could say what he thinks *sōphrosunē* is (159a6–7). Charmides answers "perhaps" (159a8), but still refrains from answering. He attempts to answer only once Socrates, using the imperative "say" (*eipe*), politely orders him to give his opinion so that those present could guess whether he possesses *sōphrosunē* (159a9–10). Even then,

90. Scholars have interpreted Charmides' blush variously. Some suggest that it indicates his *sōphrosunē*. For example, Gonzalez, *Dialectic and Dialogue*, 42–43, argues that Charmides' blush implies that he is *sōphrōn*, since "if he asserts that he has temperance, this assertion will exhibit a pride that contradicts the possession of what he claims to have. If, on the other hand, he denies that he has temperance, this denial will wrong both himself and his cousin and thus show him to be lacking in virtue." Tuozzo, *Plato's Charmides*, 156, argues that Charmides' blush indicates his sincerity and a sort of *sōphrosunē*. Tuozzo, 162, additionally claims that it indicates Charmides' embarrassment as he is expected to confirm Critias' praise and therefore praise himself. Lampert, *How Philosophy Became Socratic*, 170, argues that Charmides thinks he possesses *sōphrosunē* and that his "blush shows he possesses the *sōphrosunē* of one of the definitions he will offer." In section "The Opinion of a Few about You," I will argue that Charmides' blush has to do with his consideration of the opinions of the crowd about *sōphrosunē* in youth like him.

however, Socrates says "at first he hesitated and altogether did not want to answer" (159b1–2).[91] In addition to his earlier refusal to answer whether he has *sōphrosunē*, his subsequent reluctance to say what he thinks *sōphrosunē* is may very well also be the result of his consideration of the opinion of the crowd about him. This becomes more evident as the conversation progresses.[92]

Charmides' three subsequent attempted answers, we will see, are indeed based on his consideration for the opinion of the crowd. His first proposal is that *sōphrosunē* means doing things orderly and quietly/calmly. Socrates' inquiry will reveal that it is a common opinion, and that Charmides interprets it as mere slowness (to be discussed in the next section "The Opinion of the Many"). This proposal is already embodied in his hesitancy and slowness to answer what he thinks *sōphrosunē* is despite knowing how to speak Greek (159a6–b2). Charmides' second proposal is that *sōphrosunē* means *aidōs*, which is an ambivalent concept referring to a sense of shame or respect. We will see that this is what Charmides thinks people see in him as he defers to authority (to be discussed in the section "The Opinion of a Few about You"). It is evident also in his blushing and considering the opinion of others while initially avoiding answering whether he has *sōphrosunē* (158c5–d6).[93] His first two proposals, we will see, are based on common opinions concerning the sense in which an aristocratic youth, as he is, should demonstrate *sōphrosunē*.

The problem that arises from Charmides' focus on his external appearance in the eyes of his fellow noblemen is the neglect of his own soul. Charmides never takes the initiative to think for himself about what *sōphrosunē* is. He does not even pretend to own his third proposal, belonging as it does to Critias. This embodies his overall wish to wash his hands entirely of the conversation (159b1–2), as he thus motivates Critias to take over (to be discussed in the last section of the chapter "Thinking for Yourself").

Thus, Charmides' three proposals will be shown to be based on other people's opinions, and therefore show his failure to think for himself about

91. Καὶ ὃς τὸ μὲν πρῶτον ὤκνει τε καὶ οὐ πάνυ ἤθελεν ἀποκρίνασθαι· (159b1–2). Moore and Raymond, *Charmides*, 57 n. 66, rightly indicate a semantic similarity between the verb "hesitate" (*oknein*, 159b1) and the word *hēsuchia* which Charmides later proposes to be the meaning of *sōphrosunē*. They refer for example to Thucydides' *Histories*, 1.120.3–4, and to Spartan brevity in speaking.

92. Levine, *Profound Ignorance*, 99–100, argues similarly that Charmides is reluctant to converse, as he is "unwilling or unable to stand before the mirror of public scrutiny." McAvoy, "Carnal Knowledge in the *Charmides*," 101, also indicates that Charmides is unwilling to converse and thus eventually retreats "into other people's opinions and the silence of the observer."

93. Tsouna, "Subject of Plato's *Charmides*," 50, argues similarly that Charmides possesses quietness and shame, which he therefore later proposes as the meaning of *sōphrosunē*.

the meaning of *sōphrosunē*. Throughout their conversation Socrates attempts to motivate Charmides to think for himself about what *sōphrosunē* is, but Charmides never makes a true effort to break free from society's expectations. How does this lopsided dramatic interaction between Socrates and Charmides serve Plato in conveying his philosophical ideas concerning *sōphrosunē*? Through this interaction Plato gradually allows his reader to learn why Charmides is deficient in *sōphrosunē*, and to extract that being mentally active is essential for being *sōphrōn*.

The Opinion of the Many

Although reluctant to engage in the conversation, Charmides finally does attempt to answer what *sōphrosunē* is. His answer, however, is based on a culturally popular, aristocratic opinion concerning the way noble youth are expected to behave. Nonetheless, Socrates' ensuing inquiry is intended to encourage Charmides to think actively about the meaning behind this opinion and to examine whether it is correct (158e6–160d4). Those in the palaestra who are listening to this conversation are also expected to examine this opinion, which they probably hold as aristocrats who have time to spend in leisurely pursuits, and therefore to reevaluate whether Charmides possesses *sōphrosunē*. The conversation between Socrates and Charmides involves many peculiarities, but through their interaction Plato provides a glimpse into Charmides' soul. We learn not only that he is conventional, but that as a consequence he is also slow and unperceptive.

Socrates requests that Charmides will form an opinion about what *sōphrosunē* is, based on a feeling that *sōphrosunē* must elicit in him, if he has it (158e6–159a5). Socrates thus directs Charmides to base his answer on introspection. Charmides then answers that *sōphrosunē* seems to him to mean doing everything orderly (*kosmios*) and calmly (*hēsuchē*),[94] as walking in the roads, conversing, and other such things. In sum, he says, it is a sort of calmness (*hēsuchiotēs*). The ensuing process of Socrates' examination indicates that Charmides does not draw this proposal from his own introspection, but from common opinion rooted in the traditional aristocratic education.

Socrates turns to examine whether acting calmly is *sōphrosunē*, and conspicuously ignores other components of Charmides' answer. He ignores Charmides' claim that *sōphrosunē* means acting "orderly" (*kosmios*). This is a peculiar move by Socrates, as the concept "order" was used by writers of

94. The word *hēsuchia* may be translated variously as calmness, quietness or tranquility. In order to stress that the concept can be used to indicate a state of the soul, I will translate it as calmness.

the fifth-century BCE in association with *sōphrosunē*, and in some cases as its synonym.[95] Socrates also ignores the examples that Charmides gives, walking in the roads and conversing. Later on we will see that he strangely brings these components back to his final refutation of Charmides' answer (160c2–d4).

Socrates' inquiry, therefore, focuses on only part of Charmides' answer, the concept *hēsuchia*, calmness. Socrates explicitly emphasizes that people say (*phasi*) that those who are calm are *sōphrones* (159b7–8). We may thus suspect that Charmides' answer comes not from himself so much as from a culturally popular opinion.[96] The concept *hēsuchia* notably appears in writings of the fifth-century BCE referring to peace and quiet both in one's personal life and in the political state of a city.[97] It was also associated by the Greeks with *sōphrosunē*.[98] Traditionally it was understood as virtue of good, noble youth, who were expected to demonstrate quiet behavior and to refrain from speaking hastily.[99]

Charmides' answer would, therefore, seem to the crowd in the palaestra to indicate that he is an educated, aristocratic youth. However, Plato sets his dialogue at a time in which the concept *hēsuchia* appears in Greek usage with an additional negative sense. At the outset of the Peloponnesian War the Greeks use the concept *hēsuchia* to refer negatively to Sparta's slowness to act, because of being overly cautious and unduly inactive in its foreign relations. This is in contrast to the Spartan value of *hēsuchia* as indicating being deliberate, moderate and cautious about domestic change and foreign entanglements.

95. The concepts "order"/"orderly" (*kosmios, kosmiōs*) and *sōphrosunē* were used in some cases as synonyms according to Rademaker, *Sōphrosynē and Rhetoric*, 236–7, 257, and according to North, *Sōphrosynē*, 18, 111. It should be especially noted that a strong connection between the two concepts is made in Plato's *Gorgias*, 506–8, about which see discussions by Rademaker, 314–16, and North, 189–92.

96. Other scholars have also observed that Charmides' proposal is based on a popular opinion, e.g.: Schmid, *Plato's Charmides*, 22–23; Moore and Raymond, *Charmides*, 57; Levine, *Profound Ignorance*, 100, and n. 28 in 111–12.

97. Gocer, "*Hesuchia*," 17 n. 2.

98. According to North, *Sōphrosynē*, 15, 18, during the sixth and fifth centuries BCE *sōphrosunē* gained a class-related meaning, and it was linked to the concept *hēsuchia* which was traditionally a Dorian aristocratic value. In fact, North, 183, claims that all of Charmides' proposals are traditional Dorian and aristocratic opinions. See also Moore and Raymond, *Charmides*, 57, on the meaning of *hēsuchia*.

99. Rademaker, *Sōphrosynē and Rhetoric*, 6, 227–8, 265–6, 326–9, indicates that an educated aristocratic youth was expected to demonstrate *sōphrosunē*, which is associated with *hēsuchia*, a quiet and self-restrained behavior. Rademaker claims rightly that this explains why the young Charmides raises this concept as a proposal for what *sōphrosunē* is. Carter, *Quiet Athenian*, 57–58, also argues that the connection made between *sōphrosunē* and *hēsuchia* reflects traditional education of noble youth at the time of the setting of the dialogue *Charmides*.

In this context, a group of Athenian aristocrats who were pro-Spartan valued the same caution and avoided involvement in the Athenian democracy due to their opposition to the imperialistic policy and especially the war against Sparta.[100] We will see that Socrates' inquiry also suggests a negative sense for *hēsuchia*, which implies that Charmides acts with difficulty and slowness.

Socrates emphasizes the need to examine Charmides' proposal, despite being based on a culturally accepted opinion (159b8).[101] As he begins, at first he associates beauty with *sōphrosunē* (159c1–2), as he had done previously in his fictitious medical story (discussed above, in section "The Whole and Its Parts"). He asks whether various activities appear to be beautiful when they are conducted calmly. Socrates divides the activities into two groups, one relating to the body and the other to the soul (*kai ta peri tēn psuchēn kai ta peri to sōma*, 160b1–3). The first group includes activities with distinctive physical appearance: writing, reading, playing the cithara, wrestling, boxing, exercising in the combat sport that the Greeks called *pankration*, running and jumping (159c3–d2).

Already in his questions about the first two examples Socrates deliberately gives the concept "calmness" a negative sense of slowness:

> Which of the two, then, is more beautiful to do while being with the school teacher, to write the same letters **quickly or calmly**?
>
> Quickly.
>
> And what about reading? In a **quick or slow** way?
>
> In a quick way.[102] (159c3–7)

100. See Carter's analysis, *Quiet Athenian*, 27–51, of Thucydides' description of Sparta's cautious and inactive attitude to foreign relations (*Histories*, 1.69.4–71.1, 80.1–3). The concept *hēsuchia* is also linked to the politically charged concept *apragmosunē*, which means quietism and minding one's own business (*Histories*, 1.70.8.5). Not coincidentally, Charmides' third proposal is one that he previously heard from Critias, that *sōphrosunē* means doing your own things. As we will see, in his inquiry about this proposal Socrates uses the word *polupragmosunē*, the antonym of *apragmosunē*. This may be intended to remind the reader of a political tension at the time between aristocrats and democrats. Carter, *Quiet Athenian*, 27–51, indicates that some Athenian aristocrats were described as *apragmones*, as they did not get involved in politics due to their opposition to Athens' foreign imperialistic policy and the war with Sparta (Thucydides, *Histories*, 2.40.2, 63.2, 64.4). See discussion in the last section of this chapter, "Thinking for Yourself," and especially in nn. 132–36. See also: North, "Period of Opposition," 7; Crane, "Fear and Pursuit of Risk."

101. Carter, *Quiet Athenian*, 57–58, observes rightly that Socrates examines the literal sense of Charmides' proposal, and not its cultural sense.

102. Πότερον οὖν κάλλιστον ἐν γραμματιστοῦ τὰ ὅμοια γράμματα γράφειν ταχὺ ἢ ἡσυχῇ;
Ταχύ.

Socrates' questions present an eristic choice between opposites. As he moves from the first question about writing to the second question about reading, he replaces the word "calmly" (*hēsuchē*) with the word "slowly" (*bradeōs*). This exchange of the two words allows him to present "calmness" as merely opposite to "quickness," although in Greek "calmness" and "Slowness" overlap in meaning in some cases but differ in others. He asks whether conducting an activity quickly appears to be more beautiful than conducting it slowly and therefore calmly.[103]

Charmides agrees to the association of calmness (*hēsuchia*) with being physically slow. This may be because he considers the opinion of the aristocratic audience, who likely interprets *hēsuchia* as being cautious and therefore slow to act rather than hasty. Charmides, therefore, does not pick up on the possibility that *hēsuchia* can refer to something other than a degree of speed, that it might be a mental state, and that actions may be conducted quickly and calmly simultaneously. As the examination continues, Socrates is piling on negative associations with calm actions. He concludes that every action relating to the body (159c13–d2) is beautiful (*kalos*) when it is conducted quickly and sharply (*oxeōs*, 159d1), but ugly (*aischros*, 159d2) when conducted with difficulty (*mogis*, 159d2) and calmly. Socrates clearly uses the distinction between "beautiful" and "ugly" since Charmides and the crowd in the palaestra focus on Charmides' attractive appearance.[104] He thus motivates them to look beyond the static beauty of the body, to the dynamic beauty of actions.

Socrates then turns to examine activities of the soul: learning, teaching, recalling and remembering, being witty, perceiving, investigating, deliberating and discovering (159e1–160b6). They conclude that a mental activity conducted quickly, vigorously (*sphodra*, 159e6,10) and easily (*rasta*, 160b1) is worthy of praise, while an activity conducted slowly and therefore calmly is not (*ouch . . . epainou dokei axios einai*, 160a9-10). Once again, Charmides

---

Τί δ' ἀναγιγνώσκειν; ταχέως ἢ βραδέως;
Ταχέως (159c3–7).

103. Other scholars have observed the peculiarity in Socrates' treatment of the concept *hēsuchia* merely in the sense of slowness. E.g.: Brown, "Plato's *Charmides*," 104–19; Levine, *Profound Ignorance*, 102; Moore and Raymond, *Charmides*, 58–59.

104. The distinction made by Socrates between "beautiful" (*kalos*) and "ugly" (*aischros*) is understood and translated variously by scholars, e.g.: Moore and Raymond, *Charmides*, 11, translate the words as admirable and shameful. Gonzalez, *Dialectic and Dialogue*, 44, translates the words as good and bad. While the Greeks did use the two words also in these senses, I argue that attending to the dialogue's drama has implications even for how to translate these words. Socrates' vocabulary emphasizes the distinction between the beautiful and the ugly since the crowd in the palaestra focuses on Charmides' attractive appearance, and consequently Charmides also focuses only on his own external appearance.

does not pick up on the possibility that calmness might concern something other than a degree of speed, and that the mental actions, as physical ones, may be conducted quickly and calmly simultaneously.

Socrates' concluding refutation includes several distorted claims that do not follow logically from his examination. First, he concludes that *sōphrosunē* would not be some kind of calmness, and that the *sōphrōn* life would not be calm, as calmness is not beautiful while *sōphrosunē* is (160b7–9).[105] That a life of virtue would not be calm is an outrageous claim, yet Charmides is not alarmed. Second, although throughout the examination Socrates does not indicate the existence of beautiful, calm actions, he concludes that one of two options follow, either that calm actions are never *sōphrōn*, or that only a few of them are (160b9–c3). He thus grants the existence of a few beautiful, calm actions, but we are given to infer that *sōphrosunē* is always beautiful. Charmides does not indicate that he notices that this conclusion does not follow logically from their examination.

Socrates next brings back into the refutation those components of Charmides' proposal which he had ignored during his examination (160c6–7). He mentions the activities that Charmides originally raised, walking in the roads and talking, concluding that even in their case acting calmly should be considered as *sōphrosunē* no more than acting quickly. Socrates then also brings back the concept of order (*kosmios*). Modern editors indicate a difficulty in the syntax and suggest omitting the word *kosmios* as they supplement their argument with the claim that Socrates did not address this concept throughout his inquiry.[106] However, the omission of the word does not seem justified. In these lines (160c6–7) Socrates brings back the other components that he ignored from Charmides' answer as well, namely the examples of walking, conversing and other such things. Thus, Plato allows us to learn that Charmides is unperceptive or unwilling to call out Socrates' peculiar inquiry that ignores some components of Charmides' proposal on the one hand, but on the other hand brings them back to the final refutation. Socrates, therefore, concludes that a calm, well-ordered life would not be more *sōphrōn* than an uncalm life. He finally presents his distorted conclusion in an eristic formulation:

105. Οὐκ ἄρα ἡσυχιότης τις ἡ σωφροσύνη ἂν εἴη, οὐδ' ἡσύχιος ὁ σώφρων βίος... (160b7–9).

106. The entire manuscript tradition shows the word *kosmios* in the sentence ὁ ἡσύχιος βίος κόσμιος (160c7). Due to the resulting difficulty in the syntax, two possible corrections have been suggested: either omit the word *kosmios*, or add before it the word *kai* as done by the Coislianus. All modern editors suggest omitting the word, see for example Burnet, *OCT*, who follows Heindorf. See also Moore and Raymond, *Charmides*, 59 n. 73, and 61 n. 77, and van der Ben, *Charmides of Plato*, 27–28, who indicate in this context that Socrates does not address the concept *kosmios* during his inquiry.

quick actions are no less beautiful than calm actions (A is no less F than B is, 160d1–3). Charmides once again does not resist the peculiarities in Socrates' conclusions.

While Socrates does not examine the concept of order, the reader may wonder what kind of order Charmides associates with *sōphrosunē* and with the seemingly aimless activities that he mentions: walking to where? Talking about what? A sense of order is expected in deliberate activities with an intentional purpose. Since Socrates ignores this concept, we may speculate whether it is in fact directly related to the philosophical content that Plato intended to convey concerning the meaning of *sōphrosunē*. However, this can be appreciated only upon completion of the analysis of the whole dialogue. In the concluding chapter I will argue that the concept "order" is in fact essential for understanding what Plato wished to convey through his dialogue concerning *sōphrosunē*.

We have seen that Socrates asks Charmides to examine what *sōphrosunē* is according to a feeling that it might elicit in him, if he indeed has it. At first, Charmides is reluctant to participate in the conversation. He finally raises a proposal, but instead of being based on any introspected feeling, it is based on a culturally popular opinion that *sōphrosunē* is calmness. Socrates, nonetheless, examines Charmides' understanding of the meaning of this opinion, using various peculiar eristic and rhetorical manipulations. Socrates asks questions and employs various eristic and rhetorical techniques throughout his examination. He ignores components of Charmides' answer and returns to them in his final conclusions. He presents a choice between opposites. He exchanges between words that are seemingly merely synonyms, and thus gives the concept "calmness" a negative sense. He presents his invalid concluding refutation in the eristic form "A is no less F than B is"; and in general, Socrates presents distorted conclusions that do not follow logically from his already peculiar examination.[107]

Charmides does not call Socrates out on these manipulations, nor on his outrageous conclusion, that calm actions seem negatively slow and that therefore a virtuous life would not be calm. He allows Socrates to interpret

---

107. Tuozzo, *Plato's Charmides*, 45, claims that in the dialogue "elenchus takes a specifically educative form." Tuozzo, 44–51, expounds on his interpretation of the refutations and consequential *aporia* with which the dialogue ends up, claiming that they are intended to positively lead Socrates' interlocutors to a deeper insight into the truth. While I agree that Plato intended his reader to learn from the sequence of refutations, I disagree with Tuozzo's claim (45, 50) that Socrates succeeds in part in educating his interlocutors. I argue that the characters in the dialogue do not progress at all. They consistently exemplify their focus on, or disregard of, either beauty or wisdom or both. The readers, however, can learn where they err because of their consistent behavior and its consequences.

the concept "calmness" through a narrow focus on external appearance, that is, on whether an action appears fast or slow. Socrates and Charmides do not address the possibility that calmness may concern the state of one's soul, and therefore could influence the effectiveness of an action regardless of the speed at which it is conducted.

Plato uses this strange interaction between Socrates and Charmides to provide us a glimpse into Charmides' soul. We learn that Charmides himself is hesitant, slow and unperceptive, as he is either unable or unwilling to call out Socrates' peculiar way of inquiry and conclusions. If, as the outcome of their peculiar interaction indicates, acting slowly and with difficulty is indicative of lacking beauty, Charmides should be considered ugly,[108] and if beauty is indicative of *sōphrosunē* Charmides should be considered as deficient in *sōphrosunē*. Will Charmides do better in his next attempt?

The Opinion of a Few about You

Socrates asks Charmides to make a second attempt at answering what *sōphrosunē* is (160d5–e1). He directs him once again to base his answer on self-examination. Charmides, however, draws his proposal from the opinion of the audience about his appearance. Although Socrates' examination of this proposal is short (160d5–161b3), it provides us with another glimpse into Charmides' soul. We learn that while he concerns himself with the opinion of his fellow elitists about him, he defers to authority and does not put in the effort to form his own opinions.

Socrates asks Charmides to concentrate more than before and to look into himself (*eis seauton emblepsas*, 160d5–6). He asks him to think what kind of a person *sōphrosunē* makes him, and what sort of a thing would produce such a person (160d7–8). He also asks that Charmides say his thoughts well and courageously (*eipe eu kai andreiōs*, 160d8–e1). As in his previous attempt, however, Charmides does not follow Socrates' instructions.

At first, Charmides pauses (*epischōn*, 160e2). Since the previous examination concluded that acting calmly, slowly and with difficulty is ugly, we may speculate whether Charmides' current pause should be considered ugly. A pause could indicate that one takes a moment for thoughtful concentration, but we soon learn that Charmides does not make an effort to think for himself about Socrates' question, but uses his time to think of the opinion of others

---

108. Levine, *Profound Ignorance*, 146, argues that Charmides seems to be beautiful and ugly at the same time, as he is physically beautiful but his soul is ugly. Levine thus makes an interesting association between Charmides and the familial line of Critias, whose father is actually named Callaischrus, which literally means beautiful-ugly.

about him. Socrates relates that Charmides examined the matter by looking at himself in quite a manly way (*panu andrikōs pros heauton diaskepsamenos*, 160e2–3). This clearly stands in contrast to the instruction that was given to him. While Socrates asks him to look *inside* himself (**eis seauton** *emblepsas*, 160d5–6) Charmides looks *at* himself (**pros heauton** *diaskepsamenos*, 160e2–3). Plato thus uses wordplay to demonstrate that Charmides is unperceptive of nuances and that he continues to focus on his physical appearance.

Furthermore, Socrates asks Charmides to answer well and courageously (*eu kai andreiōs*), but Charmides' actions are described as "manly" (*andrikōs*).[109] The two adverbs, courageously and manly (*andreiōs, andrikōs*), stem from the same root, but the first is used here to refer to a virtuous behavior, acting courageously, while the second is used to describe Charmides' physical appearance, in a manly way as he looks at himself.[110] The fact that once again Charmides does not follow Socrates' instructions implies that his second attempt at answering what *sōphrosunē* is will fail to satisfy as well.

Charmides' answer is that *sōphrosunē* causes a person to be ashamed/feel shame (*aischunesthai*, 160e3), and makes a person be shameful (*aischuntēlon*, 160e4). Charmides concludes that *sōphrosunē* is *aidōs* (160e4–5). Once again he raises concepts that the Greeks associated with *sōphrosunē* in youth. The word *aischuntēlon* was used to mean shame and therefore also modesty. The word *aidōs* was used ambivalently to refer to "shame" or "respect." It was understood as an emotion that has to do with the evaluation of public opinion, arising from either concern for one's self-image or from recognition in someone else's positive status.[111] Shyness and respect were understood to imply

109. The Greeks often connected physical appearance and manliness. See, e.g., Donlan, "Origin of *Kalos kagaqos*," 370–2, on the importance of physical beauty for the heroic warrior in Homer, and on the aristocratic ideal of men's physical beauty.

110. The passage has been interpreted by scholars variously, but commonly to suggest that Charmides makes an effort to look inside himself. McCoy, "Philosophy, *Elenchus*, and Charmides," 142, claims that Charmides makes a serious attempt to answer, and courageously investigates the issue with regard to himself. Lampert, *How Philosophy Became Socratic*, 172, claims that Charmides looks inside himself and states his answer courageously. Tuckey, *Plato's Charmides*, 24–25, 93, claims that Charmides' second proposal is an advance because it focuses on "an inner state of mind," as opposed to his previous proposal that focused on "outward manifestation." Levine, *Profound Ignorance*, 150 n. 3, raises the possibility that Charmides looks merely at himself. However, he argues that Charmides looks into himself, and therefore that as opposed to the audience, he interprets his own blush in a deeper sense than the external physical appearance (117–18). While I disagree with Levine on this point, my analysis shares similarities with many other points he makes, as he too observes that Charmides' proposals are based on traditional, cultural opinions rather than on his own attempt to think for himself.

111. We would have expected Charmides to use the word shyness (*aischunē*), a noun fitting the root of the two former words that he uses (*aischunesthai, aischuntēlon*). The use

sōphrosunē in youth, in the sense of modesty, self-restraint and deference to authority, in various social circumstances.[112]

Socrates says that Charmides pauses and in a manly way looks at his physical appearance. We may suspect that Charmides considers the audience's opinion about his appearance and why he appears to them *sōphrōn*. We may infer what the audience sees in him from Socrates' earlier descriptions. When Socrates asks Charmides whether he thinks he has *sōphrosunē*, Charmides in reaction blushes. Socrates says that this makes him look even more beautiful, and that this shyness (*to aischuntēlon*) befits his age (158c5–7). Charmides' following reluctance to answer whether he has *sōphrosunē* may be interpreted by the audience as being modest since he does not arrogantly claim to possess this virtue, and at the same time as being respectful to those who think that he possesses this virtue. We may suspect, therefore, that Charmides bases his second proposal for what *sōphrosunē* is on the opinion of the audience concerning the way he, as a noble youth, looks and behaves.[113]

As Socrates turns to examine Charmides about his proposal, he begins, as in the previous examination, by associating *sōphrosunē* with beauty. He asks Charmides whether they did not just agree that *sōphrosunē* is something

---

of these words in context of *aidōs* probably allows Plato to emphasize the ambivalence of the word *aidōs*. Cf. Cairns, *Aidōs*, 104, 373. For the usage of the ambivalent concept *aidōs* by the Greeks see especially Cairns' introduction, 1–47.

112. See Cairns, *Aidōs*, 314–15, on the connection made by the Greeks between *aidōs* and *sōphrosunē* with regard to modest youth. Skinner, *Sexuality in Greek Culture*, 15, indicates that in pederastic relationships the beloved youth (*erōmenos*) was expected to develop a sense of distinction between shame and honor in preparation for his future domestic and civic life. North, *Sōphrosynē*, 183, argues that Charmides' proposal of *aidōs* is influenced by Dorian ethical tradition. Schmid's interpretation, "Socratic Moderation and Self-Knowledge," 339, is that the concept "came out of the aristocratic Dorian culture, culture with a shared code of appropriate behavior and what anthropologists call a shame ethic." Humble, "*Sōphrosynē* and the Spartans," 339, 341–3, discusses *aidōs* and *sōphrosunē* in Spartan education according to Xenophon, *Constitution of the Lacedaimonians* 3.1–5. Humble indicates that the two concepts together were part of the aim of Spartan education of youth between ages fourteen and seventeen. See also: Raymond, "*Aidōs* in Plato's *Charmides*," 34 n. 20; Moore and Raymond, *Charmides*, xxx, 61–62.

113. Levine, *Profound Ignorance*, 117, also observes that Charmides considers why others think he has *sōphrosunē*. Lampert, *How Philosophy Became Socratic*, 172, claims that Charmides' two first answers are based on conventions, and that his shame causes his outward decorum (calmness). See also Cairns, *Aidōs*, 4, 373, on the relation of *aidōs* to appearances, and on Charmides' second proposal in relation to his earlier blush and overall behavior. In contrast, Tuozzo, *Plato's Charmides*, 162, suggests that Charmides is embarrassed about the failure of his first proposal, and that this leads him to raise his second proposal that *sōphrosunē* is *aidōs*, which he understands as modesty. Moore and Raymond, *Charmides*, 62, propose a similar interpretation. Their interpretation, however, is based on a speculation, as we are not given any indication that Charmides is truly embarrassed following the failure of his proposal, as he is not blushing like earlier.

beautiful (160e6–8). Once Charmides agrees, Socrates associates *sōphrosunē* with being good as well. He asks whether *sōphrones* men are also good (160e9–10), and whether something would be good if it did not produce good people (160e11–12).[114] Charmides agrees to these questions too, and Socrates concludes that *sōphrosunē* is not only something beautiful but also good (*ou monon oun ara **kalon**, alla kai **agathon** esti*, 160e13–161a1). Charmides has no reason to reject the connection made here between "beautiful" and "good." The two words were often used by the Greeks interchangeably, and they were also used together in the compound epithet "beautiful and good" (*kalos kagathos*) that the aristocrats ascribed to themselves (discussed above, in the section "Does It All Stay in the Family").

In the inquiry about Charmides' previous proposal Socrates used the epithet "beautiful," probably because beauty is a topic that attracts the young, beautiful Charmides and those who are impressed by his physical appearance. It also served to reveal that Charmides focuses on the external appearance of actions and behaviors. If Socrates had asked Charmides now whether *aidōs* is something beautiful, Charmides would have likely approved. This is because, as we have seen, his blush and shame is considered to befit his age and to make him appear more beautiful. Socrates now attempts to make Charmides look deeper into what makes people good by referring to the other epithet that aristocrats ascribed to themselves, "good." We should infer that *sōphrosunē* does not simply refer to the static beauty of a blush resulting from the emotion *aidōs*, or to external appearance of shame and respect, but to something more deeply constitutive of a person. By the end of the section, we will see that while Socrates' examination of Charmides' first proposal implied that Charmides

---

114. The question goes as follows: Ἆρ' οὖν ἂν εἴη ἀγαθὸν ὃ μὴ ἀγαθοὺς ἀπεργάζεται; (160e11). Murphy, "More Critical Notes," 1000–1002, indicates that some scholars wrongly proposed to emend the text in various ways, in order to avoid an alleged textual problem due to the fallacies it leads to in the argumentations. He explains that from the idea that something that does not make people good means that it is not good (160e11), and from the earlier indication that those who are *sōphrones* are good (e9), one cannot conclude validly that *sōphrosunē* is something good (e13). Murphy seems to me to rightly claim that Plato probably does not intend to present a valid argument. Moore and Raymond, *Charmides*, 13 n. 44, further explain that we would have expected the question to be whether a thing would not be good if it produces good people, similarly to the phrase which appears later in 161a8–9. Raymond, "*Aidōs* in Plato's *Charmides*," 26–27, discusses this problem as well. He argues that such a correction by relocating the negation *mē* before the word *agathon* in 160e11 would not solve the problem. He claims that the final refutation of Charmides' proposal does not rely on the fallacious move in these lines (160e9–13), but on Charmides' failure to challenge an "equivocation on 'good'" (27–9), and on Charmides' attitude towards the Homeric authority (29–30). Raymond therefore attempts to provide his own dramatic and philosophical explanation for Charmides' proposal and its refutation. See more on his interpretation below, in n. 116.

is not beautiful, his examination of Charmides' second proposal implies that he is not a good person. Thus, the move from describing *sōphrosunē* as something beautiful to describing it as something good that creates good people is intended to imply that Charmides is not truly *kalos kagathos*, despite Critias' claim.[115]

Charmides' youthful shame and consequent blush make him look even more beautiful, but do they make him a good person? Socrates provides only one example for shame as something that is not good, but it suffices to refute Charmides' proposal. Let us now see why. Socrates asks whether Charmides does not believe Homer, who says that shame (*aidōs*) is not good for a man in need (161a2–4).[116] While Socrates' question focuses on one sense of *aidōs*, namely shame, the phrasing of the question about an authority figure in a leading way causes Charmides to exemplify the other sense of *aidōs*, respect for or deference to authority. Socrates deliberately asks Charmides whether he does not believe Homer in order to allow us a glimpse into his soul. Charmides' expected answer clearly shows that he cannot object to an authority as great as Homer,[117] just as earlier he could not answer whether or not he

115. Other interpretations for the reason that Socrates moves from the adjective "beautiful" to the adjective "good" were suggested, for example, by Raymond, "*Aidōs* in Plato's *Charmides*," 27–29, and Tuozzo, *Plato's Charmides,* 164.

116. The sentence goes as follows: αἰδὼς δ᾽ οὐκ ἀγαθὴ κεχρημένῳ ἀνδρὶ παρεῖναι; (161a3). The line is borrowed from Homer, *Odyssey,* 17.347. Odysseus returns to Ithaca and enters the palace disguised as a beggar and with a view to taking revenge on the suitors courting Penelope and to retaking his kingdom. Odysseus' son, the young Telemachus, recognizes him and sends Eumaeus with food to tell Odysseus to beg from the suitors, as shame is not a good thing for a man in need. Scholars have debated over the reason that Plato uses this quote. Raymond, "*Aidōs* in Plato's *Charmides*," 27–28, 38, 40–43, compares Charmides to Telemachus, as one who needs to overcome his shame and deference to authority in order to become *sōphrōn*. Tuozzo, *Plato's Charmides,* 164–65, suggests that Telemachus' advice to his father is intended to imply that he should not be ashamed to claim his own kingdom. Similarly, Charmides should conclude that he must not neglect his concern from himself as he addresses the question what *sōphrosunē* is. Tuozzo's interpretation, therefore, indicates that Charmides tends to focus on others' opinions. Moore and Raymond, *Charmides,* 64, suggest a similar interpretation. Cf. also Levine, *Profound Ignorance,* 123. Joosse, "*Sōphrosunē* and the Poets," 577–9, compares Socrates' famous "beggarly appearance" with Odysseus' beggarly disguise. See also above n. 21 on scholars' comparison between Odysseus' return to Ithaca and the description of Socrates' return to Athens at the opening of the dialogue, and below n. 153 on the connection between Socrates' quotation from Homer's *Odyssey,* and Critias' later quotation from Hesiod.

117. That Charmides cannot object to the authority of Homer without appearing to lack *sōphrosunē* is suggested by many scholars. Burger, "Socrates' Odyssean Return," 224, claims that while Socrates encourages Charmides to look into himself, he also "undercuts" this effort as he provokes Charmides' respect for the authority of Homer. See also: Raymond, "*Aidōs* in Plato's *Charmides*," 38; McCoy, "Philosophy, *Elenchus*, and Charmides," 144–6; Levine, *Profound Ignorance,* 120–127.

possesses *sōphrosunē* lest he would annoy some people or imply that others are liars.[118]

Although Charmides does not reject the claim ascribed to Homer that shame is not good sometimes, he also does not take back his own proposal that shame is something good. This is probably because his proposal is based on the audience's opinion about him and about the way youth are expected to behave. Charmides finds himself stuck between two authorities, that of Homer and that of the adult audience. He thus agrees that shame is both good and not good (161a6–7). It should be noted that the audience might still think that Charmides' answers demonstrate modesty and respect (*aischuntēlon*, *aidōs*) for authority as expected of youth, and that he therefore possesses *sōphrosunē*. However, Charmides' deference to authority does not allow him to form and express his own opinions. At the beginning of this examination Socrates instructs him to answer courageously (160d8–e1), but it seems that Charmides fears objecting to authority, probably because he is concerned for his reputation. A fear of bad reputation seems to have been one ancient interpretation for *aidōs*.[119] Plato thus deliberately makes the reader think of the role of education. Charmides, as an aristocratic youth, is expected to be obedient, but this does not prepare him for adulthood and the political life, where he would need to have already learned how to think for himself.[120]

Charmides' proposal fails to satisfy. This is because he continues to focus on other people's opinions, as he is concerned for his public appearance. Socrates encourages him to examine critically the opinions of others, but Charmides consistently avoids objecting to authority. He fails to examine critically both the audience's opinion and the opinion that Socrates ascribes to Homer. He thus allows Socrates to lead him into the conclusion that shame is no more good than bad (161a11–b2). His eristic formulation "A is no more F than it is G," is slightly different than his formulation in the previous examination "A is no less F than B is" (quick actions are no less beautiful than calm ones, 160d1–3).

118. See my discussion below in the section "An Unengaged Beauty." The reluctance of the historical Charmides to speak openly seems to be indicated also in Xenophon's *Memorabilia* 3.7, where he is described as one who shrinks from speaking in the assembly and participating in politics. This is observed also by Carter, *Quiet Athenian*, 58–59.

119. See Moore and Raymond, *Charmides*, 61–62, 62 n. 79, who refer to Plato's *Euthyphro*, 12c1, and Aristotle's *Nicomachean Ethics* 4.9, 1128b11–12, where *aidōs* is interpreted as a fear of bad reputation.

120. Levine, *Profound Ignorance*, 122–7, seems to indicate rightly that Plato may be alluding here to the charge against Socrates in corrupting the youth, as his inquiry requires Charmides to challenge traditional opinions and education.

Socrates' questions suggest that *sōphrosunē* does not simply cause people to look physically beautiful, but is something good that causes people to be good rather than bad (161a8–10). While Charmides' blush and shame seem beautiful to the audience, this does not imply that he is a good person. His calmness was associated with the ugly in the previous examination. Now in addition, his shame is associated with being bad. As opposed to Critias' earlier praise that Charmides is "beautiful and good" (*kalos kagathos*, 154e3),[121] the crowd should conclude that Charmides is ugly and bad, that is, neither beautiful nor good. Is there still any hope that Charmides will improve?

Thinking for Yourself

Charmides takes the initiative for the first time, but only to raise a proposal which he had heard previously from Critias. Nonetheless, Socrates encourages him to examine this third proposal (161b4–162b8), and thereby allows us to have another glimpse into Charmides' soul. Charmides does not make an effort to think for himself.[122] Eventually he renounces his hold of the conversation by manipulating Critias, the owner of this third proposal, to take over.

Charmides suggests that Socrates will examine an opinion that he previously heard from someone, that *sōphrosunē* means "to do your own things" (*to ta heautou prattein*, 161b3–7).[123] Socrates says "You rogue, you heard this from Critias here, or from one of the other wise men" (161b8–c1).[124] Proving that he is an active listener, Critias immediately denies that Charmides heard it from him (161c2). We will later see that, once again, he lies (162c4–6).[125]

121. Tuozzo, *Plato's Charmides,* 164, argues similarly on this point that Socrates' questions in the first and second examinations seem to indicate a connection between *sōphrosunē* and being *kalos kagathos.*

122. That Charmides does not think for himself is indicated also by Schmid, *Plato's Charmides,* 77, and Levine, *Profound Ignorance,* 117–18. See also Lampert, *How Philosophy Became Socratic,* 176.

123. The phrase τὸ τὰ ἑαυτοῦ πράττειν (161b6) may be roughly translated variously, e.g.: Moore and Raymond, *Charmides,* 65, "doing one's own things"; Tsouna, "Socrates' Attack on Intellectualism," 67, "doing one's own business."

124. Καὶ ἐγώ, Ὦ μιαρέ, ἔφην, Κριτίου τοῦδε ἀκήκοας αὐτὸ ἢ ἄλλου του τῶν σοφῶν (161b8–c1).

125. Many scholars observe that Critias lies, e.g.: Levine, *Profound Ignorance,* 130–31; Moore and Raymond, *Charmides,* 66. However, they disagree about the source of the phrase "to do your own things." For example, Levine, *Profound Ignorance,* 130–31, 171, speculates that Critias had heard this proposal from Socrates in one of their past philosophical conversations, but misunderstood its meaning. He therefore sees the dialogue as part of the defense against the charge that Socrates corrupted the youth. Burger, "Socrates' Odyssean Return," 225–6, also argues that this was originally a Socratic formula, which

Charmides then asks why it matters from whom he heard this answer. Socrates agrees that they should examine not whose answer this is, but whether it is true (161c3–6). As we have seen in the previous sections, Socrates encourages Charmides to make a mental effort in examining the proposals that he raises, regardless of from whom he heard them. Now, however, Socrates provocatively doubts that they could find out whether "to do your own things" is *sōphrosunē*, because this phrase seems to him unclear as a riddle (161c8–d2). Describing this proposal as a riddle serves two purposes: (1) encouraging Charmides to attempt at interpreting it; and (2) motivating the owner of this answer, Critias, to join in the conversation and defend his proposal.

Socrates begins his examination about the meaning of the phrase "to do your own things" with an example concerning a teacher and his students. He then turns to ask about various activities of other arts and crafts. Finally, he asks about the well-managed *polis* and the role of the various works of the artisans in it. While the phrase "to do your own things" may be interpreted variously depending on its context,[126] we will see that Socrates' investigation is open to two possible interpretations; (1) doing things for yourself, that is, directing your activities only towards yourself, and (2) doing things by your-self, on your own, that is, allowing the possibility of directing your activities

---

appears in Plato's *Republic*, 4.434c, 441d, and suggests that each class of the city and each part of one's soul ought to do its own things/function. On the appearance of the formula in the *Republic* see also below nn 126-27, 131, 233. Tuckey, *Plato's Charmides*, 20, also ascribes this proposal to Socrates. See also discussion by Luz, "Knowledge of Knowledge." Lampert, *How Philosophy Became Socratic*, 178, argues that Critias heard from Socrates all the proposals that he raises. On the other hand, Moore and Raymond, *Charmides*, 67–68, 67 n. 101, propose various reasons to reject this interpretation. I agree with their observation that in the following lines Socrates clearly attributes the proposal to Critias, or one of the other men considered wise (161b8–c1, 162c4–6). However, Moore and Raymond, 66 and notes 94–95, take a further step and suggest that Critias is the originator of this answer. On this possibility see more in the next chapter, section "The Producers and the Recipients of Goods." North, *Sōphrosynē*, 183 n. 11, and 214, associates the phrase "to do your own things" with an older source since it is mentioned in Plato's *Timaeus*, 72a, together with the maxim *gnōthi seauton* (know yourself). In this context, she refers to Raubitschek, *Ein neues Pittakion*, 170–172, who traces the phrase to Pittacus of Mytilene, one of the seven sages (ca. 640–568 BCE). Raubitschek argues that Pittacus used this phrase in relation to the meaning of modesty, asserting that one should not strive for something beyond what one is entitled to. Raubitschek further claims that later on Critias and then Plato expanded the phrase's interpretation. On the appearance of the phrase "to do your own things" in other dialogues see below n. 126.

126. See for example discussion by Levine, *Profound Ignorance*, 132–3, and 154 notes 41–44. Levine indicates that this proposal appears in Plato's *Republic* in the context of the virtue of justice, and suggests it appears in Plato's *Laches* in the context of the virtue cour-age. See also North, *Sōphrosynē*, 183 n. 11, and 214, who indicates that in Plato's *Timaeus*, 72a, the phrase is associated once again with *sōphrosunē*.

also towards benefiting others.[127] Socrates thus moves from the interests of the individual to those of the community.[128]

Socrates clearly begins with an example that Charmides as a youth could relate to, about a teacher and his pupils:

> Does it seem to you then, that the teacher writes and reads only his own name or does he teach you, the children, yours, or did you not write the names of the enemies no less than your own and your friends' names? (161d6–9)[129]

Socrates' lengthy question includes two parts, each presenting an eristic choice between two options, A and A+B. With each added option, Socrates gradually demonstrates that the teacher supposedly does not do only his own things, because he teaches much more than merely his own name. In the first part of the question Socrates gives a choice between teaching how to write and read (A) only his own name as opposed to teaching (A) his own and (B) the children's names (thus the choice between A and A+B). In the second part of the question two further options are presented, (C) the names of the enemies and (D) the names of your friends.

Socrates directs his question to a teenager, and therefore focuses on school activities which are familiar to him. However, Socrates' question already implies that even the most basic activities, as using proper names of people, have a social role.[130] Furthermore, although the question involves a basic activity, in structure it is more complex than those questions that Socrates presented in the previous two examinations. There he gave a choice between only two options, A or B. Clearly, Socrates raises the level of his sophistication as a precursor to the transition of the conversation to Critias, who is older and more experienced in philosophical conversations.

Socrates' question stresses a tension in doing things relating to others by referring to the distinction that the Greeks made between their own home and

127. These two interpretations also appear in the *Republic*, but in the context of a discussion about justice (2.370a, 4.433a). See e.g.: Donovan, "Do It Youselfer"; Tuckey, *Plato's Charmides*, 21.

128. Levine, *Profound Ignorance*, 132–8, in his fascinating, original discussion also observes two possible interpretations, one is of self-sufficiency that leads to selfishness, and the other is the communal good.

129. Δοκεῖ οὖν σοι τὸ αὑτοῦ ὄνομα μόνον γράφειν ὁ γραμματιστὴς καὶ ἀναγιγνώσκειν ἢ ὑμᾶς τοὺς παῖδας διδάσκειν, ἢ οὐδὲν ἧττον τὰ τῶν ἐχθρῶν ἐγράφετε ἢ τὰ ὑμέτερα καὶ τὰ τῶν φίλων ὀνόματα; (161d6–9).

130. Tuozzo, *Plato's Charmides,* 168, rightly indicates the absurdity in the example of reading and writing only one's name. As he puts it, "these activities involve, in their most central uses, interaction with others." Levine, *Profound Ignorance*, 134, also indicates the communal purpose of using names.

friends on the one hand, and on the other hand enemies and strangers. In this way Socrates encourages Charmides to examine one possible interpretation for the proposal "to do your own things," that is, not to meddle with others' affairs. In the following lines he asks more specifically whether by writing and reading the names of others Charmides and the other children meddled with other people's affairs (*polupragmoneuein*) and therefore were not *sōphrones* (161d11–e2).[131] Charmides answers negatively, and thus approves that meddling with others' affairs (*polupragmoneuein*, the noun is *polupragmosunē*) is opposed to being *sōphrōn*.

The eristic contrast between meddling with others' affairs and being *sōphrōn* alludes to a political tension that existed between a section of Athenian aristocrats and the democrats at the outset of the Peloponnesian War, the time of the setting of the dialogue *Charmides*. The aristocrats were discontented with the democracy, clinging to the aristocratic, traditional view that the masses are unqualified for engaging in politics.[132] They were opposed to the Athenian imperialistic policy and to the war with Sparta, which clearly seemed aggressively interventionist and meddling in other cities' affairs (Thucydides, *Histories*, 1.70.1–71.1). In reaction, some aristocrats either withdrew from participating in politics, or strove to change the foreign policy to a quiet and non-interventionist one (*apragmosunē*), similar to that of Sparta.[133] In response, the democrats criticized quiet and disengaged attitudes (Thucydides, *Histories*, 2.40.2, 2.63.2, 64.4).[134] The word *apragmosunē* was

131. In the *Republic* 4.433a, "to do your own things" and meddling with others' affairs are discussed in context of the virtue justice. See Donovan, "Do It Yourselfer," 3.

132. Adkins, "*Polu pragmosyne*," 324–27, suggests that as the aristocrats lost their political superiority under the democracy, they began using terms such as *polupragmosunē* as gibes in order to restrain and deter the masses from engaging in politics. In this context, the word *polupragmosunē* was used to indicate that the lower classes are unqualified to engage in politics and therefore to involve themselves in other's affairs. See also next n. 133.

133. Other scholars have also observed that Plato invokes here the aristocratic tendency for political noninvolvement and quiet inactivity (*apragmosunē*), e.g.: Wolfsdorf, "Hesiod, Prodicus, and the Socratics," 2–3; Moore and Raymond, *Charmides*, 39 n. 6, and 67; North, *Sōphrosynē*, 113; Rademaker, *Sōphrosynē and Rhetoric*, 330. On the various uses of the two contrasting Greek words, *apragmosunē* and *polupragmosunē*, see: Ehrenberg, "*Polypragmosyne*," 46–47; Buis, "Apragmosyne," 68–69, and "*Polypragmosyne*," 741–2; Adkins, "*Polu pragmosyne*," who discusses *polupragmosunē*, *apragmosunē*, and the phrase "to do your own things," as it appears in Plato's dialogues; Donlan, *Aristocratic Ideal*, 87–95, 122, 136, 143, on the move from a perception of military *aretē* to quietism. See also discussion below n. 136.

134. Carter, *Quiet Athenian*, 27–47, 49, argues that Thucydides, *Histories*, has Pericles negatively describe as *apragmones* two Athenian groups. In his funeral speech he describes those who avoided participating in politics altogether (2.40.2). In his third and last speech intended to defend himself and his policy and to encourage the Athenians to

also used together with, or as a synonym for, the words *hēsuchia* (quitesim, calmness) and *sōphrosunē*, to describe Spartan qualities. However, as we have seen previously (in section "The Opinion of the Many"), these Spartan qualities were also criticized as they were interpreted as slowness to act in times of need at the outset of the Peloponnesian War (Thucydides, *Histories*, 1.69.4, 70.8, 71.1, 1.80.1–3).[135]

As we have seen, in his first two attempts at answering what *sōphrosunē* is Charmides suggests that it is *hēsuchia* and *aidōs*. This is because as a youth Charmides was expected to behave calmly, quietly, and to defer to authority in various social circumstances. Plato's reference to the issue of "meddling in others' affairs" is intended to remind his reader that aristocratic adults also exemplified some kind of quietism, but in the civic and political sphere.[136] However, Socrates' question about basic activities of the teacher and youth in school, the reading and writing proper names, indicate that doing things which relate to other people does not in itself imply meddling with others'

---

continue with the war, Pericles refers to another group, a section of aristocrats who advocated giving up the empire and changing the foreign policy to a quiet and non-aggressive one (2.63.2, 64.4).

135. Carter, *Quiet Athenian*, 27–47, 49, explicates the descriptions in Thucydides' *Histories* of Spartan *hēsuchia* and *apragmosunē* in foreign relations as slowness (see also above n. 100), and which is associated with *sōphrosunē* (1.80.1–3). This stands in contrast to the Athenian daring and aggressive attitude (1.69.4, 70.8, 71.1). North, *Sōphrosynē*, 120–22, and "Period of Opposition," 7, indicates that *apragmosunē* and *hēsuchia* were distinctive Spartan and oligarchic characteristics that were associated with *sōphrosunē*. See also Gomme, *Historical Commentary on Thucydides*, 1.32.4, 1.84.1. Donlan, *Aristocratic Ideal*, mentions the Athenian aristocrats' negative view of *polupragmosunē* and their preference for *apragmosunē*, withdrawal from politics into a quiet life. Rademaker, *Sōphrosynē and Rhetoric*, 201–21, discusses the criticism of Spartan *sōphrosunē* as a cautious policy and avoidance of risks which resulted in slowness to act when necessary. Rademaker, 225–33, also discusses the descriptions in Aristophanes' comedies of the *sōphrosunē* of some citizens as *apragmosunē*, noninvolvement in politics and lawsuits. Adkins, "*Polu pragmosyne*," 311–20, discusses the aristocratic criticism of the democrats and Athens' foreign policy as exemplifying *polupragmosunē*, and their negative view on *polupragmosunē* in internal and external relations. See also previous nn 132, 133.

136. Carter, *Quiet Athenian*, 47–50, 58–59, argues that Critias represents an adult member of a section of pro-Spartan aristocrats that advocated *apragmosunē* and that this is why in the dialogue Critias proposes synonyms of *apragmosunē* as the meaning of *sōphrosunē*. Carter also understands in this context the description in Xenophon's *Memorabilia* 3.7, of Charmides as a young, competent man who shrinks from public speaking and participating in politics. North, *Sōphrosynē*, 113, 115–16, 120, 183, claims similarly to Carter, that the proposal "to do your own things" is equivalent to the Dorian, Spartan oligarchic excellence *apragmosunē* and which is contrasted to *polupragmosunē*. Rademaker, *Sōphrosynē and Rhetoric*, 228, argues that quietness and shame are characteristics of *sōphrosunē* in boys, while avoiding others' affairs is of adults.

affairs. He gradually implies that Charmides' focus on others' opinions is, and this prevents him from thinking for himself.[137]

Furthermore, we may observe that the formulation of the second part of the question about the teacher (161d8–9) is similar to the concluding eristic refutations that Socrates employed in his examinations of Charmides' two previous proposals. As we have seen, in the first examination he concludes that "A is no less F than B is" (quick actions are no less beautiful than calm ones, 160d1–3). In the second examination he concludes that "A is no more F than it is G" (shame is not more good than bad, 161a11–b2). Now, in his examination of Charmides' third proposal, Socrates uses a similar eristic formulation, but he does so already as part of his first complex question. He introduces the formulation "doing C no less than doing A+B+D" (writing the names of enemies no less than the names of the teacher, the children and their friends, and thus doing A+B+C+D). Socrates thus does not conclude a final refutation. In this way he attempts to encourage the owner of the answer, Critias, to join in the conversation in order to provide his own interpretation for this so-called riddling answer.

Socrates next examines the phrase "to do your own things" with regard to further arts and crafts.[138] He thus addresses the role of the activities of the artisans in the *polis*. He asks whether a *polis* would be well-managed if each person would make and do (*ergazesthai te kai prattein*) everything for himself including weaving, washing, cutting shoe leather, and creating the oil-flask and strigil (161e10–162a2). This question implies not only that making and doing everything for yourself by yourself is unreasonable, but also that each *technē* is used for the benefit of others rather than merely of yourself. Charmides agrees that managing a city with *sōphrosunē* would imply managing it well, and therefore that doing everything for yourself and by yourself would not be an act of *sōphrosunē* (162a2–9).

It should be noted that previously Socrates had asked Charmides twice whether "to write" and "to read" mean doing something (161d3–4, e3–5). Now he asks whether performing activities of various arts and crafts (*technai*) such as healing, building and weaving mean doing something (161e7–9).

---

137. That this was a tendency of the historical Charmides is indicated also by Socrates' address to Charmides in Xenophon's *Memorabilia* 3.7.9. Socrates warns Charmides to beware not to make the mistake many do, neglecting examining themselves while focusing on others' affairs. See also discussion by Tuozzo, *Plato's Charmides*, 88.

138. Carter, *Quiet Athenian*, 58–59, claims that Socrates deliberately "chooses to misunderstand the sense of this definition." In the next chapter I will argue that Socrates interprets the proposal "to do your own things" in context of arts conducted by artisans because by this proposal Critias expresses his aristocratic aversion to practices associated with the lower classes.

These questions may seem peculiar, but they encourage Charmides to think about what the verb "do" designates in the phrase "to do your own things." Socrates' two main questions, about the teacher and the pupils and about the well-managed *polis*, utilize an already existing ambiguity in the phrase "to do your own things." Do the pupils do their own things while reading and writing their own and others' names? On the one hand, the answer seems to be yes, because the activity of writing and reading is their own. On the other hand, what they are writing and reading about is something beyond their own selves. Thus, one sense of "to do your own things" is doing activities on your own. The second sense of "to do your own things" is that your own activities are being directed only towards yourself. The same implicit distinction is present in the example of a well-managed *polis*. The activities of each craftsman are by definition his own activities, but these activities provide goods or services for others as well.

The reader should conclude that while the craftsman does his own mental and physical activities, thereby benefiting others, Charmides, who does not think for himself, does not make any mental effort of his own and therefore does not benefit others. Charmides may receive goods and services made by various craftsmen, or may even manipulate people by means of his beauty and status into giving him what he wants. However, no one can think, search, examine and understand for him. He must be independent and mentally active in his soul in order to learn what *sōphrosunē* is and to acquire it, as well as in order to contribute to a well-managed *polis*. Moreover, we may ponder whether Charmides' consistent focus on others' opinions about him should be considered meddling with others' affairs rather than doing his own things.

We now come to the finale of Socrates' conversation with Charmides, which leads Critias to take over. Socrates ends his examination of Charmides' soul without a conclusive refutation of the proposal "to do your own things." Instead, he provokes Critias, its owner, into taking hold of the conversation. He says that the person who suggested that it is the meaning of *sōphrosunē* spoke as in a riddle (162a10–11), and he asks whether Charmides heard this answer from someone simple or foolish. Charmides answers that on the contrary, he heard it from someone who seems quite wise (162b1–3). It is thus confirmed that Critias is considered by others to be wise. Socrates says once again that this proposal seems to him enigmatic (*ainigma*), and that it is difficult (*chalepon*) to know what it means (162b4–6).

Charmides also plays a role in motivating Critias to take over the conversation. When Socrates asks him directly whether he can tell what "to do your own things" means, Charmides answers that he does not know what it is. He adds that nothing prevents that even its owner does not know what he himself meant (162b8–10). We are told that "at the same time he said this he smiled and looked towards Critias" (162b10–11).[139] By looking at Critias, Charmides clearly gives away the truth, that Critias is indeed the owner of this proposal. A few lines later, Socrates explicitly tells his silent listener "it seemed to me that what I suspected was more than anything true, that Charmides heard from Critias this answer about *sōphrosunē*" (162c4–6).[140] Charmides also shows disrespect towards his guardian by mocking him that he might not know the meaning of his own proposal. We should therefore wonder whether Charmides' initial consideration of the crowd's opinion (158c5–d6), and his later reluctance to challenge Homer's authority (161a2–4), are a result of genuine demonstration of respect (*aidōs*) towards them.[141]

Charmides admits his ignorance concerning the meaning of "to do your own things," though he does not yet admit his ignorance concerning the meaning of *sōphrosunē*.[142] Socrates finally reveals that "Charmides. . .not wanting to hold the conversation but that the person of the answer would, motivated him, and indicated that he himself had already been examined" (162c6–d1).[143] We now see that Charmides' third and final proposal is intended to bring an end for his part in the conversation. He raises a proposal that he previously heard from Critias in order to motivate him into taking over the conversation. He thus completely abstains from thinking for himself and expressing his own opinions in public. Ironically, the last proposal he raises is "to do your own things," which may be interpreted as implying, at least in part, thinking for yourself. We may finally gather that at the opening of the dialogue Critias manipulates Charmides into joining the conversation with the false assertion that Socrates is a doctor for his headache, because he knows that Charmides would otherwise not want to participate in it.[144]

Socrates examines Charmides about the three proposals that he raises, and thereby undresses his soul. We learn in various ways that Charmides

---

139. Οὐκ οἶδα μὰ Δία ἔγωγε, ἦ δ' ὅς· ἀλλ' ἴσως οὐδὲν κωλύει μηδὲ τὸν λέγοντα μηδὲν εἰδέναι ὅτι ἐνόει. Καὶ ἅμα ταῦτα λέγων ὑπεγέλα τε καὶ εἰς τὸν Κριτίαν ἀπέβλεπεν (162b9–11).

140. δοκεῖ γάρ μοι παντὸς μᾶλλον ἀληθὲς εἶναι, ὃ ἐγὼ ὑπέλαβον, τοῦ Κριτίου ἀκηκοέναι τὸν Χαρμίδην ταύτην τὴν ἀπόκρισιν περὶ τῆς σωφροσύνης (162c4–6).

141. This point is also observed by Levine, *Profound Ignorance*, 139–40.

142. Levine, *Profound Ignorance*, 140, also points to this, although his final analysis slightly differs from mine. Worth quoting is Levine's accurate claim that "Charmides' admission of ignorance is no true knowledge of ignorance."

143. ὁ μὲν οὖν Χαρμίδης βουλόμενος μὴ αὐτὸς ὑπέχειν λόγον ἀλλ' ἐκεῖνον τῆς ἀποκρίσεως, ὑπεκίνει αὐτὸν ἐκεῖνον, καὶ ἐνεδείκνυτο ὡς ἐξεληλεγμένος εἴη· (162c6–d1).

144. Levine, *Profound Ignorance*, 161, concludes differently that Critias' praises of Charmides were "misconceived and excessive."

focuses on the opinion of his fellow aristocrats concerning his external appearance and reputation. Consequently he neglects his soul as he avoids thinking for himself. Charmides might appear to the audience as a *sōphrōn* youth, because he exemplifies quietism and deference to authority as was expected of an educated youth. However, Socrates' examination of Charmides' first proposal implies that Charmides' slowness is ugly. Socrates' examination of his second proposal implies that his shame makes him a bad person because his deference to authority does not allow him to independently formulate and express his own opinion. The third and final examination implies that Charmides does not do his own things as he refrains from thinking for himself. His focus on others' opinions may be perceived as meddling with others' affairs, and his disrespect to Critias' authority, his guardian, is revealed. Clearly, Charmides is not as *sōphrōn* and *kalos kagathos* as Critias described him.

Througout the conversation Socrates encourages Charmides to take into account both the internal and the external aspects of human conduct, but Charmides focuses on the opinion of the audience about his external appearance and as a result neglects his own soul. To conclude, this lopsided dramatic interaction between Socrates and Charmides serves Plato in conveying that being mentally active is an essential aspect of being *sōphrōn*.

3

Being Outwardly Active

Then, I said, we are no longer abiding by the claim that the person who lives knowledgeably/understandingly is happy. Because those who live knowledgeably/understandingly are not agreed by you to be happy, yet you seem to me to define the happy person as living knowledgeably/understandingly about some things.

—Plato, *Charmides*, 173E6–10

Then how will *sōphrosunē* be beneficial, if it is an artisan (*dēmiourgos*) of no benefit?

It seems, Socrates, that it will never be.

—Plato, *Charmides*, 175A6–8

An Unproductive Babbler

Socrates' initial suggestion is to undress Charmides' soul (154e5–6), but in the middle of the dialogue, he turns to examine Charmides' guardian, Critias. The seemingly unplanned conversation with Critias spans almost half the dialogue (162c1–176d5)—twice as long as the conversation with Charmides. This section is not only longer, but also requires from the reader more concentration, since Critias turns out to be a tougher nut to crack.

Plato, we will see, presents Critias as a foil to Charmides. In the previous section we learned that Charmides is an aristocratic youth who focuses on his external appearance in the eyes of the audience, but neglects his soul. Socrates' conversation with him conveys that being mentally active is essential for being *sōphrōn*. In this chapter, we will learn that Critias, in contrast, is an aristocratic adult who focuses on his intellectual, mental activity, but devalues practices that he associates with the lower class. Socrates' conversation with Critias, we will see, conveys that, along with mental activeness, outward practices are an essential aspect of being *sōphrōn*.

Critias' care for the literary field gradually becomes evident. When Charmides seeks for a way out of the conversation, he easily manipulates Critias to take over by raising a proposal that he previously heard from him, "to do your own things." Charmides is unable to explain the meaning of the proposal, and says to Socrates that even its owner probably does not know what he meant (162b9–10). Charmides thus succeeds in provoking Critias into taking hold of the conversation. Critias gets "angry at him as a poet on an actor who presented his works badly" (162d2–3).[145] The description of Critias as a poet implies that he has a tendency for the literary, and that he is either the originator of this proposal or at least the originator of a novel interpretation of it.[146]

We are gradually led to believe that Critias' literary competence has a wide reputation. Critias angrily tells Charmides that the fact that he does not know the meaning of the proposal does not entail that its owner does not know it either (162d4–6). His anger very likely indicates that he cares for his reputation. Socrates explicitly says that Critias could barely hold himself back as he was waiting for the opportunity to compete with Charmides, and to receive respect from him and the others at present (162c1–4), we are to understand, by proving his better literary skills. Later on, Socrates also indicates that Critias hides a puzzlement he experiences because he is a man who usually is held in high esteem (*eudokimōn hekastote*, 169c6–7).[147] Thus, a connection is made here between Critias' literary competence and his care for his reputation.

Socrates then encourages Critias to take hold of the conversation by boosting his confidence in his literary competence. He says that it is no

145. ὁ δ' οὐκ ἠνέσχετο, ἀλλά μοι ἔδοξεν ὀργισθῆναι αὐτῷ ὥσπερ ποιητὴς ὑποκριτῇ κακῶς διατιθέντι τὰ ἑαυτοῦ ποιήματα (162d2–3).

146. See above discussions in nn. 31, 32, and 125.

147. Burger, "Socrates' Odyssean Return," 225, claims that Critias' anger shows that he loses self-control due to his frustrated ambition to excel in the eyes of the crowd.

wonder that Charmides does not know the meaning of this proposal because of his age, but that it is appropriate that Critias would know it because he is older and cares for this subject (162d7–e2). Socrates then explicitly asks whether Critias agrees to take over the conversation and to defend his definition of *sōphrosunē* (162e2–6). Critias who was waiting for the opportunity (162c1–4) agrees, and Socrates' examination of his soul begins. Their ensuing conversation, however, shows that Critias' literary skills are limited. He does not know more than his ward Charmides does about what *sōphrosunē* is, and as Charmides, though for different reasons, he is unable to learn what it is.

The conversation with Critias is complex and branched because of two related reasons. First, Critias' literary acrobatics obscure his view that *sōphrosunē* concerns social class differences, and that the proper social role of the lower class is to work for the upper class. It thus takes Socrates a lengthy examination to unmask Critias' exploitative intentions. Second, Critias' arguments suggest distinctions between words, but these distinctions are merely stipulative and sophistic. He fails to make practical distinctions between words and between phrases when it is necessary. Socrates introduces into the conversation different words relating to the mental activity and uses them to create distorted formulations for Critias' proposal. Critias uses these words and phrases indiscriminately to support his view of social hierarchy. Consequently, the conversation becomes branched with inconsistent variations of Critias' proposal for what *sōphrosunē* is.

This has led scholars to disagree concerning the number of proposals that Critias raises for what *sōphrosunē* is, and concerning what these proposals are.[148] My analysis, however, focuses on understanding Socrates' examination

---

148. While scholars agree that Charmides raises three proposals for what *sōphrosunē* is, they disagree over the number and content of the proposals raised by Critias. See for example discussion by Schmid, *Plato's Charmides*, 153–58, on the structure of the dialogue "depending on what are taken to be the definitions in the dialogue" (154). Schmid, 40, suggests that the conversation with Critias includes three steps that ascend to the ideal definition "the knowledge of what one knows and what one does not know" (167a7), and three steps that descend in criticizing it. Tsouna, "Subject of Plato's *Charmides*," 51 n. 47, indicates that her numbering of the proposed definitions differs from Schmid's. Tuckey, *Plato's Charmides*, 21–27, suggests that Critias defends four proposals, while the discussion over the third one results in several variations. Rutherford, *Art of Plato*, 90, claims that Critias proposes six definitions, as does Notomi "Origin of Plato's Political Philosophy," 246. Halper, "Is Knowledge of Knowledge Possible," 309, argues that Critias' final definition is "knowledge of itself and of other kinds of knowledge," while other scholars, as Tuckey for example, argue that his final proposal is "knowledge of good and bad." The disagreements among scholars also concern Socrates' recapitulation of Critias' first argument (163d1–3), which some scholars consider as a distinct definition for *sōphrosunē*, see below n. 161. I will argue that this variation is raised merely as part of Socrates' examination of Critias' soul. Tuozzo, *Plato's Charmides*, 190–91, offers his own understanding of the

of Critias' soul.[149] I divide the conversation into six examinations, with each examination allowing the reader a glimpse into Critias' soul. In three examinations Socrates asks Critias what *sōphrosunē* is. Critias' answers reveal that he is more capable verbally than Charmides. However, in assuming that productive practices are characteristic of just one class, Critias is blind to the centrality of productive practices in all human experience, including in his own language. He fails to take into account the two aspects, the internal and the external of human conduct, together. In the middle of the conversation, Critias experiences an embarrassing *aporia* which he attempts to hide. Following this *aporia*, Socrates conducts three additional examinations of Critias' soul. In order that the discussion will progress, he agrees to assume that Critias' proposals are possible, and he examines Critias about the benefit that *sōphrosunē* produces. Socrates' conversation with Critias does not end with an aporia, but with the much worse result that *sōphrosunē* would not produce any benefit. Thus, Critias is unable to save his contorted aristocratic world-view of social hierarchy.

Socrates' inquiry provides us glimpses into Critias' soul. We learn about his many flaws, but we will see that his major failing is his inability to discern the morally good.[150] My analysis will attempt to explain how the dramatic interaction between Socrates and the unproductive babbler Critias serves Plato

structure of Socrates' conversation with Critias. With regard to the inquiry about Critias' proposal that *sōphrosunē* is self-knowledge, Tuozzo distinguishes the Critian formulation as "knowledge of itself and of other knowledges" from the Socratic formulation as knowing what a person knows and what he does not know.

149. Levine, *Profound Ignorance*, also does not seem to occupy himself with numbering the proposals raised by Critias.

150. Only a few scholars suggest that Critias' character in the dialogue is not completely negative. Tuozzo, *Plato's Charmides*, 6, 53–66, argues that Plato's presentation of Critias should be distinguished from the biased tradition supported by Xenophon that Critias was simply a cruel tyrant. Tuozzo indicates that another tradition existed, which saw good aspects in Critias. This is reflected for example in a scholium to Aeschines that mentions a memorial inscription set after Critias' death (Diels and Kranz, *Die Fragmente der Vorsokratiker*, 88A13). Tuozzo, "What's Wrong with These Cities," 324, claims that although Critias has many negative characteristics including ignorance, he has "intellectual gifts." See also Tuozzo, "Greetings from Apollo." Tsouna, "Socrates' Attack on Intellectualism," 66, argues that in the dialogue Critias is presented with both positive and negative characteristics. Tsouna, 75–77, argues that "Critias' intellectualism goes wrong" and becomes an object of refutation. She also indicates, 68–69, that Critias clearly lacks the virtue *sōphrosunē*, and despite his intelectualism "his soul is diseased" and needs Socrates' Thracian charm. While I agree with her observation that Critias focuses on the intellect, I believe that the analysis of the conversation with him requires more attention to the dramatic aspects of the dialogue, which consequently indicates that Critias is not a positive character, although his intellectualism appears to be attractive in the eyes of the crowd who listens to him in the palaestra.

in conveying his philosophical ideas concerning *sōphrosunē*. We will see that Plato intends to convey that along with mental activeness, outward practices are an essential aspect of being *sōphrōn*, and therefore for living the moral life.

The Producers and the Recipients of Goods

Critias replaces Charmides in the conversation, and attempts to defend his own suggestion that *sōphrosunē* is "to do your own things" (162e6–164d3). Critias is verbally more skilled than Charmides, and makes a distinction between the verb "do" (*prattein*) and the verb "make" (*poiein*). His distinction, however, is merely stipulative and sophistic. He intends to differentiate two social classes, the upper class of aristocrats who care only for their own interests, and the working class of artisans who work and "make" things for others. Socrates' examination reveals that Critias focuses on the artisans' products, and understands "benefit" and "goodness" as something external to the soul.

As we have seen in the previous chapter, Socrates asks Charmides whether to perform activities of various arts and crafts (*technai*) is "to do" (*prattein*) something. Now, he asks Critias:

> Tell me, do you also agree to what I was asking just now, that all artisans [*demiurgoi*] make [*poiein*] something?[151] (162e7–9)

Although Socrates claims that he is now asking Critias the same question that he had previously asked Charmides, his formulation involves subtle though significant changes. He asks about the artisans rather than the arts, and he uses the word "make" (*poiein*) instead of "do" (*prattein*). It is apparent that these changes are intended to provoke Critias, as Critias immediately argues for the need to distinguish between "make" and "do."

Critias agrees that the artisans make something, and that they create not only their own things but also others' things (162e7–163a4). Since Critias initially claimed that *sōphrosunē* is doing your own things, Socrates wonders how the artisans could be *sōphrones* if they make (*poiein*) things that belong to other people (163a4–9). Critias answers:

> Have I agreed . . . that those who do [*prattontes*] the things of others are *sōphrones*, if I agreed that those who make [*poiountas*] are?[152] (163a10–12)

---

151. καί μοι λέγε, ἦ καὶ ἃ νυνδὴ ἠρώτων ἐγὼ συγχωρεῖς, τοὺς δημιουργοὺς πάντας ποιεῖν τι; (162e7–9).

152. Ἐγὼ γάρ που, ἦ δ' ὅς, τοῦθ' ὡμολόγηκα, ὡς οἱ τὰ τῶν ἄλλων πράττοντες σωφρονοῦσιν, εἰ τοὺς ποιοῦντας ὡμολόγησα (163a10–12).

Critias distinguishes "those who do" from "those who make." Those who do would not be *sōphrones* if they do things that belong to others. Those who "make" would be *sōphrones* although they make things of others.

It seems, on the face of it, that Critias is more perceptive than Charmides about the subtle differences between words. Socrates' first examination of Charmides' soul showed that Charmides does not differentiate between the words "calm" and "slow" (159c3–7). He thus allows Socrates to attribute a negative sense of slowness to "calmness." Socrates' second examination showed that Charmides agrees that *sōphrosunē,* which is something beautiful, must also be something good that produces good people (160e6–12). Charmides does not question whether beauty and goodness differ from each other but accepts them as a package deal. Socrates' third examination raises the question whether performing activities (*to ergōn apergazesthai*) of various arts and crafts is "to do something" (161d3–4; *prattein dēpou ti estin,* 161e6–9). He also asks about "making" and "doing" in the same context (*ergazesthai te kai prattein,* 161e10–162a2). Socrates' questions emphasize the need to examine what the verb "do" applies to in the phrase "to do your own things." As we have seen, however, Charmides does not distinguish two senses that may be given to the phrase: doing things on your own and doing things for yourself. By contrast, Critias shows that he is more perceptive about meanings of words by distinguishing the verb "do" (*prattein*) from the verb "make" (*poiein*). However, we will now see that his distinctions are merely stipulative and intended to distinguish two social classes. In the next sections it will be apparent that Critias is as unperceptive as Charmides, and fails to make distinctions between words when truly needed.

Socrates attempts to clarify what Critias means (163b1–3). He asks whether Critias does not consider the words "make" (*poiein*) and "do" (*prattein*) as the same thing, that is, as synonyms. Critias answers that he even distinguishes the word "make" (*poiein*) from the word "work" (*ergazesthai*). The Greeks occasionally used the words *poiein, prattein* and *ergazesthai* interchangeably, to refer to the general performance of an action (see *LSJ*). Why does Critias distinguish among them, and what does he think each of them designates?

Critias' explanation demonstrates that he is more skilled and knowledgeable than Charmides in the literary, poetic field. He says that he learned from Hesiod that "work is no disgrace" (*ergon [d'] ouden einai oneidos,* 163b4–5). He draws this sentence from Hesiod's poem *Works and Days* (311), wherein Hesiod associates idleness with neediness and shameful situations (308–319). It is likely that Critias deliberately chooses to refer to this citation because six lines later (317) Hesiod exploits the Homeric sentence "shame is not good for a man in need," which Socrates mentioned earlier during his conversation with Charmides. Socrates used this Homeric sentence to imply that shame is not appropriate in certain situations. Critias, on the other hand, uses Hesiod's sentence "work is no disgrace" to argue that some situations and activities are in and of themselves shameful and disgraceful.[153]

Critias argues that by the sentence "work is no disgrace" Hesiod did not refer to the artisans' acts of "making" (*poiein*), because the thing made (*poiēma*) by them may at times become disgraceful whenever it is not produced in accordance with beauty. Critias' interpretation suggests that Hesiod's sentence does not refer to any kind of work whatsoever.[154] To his support, Critias provides three examples of activities associated with the working class. He presents them in a decreasing order of their reputation. He begins with cutting shoe leather, an example previously given by Socrates (161e10–162a2), but continues with selling salty fish and managing a brothel (163b7–8). Critias clearly deprecates the reputation of the shoe maker by presenting his activity

153. Joosse, "*Sōphrosunē* and the Poets," 587–90, rightly suggests that Critias implicitly reacts to Socrates' earlier citation of Homer, "shame is not good for a man in need," which I discussed above, in n. 116. Joosse, 587, claims that Critias "turns the dialectic between him and Socrates into a poetical rivalry as well and into a rivalry of interpretation." Critias thus implies a different interpretation for shame. Socrates refers to *aidōs* in the context that Homer uses it, Odysseus' need to overcome his shame. Critias, on the other hand, implicitly refers to *aidōs* in the context used by Hesiod, Hesiod's admonishment to his brother Perses from shameful and disgraceful situations brought about by idleness. According to Joosse, Critias thus uses the Hesiodic interpretation to claim that some situations and activities are disgraceful. See also discussion below, nn. 154 and 165.

154. Some scholars argue that Critias hereby misinterprets Hesiod. Schmid, *Plato's Charmides*, 33–34, says that as opposed to Critias, Hesiod refers to a "division of labor in society, in which all classes are seen to contribute to the common good." See also Joosse, "*Sōphrosunē* and the Poets," 583–84 n. 19. Joosse, 584–86, claims in contrast, that Critias nonetheless has some grounds for his arguments. Critias uses Hesiod's vocabulary and synonyms of his vocabulary. Joosse, also claims that this may also be Plato's response to the accusation by Polycrates and others that Socrates supported the idea that "anything one does is irreproachable." On Joosse's consequent indications concerning the dating of the dialogue see above n. 1. On Xenophon's defense of Socrates from the accusation of misusing Hesiod (*Memorabilia* 1.2.56–7), see in addition Graziosi, "Hesiod in Classical Athens," 120–24, Tuozzo, *Plato's Charmides*, 174–76, and Moore and Raymond, *Charmides*, 72–73. Levine, *Profound Ignorance*, 163 and 191 n. 14, suggests slightly differently, that Critias attempts to avoid a criticism that existed at the time concerning Socrates' use of Hesiod's verses and concerning the claim that no work whatsoever is a disgrace. Lampert, *How Philosophy Became Socratic*, 182, argues that Critias heard from Socrates an interpretation for Hesiod's saying and misconstrues it. It should be noted that Plutarch, *Lives: Solon* 2.3, in a discussion on Solon's reasons to become a merchant, uses Hesiod's verse to claim that in those days work was no disgrace. We may speculate whether Critias' interpretation stands in contrast to the Solonian tradition. I will argue that Plato deliberately insinuates such a contrast in my concluding chapter, section "The Status of Being Wise and Beautiful."

together with activities that suggest sour smell and sour morality. He thus undermines the reputation of required middle-class occupations by hinting that the products of all artisans may be disgraceful.[155]

Critias invokes Hesiod's authority in order to make his argument appear more convincing, but in the process he manipulates Hesiod's words. Hesiod refers to "work" (*ergon*) while Critias' definition of *sōphrosunē* refers to "doing" (*prattein*). Critias, therefore, argues that Hesiod calls things that are made (*ta poioumena*) in a beautiful and beneficial way "works" (*erga*), and calls the "acts of making" (*poiēseis*) such works by the names "working" (*ergasia*) and "doing" (*praxis*). We would expect the product of "doing" (*praxis*) to be the word "deed" (*pragma*) which comes from the same root *prag-*, however, Critias' interpretation suggests that "work" (*ergon*), the product of "working" (*ergasia*), is also the product of "doing" (*praxis*). Critias thus distorts the natural relation that exists between words that are based on a common root, and forces his distortion on Hesiod as well by thrice using the word "must" (*chrē*, 163b8, c5, 6). He says that Hesiod must have distinguished "doing" (*praxis*) and "working" (*ergasia*) from making (*poiēsis*, 163b9–c1), and that he must have thought, as any sensible man should, that doing your own things is *sōphrosunē* (163c6–8). We may recall that Socrates also mentioned several authorities: Zalmoxis and the Thracian doctors (156d5); good Greek doctors (156b5, d7); and Homer (161a2–4). However, Socrates, who attempted to make Charmides think critically, does not force him to accept any particular interpretation. He asks questions while Charmides may agree or disagree. In fact, in this way Charmides' disengaged attitude is revealed.

Critias' argument reflects his aristocratic, class-related view of *sōphrosunē*. He distinguishes two social classes, those who make (*poiein*) and those who do (*prattein*). Those who "make" (*poiein*) are clearly artisans (*demiurgoi*), and what they make (*poiēma*) sometimes becomes disgraceful. Critias deliberately adds that beneficial things belong to oneself (*oikeia*), but harmful things belong to others (*ta de blabera panta allotria*, 163c4–6).[156] We may infer that he implicitly claims that what the artisans make at times becomes disgraceful because they intend their products not only for themselves but mainly for others, who may use them as they please. We may further infer that Critias ascribes

---

155. Cf. Graziosi, "Hesiod in Classical Athens," 124, who argues similarly that Critias does not value the humble manual work of shoe making and thus argues that it is as disgraceful as prostitution.

156. Critias' distinction between things that belong to oneself and things that belong to others recalls Socrates' earlier distinction between writing the names of enemies (*tōn echthrōn*) and the names of friends (*tōn philōn*, 161d6–9). Joosse, "*Sōphrosunē* and the Poets," 585, argues that Critias' vocabulary is inspired by the vocabulary in the passage to which he refers in Hesiod's *Works and Days*, 306–19, especially 315.

the activity "doing" (*prattein*), and work (*ergon*) which is never disgraceful, to the upper class of aristocrats.[157] They never make things for others because they are self-employed. Ancient Athenian aristocrats did not perform crafts (*technai*) for a living.[158]

Critias distinguishes two kinds of *sōphrosunē*, of two social classes. However he devalues one of these classes, that of the artisans. His understanding of *sōphrosunē* is clearly class-related, a view often shared by aristocrats of the sixth and fifth centuries BCE.[159] Critias' distinction between two social classes will be important for understanding the whole conversation with him and of all the various aspects of his interpretation of *sōphrosunē*.

Socrates then summarizes Critias' argument with slight though significant changes:

> O Critias, I said, immediately when you began I generally understood the argument, that the things that belong and the things of one's own you call good things (*agatha*), and the acts of making (*poiēseis*) good [things or people] you call acts of doing.[160] (163d1–3)

157. Many scholars observe that Critias' argument presents his aristocratic views. Vielkind, "Philosophy, Finitude, and Wholeness," 150–1, indicates rightly that by distinguishing between the words "do" and "make" Critias expresses his aristocratic views, and differentiates between the activities of the noble and the work of the many. Burger, "Socrates' Odyssean Return," 227, argues that by this proposal Critias implicitly claims that the ruler of the city is doing his own things in the sense of treating the city and its citizens as his own possession. She claims that this idea is concealed also in Critias' later proposals. Notomi, "Origin of Plato's Political Philosophy," 247, claims that Critias' interpretations of *sōphrosunē* reflect his oligarchic views. Press, "*Charmides*," 42, and "*Elenchos* in the *Charmides*", 258, claims that Critias' definition is an antidemocratic slogan, and that his Hesiodic argument reveals his aristocratic attitude. Levine, *Profound Ignorance*, 159–72, claims that Critias' views reflect his "exclusive self-interest." Tuozzo, *Plato's Charmides,* 177, observes that Critias' distinction is between the noble and the artisans. Brennan, "Implicit Refutation of Critias," discusses the contradictions in Critias' argument, and takes Critias' linguistic distinction between "do" and "make" literally, while overlooking the fact that this distinction is merely stipulative and meant to distinguish two social classes. See also: Tuckey, *Plato's Charmides,* 21; Hyland, *Virtue of Philosophy,* 84–85; Joosse, "*Sōphrosunē* and the Poets," 586.

158. On the reputation of the crafts and manual work in Ancient Greece see e.g.: Balme, "Attitudes to Work and Leisure"; Ober, *Mass and Elite.*

159. On class-related interpretations of *sōphrosunē* in the sixth and fifth centuries BCE see for example: North, *Sōphrosynē,* 18; Rademaker, *Sōphrosynē and Rhetoric,* 75; Donlan, *Aristocratic Ideal,* 90–91.

160. Ω Κριτία, ἦν δ' ἐγώ, καὶ εὐθὺς ἀρχομένου σου σχεδὸν ἐμάνθανον τὸν λόγον, ὅτι τὰ οἰκεῖά τε καὶ τὰ αὑτοῦ ἀγαθὰ καλοίης, καὶ τὰς τῶν ἀγαθῶν ποιήσεις πράξεις· (163d1–3).

Some scholars argue that this distorted recapitulation of Critias' argument presents a new definition for *sōphrosunē*: "to do good things."[161] I contend, however, that Socrates is thus conducting his first examination of Critias' soul. Through his distorted recapitulation, Socrates intends to uncover that Critias understands "benefit" and "goodness" to be not in one's soul and activities, but in products and their instrumental use.

Critias originally used the words "beautifully" (*kalōs*) and "beneficially" (*ōphelimōs*) to describe things which belong (*oikeia*) to oneself (163c3–6). In his recapitulation, however, Socrates uses the word "good." At first he refers to good things (*agatha*), but then he uses an ambiguous sentence, "the acts of making good [things or people]" (*tas tōn agathōn poiēseis*). As we see, this sentence may refer either to the making of good things, that is, products, or to making good people. The idea that *sōphrosunē* makes good people has already been raised in the conversation with Charmides (160e9–12, discussed above, in the section "The Opinion of a Few about You"). Critias, like Charmides, does not understand *sōphrosunē* as a virtue that causes people to be good. He, therefore, does not notice that the word "good" may be used variously to refer to different objects: things or people.[162]

While Critias distinguished the verb "do" from other related words in order to distinguish the aristocrats from the artisans, he now accepts uncritically Socrates' move from the "beautiful" and "beneficial" to the "good." He does not distinguish among the adjectives "beautiful," "beneficial," and "good,"[163] we will see, because he ascribes all these descriptors to things, products, which are external to the soul, and may serve his self-interests.

After his distorted recapitulation, Socrates stresses that he is unimpressed by Critias' verbal distinctions between words. He tells him that he previously heard many distinctions between words from Prodicus (163d3–4), who was a famous sophist.[164] The mention of Prodicus in this context implies that Critias' distinctions are merely sophistic.[165] Socrates allows Critias to use

161. Tuckey, *Plato's Charmides*, 21; Moore and Raymond, *Charmides*, 73; Tuozzo, *Plato's Charmides*, 178; Notomi "Origin of Plato's Political Philosophy," 246. See in addition discussion by Schmid, *Plato's Charmides*, 154–55.

162. Cf. Tuckey's indication, *Plato's Charmides*, 21–22, that there is an ambiguity in the words "good" and "beneficial," and that Critias' and Socrates' opinions about them differ.

163. Levine, *Profound Ignorance*, 172–3, also indicates that for Critias Socrates' distinction between good and bad is similar to his distinction between benefit and harm, and that Socrates is interested in the meaning of the words.

164. Prodicus of Ceos the sophist was an expert in making distinctions between synonyms. He appears as a character in Plato's dialogue *Protagoras* (337a1–c4), and is mentioned in other dialogues as well.

165. Some scholars even argue that Critias is a sophist: Tuckey, *Plato's Charmides*, 25;

any distinctions he wants, as long as he explicitly explains what he means by each word (163d3–7). We will gradually see that Critias will fail to do so throughout the conversation. We may suspect that Charmides' proposals were refuted not because of his inability to make conceptual distinctions, but because of his misunderstanding of what each concept designates. Critias, we will see, is heading down the same path as his ward.

Socrates repeats once again his summary that is ambiguous between things and people, but as a question:

> So, the doing or making of good [things or people], or however you want to name it, this you say is *sōphrosunē*?[166] (163e1–2)

Socrates gives Critias another opportunity to prove that he is aware of the distortions in his recapitulation. Critias, however, fails to do so, and agrees that what Socrates says is what he claims. Socrates next asks whether the *sōphrōn* does good things (*tagatha*) rather than bad things (*ta kaka*), and Critias approves. Critias expects that Socrates would agree (163e4–e11), but Socrates says that they are not examining what he himself thinks but what Critias says.

Critias therefore repeats his argument in his own words, that those who make (*poiein*) good things and not bad are *sōphrones*, and that the doing (*praxis*) of good is *sōphrosunē* (163e8–11). Socrates says that nothings prevents that he is saying the truth (164a1).[167] We may already understand that Critias' formulation based on Socrates' changes holds some truth, although Critias is not aware of what it is. We can interpret his sentence in two senses: (1) that those who are *sōphrones* do good deeds and that *sōphrosunē* makes good people; or (2) that those who are *sōphrones* make good things/products and that *sōphrosunē* is the making of such good products. As the conversation

---

Lampert, *How Philosophy Became Socratic*, 189. See also discussion by Tuozzo, *Plato's Charmides*, 66–70. Socrates may be merely implying that Critias' argument is influenced by Prodicus' work on Hesiod. See O'Sullivan, *Alcidamas, Aristophanes*, 75–76, on Prodicus' theory of synonyms and Hesiod's *Works and Days*, and 78–79, on the indication that Critias takes his distinctions between synonyms in Hesiod from Prodicus. See also: Wolfsdorf, "Hesiod, Prodicus, and the Socratics," 3–6; Koning, *Hesiod, the Other Poet*, 224–26, and "Plato's Hesiod," 102–3; Joosse, "*Sōphrosunē* and the Poets," 587, especially 584 n. 19.

166. ἆρα τὴν τῶν ἀγαθῶν πρᾶξιν ἢ ποίησιν ἢ ὅπως σὺ βούλει ὀνομάζειν, ταύτην λέγεις σὺ σωφροσύνην εἶναι; (163e1–2).

167. Socrates' statement recalls Critias' rhetorical question at the beginning of the dialogue, as he asks Socrates what prevents him from pretending that he is a doctor to Charmides' headache (155b5–6), that is, what prevents him from lying. That *sōphrosunē* prevents one from pretending to know what one does not know is suggested later in the dialogue. See my discussion below, in the section "Discerning the Morally Good."

will progress it will become more apparent that Socrates intends the first sense and Critias the second.[168]

While nothing prevents that Critias' words hold some truth in them, Socrates wonders whether Critias thinks that those who are *sōphrones* do not recognize (*agnoiein*, 164a2–3) that they are *sōphrones*. Critias says that he does not think so. Socrates makes Critias confirm, as earlier in 162e7–163a5, that although the artisans make things for others, they are nonetheless *sōphrones* (164a6–7). He then asks Critias if every time a doctor makes someone healthy, that is, when he cures someone, he makes benefits (*ōphelima*) for himself and for his patient (164a9–b1). Critias agrees. As we see, Socrates has moved from using the word "good" back to using the word "beneficial."

Socrates indicates that in treating a patient the doctor would benefit not only the patient but also himself. It is not explained why the doctor benefits himself too, but in this way Socrates uses the word "benefit" (*ōphelimos*) in a way that is unspecified as to whether it refers to benefiting yourself or to benefiting others. Socrates next asks whether the doctor does necessary things (*ta deonta*, 164b3). It is also not explained why these things, either those made for oneself or those made for others, are necessary. Socrates' following question sheds light on these two unexplained issues:

> Is it, therefore, also necessary (*anagkē*) for the doctor to recognize (*gignōskein*) whenever he heals beneficially (*ōphelimōs*) and whenever he does not? And for each of the artisans, whenever he is about to be benefited (*onēsesthai*) from a work (*ergon*) that he does and when not?
> Maybe not.[169] (164b7–10)

Socrates' question suggests that it is necessity for the doctor to recognize when he heals someone beneficially, and for any artisan to know whenever he himself would be benefited. Socrates indicates once again two kinds of benefit, using two different words naturally used in Greek. He uses the adverb "beneficially" (*ōphelimōs*) which is related to the verb "to benefit" (*ōpheleō*) to refer to the way a work is being conducted, but he uses a verb with a different root for the meaning of "to be benefited" (*oneomai*). Thus, his choice of formulation deliberately emphasizes the connection between doing beneficially for the sake of others and benefiting oneself.

---

168. Schmid, *Plato's Charmides*, 34, indicates rightly that "Critias identifies the good with what benefits himself." See also Levine's interpretation, below n. 173.

169. Ἦ οὖν καὶ γιγνώσκειν ἀνάγκη τῷ ἰατρῷ ὅταν τε ὠφελίμως ἰᾶται καὶ ὅταν μή; καὶ ἑκάστῳ τῶν δημιουργῶν ὅταν τε μέλλῃ ὀνήσεσθαι ἀπὸ τοῦ ἔργου οὗ ἂν πράττῃ καὶ ὅταν μή; Ἴσως οὔ (164b7–10).

Socrates' question emphasizes the "necessity" in knowing how to do something. The first part of Socrates' question clearly indicates the mental activity required by the artisans in order to benefit others. The second part of his question links the artisan's ability to benefit others with the result of benefiting himself. We may infer that, as all artisans, by performing his work of healing others the doctor benefits himself since he earns money.[170] Socrates thus indicates a communal benefit. However, in the context of Critias' initial argument, by earning money, the artisan does his own things, but by servicing others he does not, and therefore he is socially inferior to those who are able to focus on only their own benefit.[171] Critias, however, surprisingly answers that the doctor does not need to recognize when he benefits and when he is benefited. Why?

Socrates' next question implicitly suggests that Critias' strange answer is a result of his selfish focus on the instrumental use of the artisans' products. He asks Critias:

> Thus, sometimes, I said, after he has acted (*praxas*) beneficially or harmfully, the doctor does not recognize himself how he has acted (*epraxen*). And after he has acted (*praxas*) beneficially, according to your argument, he has acted (*epraxen*) in a *sōphrōn* way (*sōphronōs*). Is it not this that you said?
> It is what I said.[172] (164b11–c3)

Critias confirms that Socrates understood his argument (164c4): the doctor does not recognize whether he acted beneficially or harmfully, and yet he may be *sōphrōn*. Socrates' questions indicate the logical problems in Critias' view: how can the artisan act beneficially if he is not aware of how he makes things?; and how can he be *sōphrōn* without recognizing that he is?

Socrates' questions attempt to encourage Critias to realize that benefit is a direct result of the mental and physical activities made by the artisan. Critias, however, is unwilling to accept it. He is not alarmed by the idea that the artisan does not recognize how he conducts an action that turns out to be beneficial.

170. See Tuozzo, *Plato's Charmides*, 181–83, who discusses various ways to understand this passage (164b7–10) while proposing his own interpretation.

171. Cf. Levine's claim, *Profound Ignorance*, 174–75, that Socrates implies an ambiguity in the word "benefit." Only at this point, Levine indicates that Critias distinguishes himself from the craftsmen. His interpretation differs from mine, as he claims that the artisan, dedicated to his art, is preoccupied with benefitting others, and in a way forgets about his own benefit. However, as my account indicates, I do not agree that Critias sees this as a case of forgetfulness.

172. Ἐνίοτε ἄρα, ἦν δ' ἐγώ, ὠφελίμως πράξας ἢ βλαβερῶς ὁ ἰατρὸς οὐ γιγνώσκει ἑαυτὸν ὡς ἔπραξεν· καίτοι ὠφελίμως πράξας, ὡς ὁ σὸς λόγος, σωφρόνως ἔπραξεν. ἢ οὐχ οὕτως ἔλεγες "Ἔγωγε (164b11–c3).

He thinks that the artisan does not need to know whether his products are used beneficially or not, but only to do what he is requested. Clearly, Critias understands "benefit" and "goodness" to be in something external to the soul, in products (*erga*). Socrates and Critias promote different world-views and the discussion, therefore, results with two different sorts of objects that one might "recognize": (1) the benefit of knowing how to conduct an activity, and (2) the benefit of the end product.

Critias, we have seen, distinguishes between the words "make" and "do," but his distinction is merely stipulative and sophistic. He intends to differentiate two social classes, the artisans who are producers of goods and the aristocrats who use these goods. Critias thinks that the artisans who serve others are inferior to the aristocrats who serve only themselves. Yet he assumes that the artisans' activities are also motivated only by the selfish desire to benefit themselves.[173] The artisans do what is necessary for their social class, which is to work for others in order to earn money. However, according to Critias, it is not necessary for the artisans to know how they conduct something beneficially, because he thinks that the benefit of a product is determined not by the way the artisan conducts his work, but by the users of the products. The artisans do not need to know whether their products and services are used beneficially or harmfully.

Critias and Socrates talk past each other because they have different world-views. Critias' view is of social hierarchy, where members of each class do whatever they are able for selfish gain, while Socrates' view is of communal benefit, where each person needs to know how to conduct his art well in order to benefit both others and himself. These two different world-views are reflected in the way they use the words "good," "beneficial," "necessary," and "recognize": good people vs. good products; beneficial ways to conduct an activity vs. beneficial products; necessity to know how to do something vs. necessity for one's social class to earn money; and to recognize how to do something beneficially and not harmfully vs. to recognize the benefit of the end product. This contributes to the complexity of the conversation, but also allows us a glimpse into Critias' soul. We learn that Critias understands value to be in the use of external things, products, for one's own benefit. He therefore does not pick up on Socrates' indication that value resides in the soul: good people recognize the necessity of knowing how to do something well in order to benefit communally. While Socrates understands Critias' errors and by means of his dialectic questions attempts at encouraging Critias

---

173. Cf. Levine, *Profound Ignorance*, 164, who rightly claims that "For Critias *benefit to himself* is the standard of measure of deeds," and 165, "for Critias *self-interest* is the measure of the good and the bad."

to recognize and correct them, he is unable to make Critias do what he is unwilling to do. Thus the two exemplify consistent dramatic characters who do not change.

While Critias is not alarmed by the idea that the artisan does not recognize how he conducts an action that turns out to be beneficial, he is alarmed by the idea that the artisan will not recognize that he is *sōphrōn*. He rejects Socrates' subsequent conclusion that after doing something beneficial and in a *sōphrōn* way, the doctor does not know that he was *sōphrōn* (164c5–d3). He abandons his proposal "to do your own things" and says that he would not be ashamed to admit that something that they had said was incorrect (164d1–2). His self-proclaimed lack of shame seems to distinguish him from the young and shy Charmides. However, that Critias is lying again will become clear later on. When he eventually reaches a point where he is unable to support his claims he shamefully hides his puzzlement (*aporia*) and does not back down from his statements.[174] Critias' next argument reveals why he thinks that the artisan must recognize that he is *sōphrōn*.

Know Your Place

Critias uses Socrates' mention of the verb *gignōskein*, in suggesting that *sōphrosunē* is *to gignōskein heauton* (164d4). The literal translation of this phrase is "to recognize oneself," or in its most familiar version in English "know yourself" (*gnōthi sauton*).[175] I use the former translation "recognize," in order to distinguish the word *gignōskein* from the forthcoming words *epistēmē* and *eidenai*, which also refer to the mental activity of knowing.[176] Critias continues to mask his opinions concerning social hierarchy by presenting his new proposal as enigmatic, and by using once again stipulative distinctions. As we will see, Critias intends to claim that the artisan needs to recognize that he is

---

174. See discussions in sections "The Practicality of *Sōphrosunē*" and "To Be or Not to Be in *Aporia*." Cf. Press, "*Elenchos* in the *Charmides*," 260, who claims that at this point Critias "still doesn't think his answer has been refuted, and he is not learning anything." Press, 261 n. 19, argues rightly that throughout the conversation Critias will not admit that his claims are refuted, and will present the next proposals as merely clarifications and refinements of his initial argument.

175. Scholars translate the word *gignōskein* as either "know" or "recognize." Schmid, *Plato's Charmides*, 43, indicates that the correct translation of the maxim *gnōthi sauton* is "recognize oneself." Levine, *Profound Ignorance*, 182, translates the word *gignōskein* as cognition. Moore and Raymond, *Charmides*, 19, translate the phrase *gnōthi sauton* as "knowing oneself," and later, 23, 167a1, translate the word *gignōskein* as "know."

176. On the translation of the word *epistēmē* see discussion below, in n. 186. On the translation of the word *eidenai* see next section.

sōphrōn because he must be aware of his place in society, and of his proper role to serve the upper class. Socrates' examination (164d3–166b4) indicates that Critias does not realize that self-knowledge should derive from self-examination. In assuming that productive practices are characteristic of just one class, Critias is blind to the centrality of practicality in all human experience, including in his own language which creates linguistic and conceptual difficulties that one cannot apply to life.

Critias argues that "recognize oneself" is god's greeting to those who enter his temple. Humans, on the other hand, greet each other with *chaire*, which may be translated as "cheer," "rejoice," or "welcome." Critias holds, nevertheless, that people are mistaken, and should greet each other instead with the commandment "to be *sōphrōn*" (*sōphronein*, 164e2). Critias therefore argues that humans' greeting "be *sōphrōn*" and god's special greeting "recognize yourself" are functionally equivalent. Critias also says that the saying "recognize oneself" is quite enigmatic (*ainigmatōdesteron*), as diviners' sayings usually are (164e6–7). This should remind us of Socrates' description of Critias' previous proposal "to do your own things" as an enigmatic riddle (162b4, Chapter 2, section "Thinking for Yourself").[177] Thus, Critias once again interprets a riddling phrase. He again makes distinctions among words (*gignōskein*, *chairein*, and *sōphronein*). Is this new distinction more profound than his previous one?

Although Critias does not mention the name of the god, we may gather that he refers to Apollo, the god of prophecy who spoke to humans in riddles through an oracle. Apollo was associated with *sōphrosunē* since Homer, and the maxim "recognize oneself" was inscribed on his temple in Delphi.[178] Critias mentions two further inscriptions from this temple, "nothing in excess" (*mēden agan*), and "a pledge and ruin is near" (*enguē para d' atē*).[179] He argues

177. The phrase "to do your own things," the saying "recognize oneself," and the virtue *sōphrosunē*, are also mentioned together in Plato's *Timaeus* 72a. See discussion by Adkins, "Polu pragmosyne," 302–3. On the appearance of the maxim *gnōthi sauton* in other dialogues see Moore and Raymond, *Charmides*, 77 n. 132.

178. North, *Sōphrosynē*, 4–5, 12–13, indicates that Apollo was associated with *sōphrosunē*, and that the sayings *gnōthi sauton* and "nothing in excess" (*mēden agan*, which we will see is also mentioned by Critias) were inscribed on Apollo's temple in the late sixth century BCE.

179. On these maxims see Parke and Wormell, *Delphic Oracle*, 386–88, and Burkert, *Greek religion*, 148. The sayings were inscribed on the temple of Apollo in the sixth century BCE. Later the maxims were ascribed to the seven sages. In fr. 7 of the remains of Critias' writings (Diels and Kranz, *Die Fragmente der Vorsokratiker*) Critias associates the phrase *mēden agan* with Chilon the Spartan sage. The maxim was also ascribed to Solon among other sages, according to Diogenes Laertius, *Vitae Philosophorum* 1.63, as discussed by Noussia-Fantuzzi, *Solon the Athenian*, 9–11, and North, *Sōphrosynē*, 11–113.

that the inscriber who added these two advisory maxims misinterpreted the greeting "recognize oneself" as a bit of advice or a recommendation. If the commandment "recognize oneself," and its equivalent "be *sōphrōn*," are not advisory but merely greetings, are they beneficial for humans or for Apollo at all?

Humans approach the god's temple, we are to understand, in order to worship him by bringing offerings and gifts. Critias' god does nothing other than simply receive these gifts.[180] We may recall that Critias' Hesiodic argument in the previous examination presented the class of aristocrats in a similar way. The aristocrats are not engaged in any work for others, but only do their own things while enjoying the products of the lower class of artisans. Thus, Critias clearly intends to distinguish three classes: the divine, aristocrats, and artisans.

While Apollo tells humans to know their place as humans and nothing more, humans tell each other to know their place, that is, their social class. We may now infer why Critias insists that the artisan must recognize that he is *sōphrōn*. Critias is inspired by the ancient interpretation of the maxim "recognize oneself" as god's reminder to humans to know their place, that is, that

---

At some point, aristocrats used the maxim to distinguish themselves from the masses according to Donlan, *Aristocratic Ideal*, 91–92. The maxim *enguē para d' atē* is translated variously, e.g.: Tuozzo, *Plato's Charmides,* 185, "Give bond, and ruin follows"; Lampert, *How Philosophy Became Socratic*, 178, "Guarantee, and you guarantee disaster"; Moore and Raymond, *Cahrmides*, 19 n. 57, 79 n. 141, "Pledge and disaster is near." See also below n. 293.

180. Tuozzo, *Plato's Charmides,* 186–88, 255, interprets Critias' description of *sōphrosunē* in the context of the maxim *gnōthi sauton* similarly to the greetings "rejoice" (*chaire*) and "be healthy" (*hugiainein*), which are intended to be "an expression of goodwill." Instead of the hedonist view that is suggested by the greeting "rejoice" (as also observed by Witte, *Die Wissenschaft vom Guten und Bösen*, 98, and Tuckey, *Plato's Charmides*, 24), self-knowledge is a fundamental good. Tuozzo claims that "Critias raises the idea that it has a more fundamentally social nature than other human goods." Tuozzo, "What's Wrong with These Cities," 346, argues that Critias' interpretation of the saying "know oneself" as a greeting indicates, contrary to the contemporary opinion, a bridge between god and humans as the god welcomes humans to his house. Moore and Raymond, *Charmides*, 79–81, also speculate similarly over the reason Critias describes *sōphrosunē* as a greeting. They suggest that the historical Critias is perhaps the originator of this interpretation. He meant that *sōphrosunē*, being a necessary condition, is "something more fundamental than any other kind of advice," but that in the dialogue "Plato reveals Critias' limited understanding of his own insight." See also Tuckey, *Plato's Charmides*, 24–25, who argues that the previous proposal "doing good" focused on the external, and now Critias moves to an advanced proposal that focuses on a state of mind. Kosman, *Virtues of Thought*, 229, suggests that in claiming that *sōphrosunē* is knowing oneself Critias proposes a more extensive suggestion than his previous one, "not merely *knowing what one is up to* nor merely *knowing oneself to be temperate* . . ." These interpretations strike me as giving Critias more credit than he deserves.

as humans they should be humble in front of the divine. However, he strips it of the moral implications of equality among humans, which results from the reminder that all humans are equally limited in comparison to god.[181] Critias thinks that the artisan should know his place in the social hierarchy, and his consequent limitations. On the other hand, he sees himself closer to the divine class of Apollo, who does only his own things for his own selfish benefit.[182] This is not surprising, since aristocrats claimed to have a special connection with the divine as direct descendants of heroes and gods.[183] Critias, like his

181. On this ancient meaning of the maxim *gnōthi sauton*, see, e.g., North, *Sōphrosynē*, 4–5, who claims that *sōphrosunē* together with self-knowledge indicated "boundary between god and man." North, 15, says that the archaic poets interpreted *sōphrosunē* as a class virtue in the sense of "knowledge of limitations." Tsouna, "Subject of Plato's *Charmides*," 52, formulates Critias' intention as "know yourselves for what you are—men but not gods, mortals but not immortals, endowed with limited cognitive capacities as opposed to the perfect wisdom of the gods." Schmid, *Plato's Charmides*, 37–38, argues that Critias separates the maxim from its original divine moral counsel that humans must act respectfully to one another. See also Tuckey, *Plato's Charmides*, 9–10. Luz, "Knowledge of Knowledge," 100, also indicates rightly that "Critias' understanding of knowledge of oneself is bereft of its moral (165d–e) and even practical content (166c)."

182. Press, "*Elenchos* in the *Charmides*", 260–61, argues that Critias' leap to the traditionally accepted saying *gnōthi sauton* indicates his attempt to square his position with the tradition due to his distress about his reputation. He further claims that Critias, however, does not use the phrase in its traditional sense "recognizing your limits as human." Press, 261 n. 26, claims that Critias means by the phrase "know what *epistēmē* you have," referring only to noble men. I agree with Press' indication that Critias continues with stressing that *sōphrosunē* has a class-related interpretation, but I contend that by the Delphic phrase he does refer to all social classes, though with the intention to differentiate between aristocrats and the artisans. See also Press, "*Charmides*," 43. Levine, *Profound Ignorance*, 177, argues similarly that Critias assumes that a person needs to know himself in order to do his own things. See other interpretations by Barker, "Problems in the *Charmides*," 29–30, and Moore and Raymond, *Charmides*, 77 n. 131.

183. Donlan, *Aristocratic Ideal*, 97–100, indicates that aristocrats claimed to be of noble birth, that is, superior over the masses because of their kinship to heroes and gods. Some scholars, however, assume that Critias is presenting an atheistic argument. Schmid, *Plato's Charmides*, 38–39, claims that Critias presents an atheistic interpretation for the religious maxim "recognize oneself." Truth and wisdom are not derived from the divine. Critias compares himself to a god, as he is able to interpret the god's greeting. Lampert, *How Philosophy Became Socratic*, 188, claims similarly that Critias presents an atheistic view. Critias frees himself from the command by his ability to explain it in his words. See also discussions by: Moore and Raymond, *Charmides*, 78 n. 136; Hazebroucq, *La Folie Humaine et ses Remèdes,* 231–33. The proposal that Critias presents atheistic views is probably influenced by the controversial attribution either to Critias or to Euripides of a fragment from the dramatic work *Sisyphus* that presents atheistic views (Diels and Kranz, *Die Fragmente der Vorsokratiker*, fr. 88B.25; Sextus Empiricus, *Against the Physicists* 1.48–54). See discussions on this fragment by: Tuckey, *Plato's Charmides*, 16; Kahn, "Sisyphus Fragment"; Tuozzo, *Plato's Charmides*, 78–86; Lampert, *How Philosophy Became Socratic*, 188 n. 174.

god Apollo, focuses on gifts and products. He even rejects the connection of *sōphrosunē* with the maxim "nothing in excess" (*mēden agan*). Is he in danger of becoming an immoderate hedonist? It seems that the character of Critias in the dialogue accords with Xenophon's account that the historical Critias was the most greedy among the oligarchs (*Memorabilia* 1.2.12).[184]

We may recall that Socrates mentioned earlier a different god, Zalmoxis, a human who became immortal. Socrates describes Zalmoxis as a healer who benefits both himself and humans. Apollo was actually also associated by the Greeks with medicine, but Critias does not mention this. Critias describes his god as a passive hedonist, being served a variety of pleasures by others, and he aspires to resemble him in this respect.

At the end of his speech, Critias says that if Socrates does not agree to his argument he can present another speech (165b3–4). This clearly indicates once again that Critias is an experienced speaker. However, Socrates is not impressed with his talkativeness. He replies that he must first examine what Critias has just said, that he searches for the answer together with him and does not know in advance whether he agrees or not. He therefore asks Critias to wait while he examines it (165b5–c2). In doing so, Socrates exemplifies a different interpretation for the maxim "recognize oneself" that derives from self-examination. Critias, on the other hand, will continue to advocate his class-related interpretation for *sōphrosunē* throughout the dialogue.[185]

Although Critias corrects his proposal "to do your own things" to "recognize oneself," his aristocratic intentions remain unchanged: he thinks that *sōphrosunē* concerns social class. Socrates turns to examine Critias' soul once again, but he does not address Critias' new argument directly. He continues to address the problem that he pointed to in his previous examination, that Critias' aristocratic view suggests that the artisan does not need to recognize

---

184. Cf. Levine, *Profound Ignorance*, 159–72, 167, and Notomi, "Origin of Plato's Political Philosophy," 237. See my conclusions concerning the characters' immoderation, below, section "Well-Ordered and Disordered Lives," subsection "Civic-Mindedness."

185. Levine, *Profound Ignorance*, 180–81, stresses a slightly different dissimilarity between the attitudes of Critias and Socrates. He claims that while Critias supposes that his proposal is correct, Socrates turns to self-examination. Some scholars suggest that Socrates and Critias each advocates his own interpretation for the phrase "recognize oneself," however they disagree on what their interpretations are. See for example Tsouna, "Subject of Plato's *Charmides*," 48–51, who argues that the Socratic interpretation of self-knowledge concerns the practice of investigating oneself with regard to beliefs about virtue, while Critias' concerns the "*epistēmē* of the value of one's actions." see also Schmid, *Plato's Charmides*, 41–42. McAvoy, "Carnal Knowledge in the *Charmides*," 64–65, 71, argues that Socrates here, and in other places in the dialogue, professes ignorance, and later on will introduce the theme of knowledge of ignorance because of Critias' refusal to admit his ignorance.

how he conducts an action that turns out to be beneficial. Socrates continues to stress that the benefit produced by *sōphrosunē*, as the benefit produced by any art, must be a direct result of mental, no less than physical, activities.

Socrates begins by asking, "if *sōphrosunē* is to recognize (*gignōskein*) something, clearly it would be some kind of knowledge (*epistēmē*)[186] and of something. Is it not right?" (165c4–6).[187] Critias agrees, and says that it is knowledge "of oneself" (165c7). Socrates' previous examination indicated the need to clarify to what each word refers. Yet, we now see that Critias treats the verb "recognize" (*gignōskein*) and the noun "knowledge" (*epistēmē*) as referring to the same object: oneself.[188] So far, Socrates and Critias used the word "recognize" (*gignōskein*) to apply to oneself. However, while Critias implies that it concerns what one's social place and role is, Socrates suggests that it concerns how one does something beneficially. Socrates encourages Critias to think of *sōphrosunē* in relation to the word "knowledge" (*epistēmē*), because the word "knowledge" may refer to the theoretical and practical understanding of how to conduct a specialized activity, derived from examination and search (i.e. research). He thus presents *sōphrosunē* and its unique "knowledge" (*epistēmē*) similarly to the arts (*technai*). He attempts to make Critias realize that productivity and practicality are not characteristics of only one social class.[189]

186. Scholars translate the word *epistēmē* variously, or alternately, as either "knowledge," or "science," although it also rendered as "understanding." E.g.: Schmid, *Plato's Charmides*, 47, "knowledge (or science) of oneself"; Levine, *Profound Ignorance*, 182, translates *epistēmē* by the word "knowledge."

187. εἰ γὰρ δὴ γιγνώσκειν γέ τί ἐστιν ἡ σωφροσύνη, δῆλον ὅτι ἐπιστήμη τις ἂν εἴη καὶ τινός· ἢ οὔ; (165c4–6).

188. Tuckey, *Plato's Charmides*, 30–31, argues that the words *gignōskein* and *epistēmē* are ambiguous. He argues that by means of these two words Socrates changes the meaning he attaches to knowledge, from knowing oneself to the craft of the self, but Critias continues without noticing.

189. Scholars variously understand Socrates' comparison between *sōphrosunē* and the arts (*technai*). For example, Tuozzo, *Plato's Charmides*, 193–94, claims that Socrates' exchange between the words *gignōskein* and *epistēmē* allows him "to explore the nature of self-knowledge by comparing it with systematic types of knowing" such as the arts. Though, Tuozzo claims, self-knowledge is not an art, but is connected to the arts and supplements them, and Critias understands that (197). Schmid, *Plato's Charmides*, 45–46, 62–4, argues that Socrates intends to reveal that Critias fails to explain the distinction between self-knowledge and the kinds of knowledge of the crafts, which are productive. See also Schmid's criticism, 125–46, of the view that virtue is craft-knowledge presented by Irwin, *Plato's Moral Theory*, 1, 71–77. See also: Tuckey, *Plato's Charmides*, 30–32; Moore and Raymond, *Charmides*, 82–83; Lesses, "Crafts and Craft-Knowledge"; Balaban, "Meaning of 'Craft' in Plato"; Wellman, "Question Posed at *Charmides*." For further discussion on the reasons that Plato makes a connection between *sōphrosunē* and the arts see my concluding chapter, section "Well-Ordered and Disordered Lives."

Critias' argument does not indicate that the maxim "recognize (*gignōskein*) oneself," or its new distorted formulation "knowledge (*epistēmē*) of oneself," entails productivity or benefiting anyone in any way. Nonetheless, Socrates' next questions suggest that it does:

> If you would have asked me now, I said, "medicine, as knowledge (*epistēmē*) of health, in what is it useful for us and what does it produce (*apergazetai*)" I would have said that in not a small benefit, because it produces (*apergazetai*) health which is a beautiful product (*ergon*) for us, would you accept this?
> I accept.
> And if you asked me about the art of building (*oikodomikē*), that is the knowledge (*epistēmē*) of building (*oikodomein*), what product I would say it produces, I would say that housing (*oikēseis*).[190] (165c10–d6)

Socrates' questions imply that the knowledge (*epistēmē*) that they associate with *sōphrosunē* applies to something productive and therefore useful (*chrēsimē*); and that it applies to a kind of practice as any kind of knowledge of the arts (*technai*) such as of healing, building etc. Clearly, Socrates presents *sōphrosunē* in comparison with *technē*, in order to stress that it has two aspects, a theoretical and a practical. He therefore asks what *sōphrosunē* would produce that makes it worthy of its reputation (165d6–e2).

A close reading indicates that Socrates' questions refer to activities or active states rather than to final products. Regarding the art of house-building he asks what product/work it makes, but his answer is the activity of housing (*oikēseis*, 165d6) rather than houses. He treats the physical activity, something which is being done, as the product. Similarly, he says that medicine produces health. Health is an active condition of the body. If *sōphrosunē* is knowledge that is directed to oneself, Critias should gather that it also applies to activities. What kind of activities? Ones that are within oneself, and that are made by oneself, and thus make oneself a good person.

Critias, however, uses the word "knowledge" (*epistēmē*) not in the sense of understanding how to conduct a specialized activity that derives from research and self-examination, but to refer to one's awareness of one's place and role in the social hierarchy. He therefore rejects Socrates' method of

---

190. Εἰ τοίνυν με, ἔφην, ἔροιο σύ· "Ἰατρικὴ ὑγιεινοῦ ἐπιστήμη οὖσα τί ἡμῖν χρησίμη ἐστὶν καὶ τί ἀπεργάζεται," εἴποιμ᾽ ἂν ὅτι οὐ σμικρὰν ὠφελίαν· τὴν γὰρ ὑγίειαν καλὸν ἡμῖν ἔργον ἀπεργάζεται, εἰ ἀποδέχῃ τοῦτο.
Ἀποδέχομαι.
Καὶ εἰ τοίνυν με ἔροιο τὴν οἰκοδομικήν, ἐπιστήμην οὖσαν τοῦ οἰκοδομεῖν, τί φημι ἔργον ἀπεργάζεσθαι, εἴποιμ᾽ ἂν ὅτι οἰκήσεις· (165c10–d6).

investigation. He claims that the knowledge (*epistēmē*) that he associates with *sōphrosunē* differs from the kinds of knowledge of the arts, and that each kind of knowledge is unique and differs from the other kinds. Instead of Socrates' example of medicine he mentions weaving, and instead of mentioning practical activities he focuses on the products that these arts produce: a building and a cloth (165e7–8). He claims that calculation and geometry, on the other hand, do not apply to products such as these (165e5–166a2). Critias clearly gives a different list of arts that is associated with aristocrats. The study of geometry was associated with the aristocratic class who had money and free time to engage in it. Calculation was used by both artisans and aristocrats. Thus, Critias implicitly intends to distinguish between practical arts that are associated with artisans and theoretical arts that are associated with aristocrats.[191]

Socrates answers that although he cannot indicate that these arts produce a product/work, he can, nonetheless, show that they apply to something other than themselves. For example, calculation applies to relations between numbers, and to odd and even numbers (166a5–7). Socrates ignores Critias' example of geometry and instead mentions the art of weighing, and says that it applies to the heavy and light (166b1–3). Socrates' mention of relations between things (odd and even, heavy and light) could be an attempt to encourage Critias to unmask his aristocratic view about the hierarchical relation between the aristocrats and the masses. Critias, however, continues to obscure his aristocratic opinion about social hierarchy with his literary disguise.

Although Critias agrees that geometry and calculation refer to something other than themselves, he insists that the kind of knowledge associated with *sōphrosunē* differs entirely from the kinds of knowledge of the arts. He claims that this knowledge does not apply to a productive activity or a product. We see once again that Critias associates productivity with the class of artisans. However, according to him, both social classes need to be *sōphrones*, that is, to recognize their place in the social hierarchy. Instead of making clear what he means by the word "knowledge," Critias blames Socrates in denying that he understands his intention and in trying to refute him (166c).[192]

Critias aspires to resemble an unproductive god who is worshiped by the artisans providing him with service and gifts. Socrates, however, emphasizes throughout the dialogue the need to take into account two aspects, the internal and the external, of human conduct. Socrates brings into the conversation

---

191. Vielkind, "Philosophy, Finitude, and Wholeness," 165, interprets the exchanges that Socrates and Critias make in each other's lists as merely additions.

192. Other interpretations for Critias' rebuke of Socrates: Levine, *Profound Ignorance*, 189, 205–6; Lampert, *How Philosophy Became Socratic*, 193; Tuozzo, *Plato's Charmides*, 200–201. About Socrates' response, see discussion in the next section.

with Critias the concept "knowledge" (*epistēmē*), because it may be used to represent the internal aspect of human conduct. In this way, he attempts to motivate Critias to think about *sōphrosunē* as something that concerns practical activities, as he compares *sōphrosunē* to knowledge of an art that applies to something practical. Critias accepts that *sōphrosunē* is some kind of "knowledge" because he assumes that both the lower and the upper classes need to know something, namely, their place in the social hierarchy. However, because he thinks that *sōphrosunē* is knowing only your social place, and is devoid of knowing how to carry out a craft, he thereby denies that *sōphrosunē* has a practical side. Critias assumes that it is only the artisans' social role to be engaged in practices. Thus, unwilling to associate the aristocratic *sōphrosunē* with practices, Critias corrects his argument once again. This leads to the appearance of a new proposal: *sōphrosunē* is "knowledge (*epistēmē*) only of itself and of other kinds of knowledge (*epistēmai*)."

The Practicality of *Sōphrosunē*

Socrates turns to examine Critias' adjusted suggestion (166d8–169c2), that *sōphrosunē* is knowledge (*epistēmē*) of itself and of other kinds of knowledge (*epistēmai*, 166c2 3, e5–6). While Socrates encourages Critias to examine critically this proposal with regard to its practicality, Critias' underlying opinion remains unchanged: he insists that *sōphrosunē* concerns social class, and continues to devalue the artisans and the practice of the arts. Consequently, Critias denies that *sōphrosunē* has a practical aspect altogether, by separating the knowledge it involves from its applicability to everyday life. For this reason, we will see, Critias' adjusted proposal fails to satisfy, and his ignorance concerning *sōphrosunē* is exposed.

Before Socrates turns to examine Critias' suggestion, he responds to Critias' reproach that he, Socrates, attempts to refute him. Socrates says that if he refutes Critias it is only because he also examines himself. He fears that he would think that he knows (*eidenai*) something that he does not know (166c7–d2). This claim foreshadows Socrates' additions to the conversation of a third word, the verb "to know" (*eidenai*), that concerns the mental activity of knowing, with its negation meaning not knowing something and the state of ignorance (*anepistēmosunē*).[193]

---

193. That Socrates' answer to Critias foreshadows the additions of these words is also observed by other scholars, for example McCabe, "Looking Inside Charmides' Cloak," 179–80.

Socrates adds that he does what he does also for the sake of others who are suitable/friends (*tōn allōn epitēdeiōn*, 166d2–4).[194] He then asks Critias whether it would not be a common good (*koinon agathon*) to all humans that each of the existing things would manifest in the way that it is (166d4–6). I suggest that Socrates' question insinuates that Critias is disinterested in the common good, and that his literary acrobatics are intended to obscure his exploitative intentions.[195] Critias, however, agrees with Socrates that this would be a common good.

Socrates then asks Critias to answer courageously, and to leave aside the question of who is being refuted (166d8–e2). He directs Critias to concentrate on the proposed argument and see what result comes out of it once it is examined. Socrates clearly encourages Critias to examine critically his own proposal. Critias agrees because, he says, Socrates seems to him to speak with measure (*metria legein*, 166e3). Critias uses a word that the Greeks associated with *sōphrosunē*.[196] We will see, however, that he does not critically examine his proposal or his underlying aristocratic views.

Critias repeats his proposal, that *sōphrosunē* is knowledge (*epistēmē*) of itself, and of other kinds of knowledge (*epistēmai*, 166e5–6). Scholars have pondered over Critias' change of formulation, from arguing that *sōphrosunē* is "to recognize oneself"/"knowledge of oneself" (*to gignōskein heauton*, 164d3; *epistēmē heautou*, 165c5–7) to arguing that it is "knowledge of itself" (*epistēmē heautēs*, 166c3); and over Critias' intention by his addition that this knowledge is also of other kinds of knowledge.[197] I contend that these two

194. Some scholars indicate the peculiarity in Socrates' choice of the ambiguous word *epitēdeios*, that means either "suitable" or "friend." Levine, *Profound Ignorance*, 206–8, indicates Socrates' move from a selective group of friends that might be suitable, in which Critias perhaps does not deserve to be included, to the notion of a common good. Lampert, *How Philosophy Became Socratic*, 194–95, argues similarly. See also translation by Moore and Raymond, *Charmides*, 22, as "friends."

195. I follow Levine's translation with slight changes, as it seems to me to grasp Socrates' intention most adequately. While Levine, 208–10, argues that the sentence refers to human beings (*tōn ontōn*, 166d6) as the souls of Charmides and Critias, I contend that it refers to Critias' tendency to obscure his intentions behind his verbal gymnastics, although this also implies that Critias' soul is corrupted. Lampert, *How Philosophy Became Socratic*, 194–6, also translates *tōn ontōn* as "beings." Schmid, *Plato's Charmides*, 74, argues that the phrase deliberately has a double meaning, and refers both to things in the world and to souls. See other interpretations for Socrates' response: Schmid, *Plato's Charmides*, 52–53; Moore and Raymond, *Charmides*, 85.

196. See North, *Sōphrosynē*, xiii.

197. Tuckey, *Plato's Charmides*, 33–37, 59, gives a survey of scholarly debate in his time over these problems. He suggests that Plato implies by the move to the proposal "knowledge of itself" that "one has knowledge of his knowledge" about self-control. Tuckey, 43–49, therefore asks what Plato's intentions are, whether science can be its own object,

83

issues may be explained once addressing the dramatic context.[198] Later on it becomes clear that Critias identifies "knowledge of itself" with "knowledge of oneself," as he claims that one who has knowledge of itself will know himself (169e1–e5). Critias' gradual move from the formulation "recognize oneself" to "knowledge (*epistēmē*) of oneself" and then to "knowledge (*epistēmē*) of itself" is not intentional. He does not intend to change his opinion, or to suggest a discussion on the epistemological possibility of "knowledge of knowledge." Critias indiscriminately and thoughtlessly accepts Socrates' exchange between the words *gignōskein* and *epistēmē*, and this leads him to apply subtle grammatical and syntactical changes to his proposal. As for his addition that the knowledge associated with *sōphrosunē* is also of other kinds of knowledge, we will gradually see that Critias at first intends to clarify that each person should know his place in the social hierarchy in relation to others, but as the conversation progresses he uses the same formulation to mean that the upper class should supervise and control the lower class.

Socrates next asks Critias whether *sōphrosunē*, assuming that it is knowledge (*epistēmē*) of knowledge, is also knowledge of ignorance/lack of knowledge (*anepistēmosunē*, 166e7–9), and Critias agrees. The two words, *epistēmē* and *anepistēmosunē*, are antonyms, but differ from each other in that *anepistēmosunē* is a character trait similarly to the word *sōphrosunē*, and *epistēmē* is not. The word *epistēmē* refers either to the result of knowledge

---

how one is able to know that one knows something, and whether knowledge is knowable. He suggests that Plato is concerned with how one recognizes one's own knowledge. Several decades later, Schmid, *Plato's Charmides*, 47, 181 n. 14, provides an updated survey of the controversy. He argues that this move makes sense to both Critias and Socrates, but for different reasons. Critias thinks that self-knowledge means "knowing that one knows a science," while Socrates is concerned with "the self in relation to moral ideals and universal human interests." Moore and Raymond, *Charmides*, 82, indicate that Socrates' examination of the proposal "self-knowledge" proceeds by asking about knowledge of what (*tis*) it is, and this leads to the new proposal "knowledge of itself." See also: Tuozzo, *Plato's Charmides*, 194–95, 198; Dyson, "Some Problems Concerning Knowledge"; McKim, "Socratic Self-Knowledge," 61–62; Annas, "Self-Knowledge in Early Plato," 134; Luz, "Knowledge of Knowledge"; Kosman, *Virtues of Thought*, 227–45.

198. Other scholars suggest that Critias' proposal should be understood within the dramatic context. For example, Desjardins, "Why Dialogues," 121–22, argues that "knowledge of knowledge" (*epistēmē epistēmēs*) should be understood in the context of the practical examples demonstrated by the dramatic action and not merely through the discursive content. However, she does not pursue a full analysis of this passage and of the dialogue as a whole. McKim, "Socratic Self-Knowledge," suggests that Critias' proposal needs to be examined within a dramatic context, but concludes, 76, (vastly different than I) that Plato criticizes the Socratic philosophical method and the limitations of self-knowledge and ignorance, in order to indicate the "need for a different method of dialectic." He argues that Plato thinks that the Socratic method is insufficient to correct the ills of society. See also McCabe, "Looking Inside Charmides' Cloak," 179, and discussion below n. 214.

or to an active mental state of understanding something, while the word *anepistēmosunē* refers to the result of ignorance or to an active mental state of being ignorant of something.[199] Why does Socrates bring the word "ignorance" into the conversation?

Socrates uses the reference to "ignorance" to bring into the conversation another Greek word that concerns the mental activity of knowing, the verb "to know" (*eidenai*). He interprets Critias' proposal as follows:

> Then only the *sōphrōn* person will recognize (*gnōsetai*) himself and will be able to examine what he happens to know (*eidōs*) and what he does not. And he will be able to test the others likewise, what one knows (*oiden*) and thinks, whether he really knows (*oiden*) it, and also what he thinks he knows (*eidenai*) but does not know (*oiden*), no one except him [could do that]. And this is what it means to be *sōphrōn* and *sōphrosunē* and to recognize (*gignōskein*) himself: knowing the things that one knows and the things that one does not know.[200] So, these are the things that you are saying? Indeed, he said.[201] (167a1–8)

Although Critias' adjusted proposal concerns the word *epistēmē*, in his interpretation Socrates uses the words *gignōskein* and *eidenai*. Socrates alternates

199. Levine, *Profound Ignorance*, 213–14, observes in his own way the strangeness in the idea of knowledge of ignorance. He indicates that ignorance is not a "disciplinary whole" and is a condition of the soul, a state in which one cannot know in full knowledge what are the things that one does not know. Levine, 222–26, 330, argues that knowledge of oneself and of one's ignorance underlies Socrates' interpretation of *sōphrosunē*. Critias, on the other hand, is ignorant of himself and unable to distinguish between different opinions. Levine, 187–88, therefore, claims that Critias understands the phrase differently, as knowing your own interests and serving your own good. Other scholars also argue that Socrates' addition of the word "ignorance" is essential for understanding Socrates' *sōphrosunē*, as is demonstrated in his assertion of his own ignorance in the *Apology*. See for example: Tuckey, *Plato's Charmides*, 64; Schmid, *Plato's Charmides*, 145. McAvoy, "Carnal Knowledge in the *Charmides*," 99, argues that the prologue of the dialogue already indicates in various ways that "the recognition of ignorance" is a central issue in the dialogue, and that it is the foundation of *sōphrosunē*. See also discussion by Tuozzo, *Plato's Charmides*, 251–52, Benson, "Note on Socratic Self-Knowledge," and my discussion in the concluding chapter, section "Well-Ordered and Disordered Lives," on why Socrates professes his ignorance.

200. Later on, in the next sections, we will see that Socrates challenges that it is possible for a person to know the things that he does not know.

201. Ὁ ἄρα σώφρων μόνος αὐτός τε ἑαυτὸν γνώσεται καὶ οἷός τε ἔσται ἐξετάσαι τί τε τυγχάνει εἰδὼς καὶ τί μή, καὶ τοὺς ἄλλους ὡσαύτως δυνατὸς ἔσται ἐπισκοπεῖν τί τις οἶδεν καὶ οἴεται, εἴπερ οἶδεν, καὶ τί αὖ οἴεται μὲν εἰδέναι, οἶδεν δ' οὔ, τῶν δὲ ἄλλων οὐδείς· καὶ ἔστιν δὴ τοῦτο τὸ σωφρονεῖν τε καὶ σωφροσύνη καὶ τὸ ἑαυτὸν αὐτὸν γιγνώσκειν, τὸ εἰδέναι ἅ τε οἶδεν καὶ ἃ μὴ οἶδεν. ἄρα ταῦτά ἐστιν ἃ λέγεις; Ἔγωγ', ἔφη (167a1–8).

among three words that he himself gradually introduced into the conversation, *epistēmē*, *gignōskein* and *eidenai*. He thus changes Critias' proposal, and Critias neither protests nor even seems to notice.

We end up with three different proposals for what *sōphrosunē* is and to what it applies to: (1) "To recognize (*gignōskein*) oneself" refers to knowledge that applies to people. (2) "Knowledge (*epistēmē*) of itself (*epistēmē*) and of other kinds of knowledge (*epistēmai*)" refers to knowledge that applies to knowledge (although Socrates previously implied differently, that *epistēmē* applies to activities). (3) "Knowing (*eidenai*) the things that one knows and the things that one does not know" refers to knowledge that applies to things or data.[202] Critias treats each of these three resulting phrases as equivalent, although we can observe that each of them is directed to a different kind of object. Critias previously presented a distinction between the words "do" and "make," and a distinction among the greetings "recognize yourself," "rejoice," and "be *sōphrōn*," but he is tone-deaf to the distinction among the three words that Socrates introduces to the conversation, which concern the mental activity, and among the resulting variations of his proposal. Is it important to distinguish among these words and variations?

Socrates then uses the expression "a third to the Savior" (167a9–b2) to indicate that they now begin a third examination. The expression refers to Zeus and his epithet "savior."[203] However, we may suspect that Critias, who does not make necessary distinctions between proposals and words, is not likely to be saved from refutation. His ignorance concerning the meaning of *sōphrosunē* is about to be publicly exposed.

Socrates suggests that they should examine again from the beginning the next two issues: whether it is possible to know the things that one knows and the things that one does not know; and then whether this would benefit us (167a9–167b4). This, however, is a new issue that they have not yet addressed. Furthermore, Socrates is about to examine a different formulation entirely: knowledge (*epistēmē*) of itself and of other kinds of knowledge (*epistēmai*) and of "ignorance" (*anepistēmosunē*). Do these two formulations refer to the same thing? Is "knowing the things that one knows" equivalent to "knowledge of

---

202. Cf. Aristotle's similar use of these words in Irwin and Fine, *Aristotle. Introductory Readings*, 341–2. See also Schmid, "Socratic Moderation and Self-Knowledge," 342, 344, who argues that moderation (*sōphrosunē*) and self-knowledge (know yourself) in this passage are a result of a philosophical and "*elenchic* process." Schmid claims that Socrates encourages Critias to realize that he does not have true knowledge about the subject, and with regard to this, he is aware of himself. Critias refuses to admit his ignorance, because he still has to learn about moderation and self-knowledge.

203. More on this phrase see e.g.: Moore and Raymond, *Charmides*, 23 n. 71; Lampert, *How Philosophy Became Socratic*, 203.

knowledge"? And is "knowing the things that one does not know" equivalent to "knowledge of ignorance"? Critias, as usual, does not question Socrates' peculiar moves.

Socrates says at this point that he is experiencing an *aporia* and that he will show Critias why (b6–8). He therefore anticipates the resulting *aporia* of this examination. Socrates goes on to demonstrate that it is absurd to assume the existence of a reflexive knowledge that also applies to other kinds of knowledge and to ignorance in the sense of "not-knowledge." Socrates mentions various human states relating to perception, emotion and cognition: seeing, hearing and the sensations of the various other senses, desire, wish, love, fear, and belief (*doxa*, 167c8–168a9). Socrates thus indicates that just like each of these examples, knowledge (*epistēmē*) is not reflexive. That is, it is not directed towards knowledge itself, but to something other than itself and something different than other kinds of cases of it.[204] For example, seeing is directed at perceiving color, but not to seeing itself and to seeing other kinds of seeing and not-seeing cases (167c8–d2). All these examples indicate the peculiarity of the formulation "knowledge of itself."

Socrates' examples, however, do not suggest that knowledge of oneself is impossible. After Critias' rebuke of him, Socrates claimed that he also examines himself, lest he would think that he knows (*eidenai*) something that he does not know. He thus examines what he himself and Critias know and what they only assume they know but do not.[205] He encourages Critias to do the same. Furthermore, previously Socrates also encouraged Charmides to reflect on himself. He asked him to look inside himself and examine what feeling *sōphrosunē* creates in him and what he thinks about it (158e6–159a4). He also asked him to look inside himself and think what kind of a person *sōphrosunē* makes him (160d5–8).

Since Critias insists that the knowledge that he links to *sōphrosunē* is not of something that can be learned but is of itself and is of other kinds of knowledge (168a6–10), Socrates asks him whether such a knowledge is of

---

204. McCabe, "Looking Inside Charmides' Cloak," discusses the various examples that Socrates presents, the claim that they are not reflexive, and whether they are transitive. See also Schmid, *Plato's Charmides*, 89–93, who divides the examples to three groups that he argues correspond with dramatic events in the dialogue. He suggests that examples relating to perception correspond with Socrates' ability, as opposed to others present in the palaestra, to direct his sight not only to the beauty of Charmides, but also to himself and to the moral. Schmid claims that the example of desire relates to Socrates' self-control when he sees into Charmides' cloak. The last group, cognition and emotion, relates to Socrates' fear that he might think that he knows something that he does not know.

205. Cf. McCabe, "Looking Inside Charmides' Cloak," 183–84, and Levine, *Profound Ignorance*, 205–16.

something at all and has some kind of power.[206] Critias approves affirmatively, and thus Socrates goes on to mention further examples of comparatives, indicating that their power is not directed towards themselves. Socrates likens the power of knowledge (*epistēmē*) to the power of comparatives, using the examples of size by the word "bigger" (*meizon*) and of quantity by the word "double" (*diplasion*, 168b5–c8). The comparative "bigger," as an example, refers to something other than itself, or else we end up with the paradox that the bigger is bigger than itself and therefore would be also smaller than itself. Socrates' examples of comparatives should be of interest to Critias, because he thinks that *sōphrosunē* is class-related, and that it involves some kind of self-recognition about one's social class in relation to others, that is, knowledge of the relations between the upper and the lower classes.[207] Finally, Socrates mentions two further examples: motion that does not move itself and heat that does not burn itself (168e9).[208]

Socrates concludes that they have yet to find anything such that its nature allows its power to be directed at itself. He claims that they would need a great man who is able to show whether such a thing is possible, and whether this thing is knowledge. He then claims that he does not trust himself to do this task.[209] He thus challenges Critias to show that knowledge of knowledge and of ignorance/not-knowledge exists or is possible, and to show whether it would be something beneficial (169a–c2).

Critias clearly fails to explain how the knowledge that he links to *sōphrosunē* could be directed towards itself, and what kind of power it would have towards itself. He is unable to explain the practicality of the proposal "knowledge of knowledge and of ignorance." He fails to realize that a person can turn his mind towards himself, his opinions, mental activities and practices. Critias fails to do so, because he uses the word "knowledge," as well as the word *sōphrosunē*, to refer to one's social class in relation to others. What practicality does knowing your social class serve? It seems that according to Critias *sōphrosunē* has no practicality in itself, especially not for the lower classes. Critias and his fellow aristocrats selfishly benefit from the artisans'

206. Shorey, "Emendation of Plato *Charmides*," suggests that the passage (168b) indicates that science/knowledge in itself is a relative term.

207. See Schmid, *Plato's Charmides*, 93–94, who offers a different interpretation.

208. Eisenstadt, "Note on *Charmides*," indicates the peculiarity of these two examples. He suggests understanding them in the context of Socrates' dramatic experience of heat, being enflamed as he looks into Charmides' cloak, and his subsequent self-movement. Schmid, *Plato's Charmides*, 98, offers a similar interpretation.

209. Levine, *Profound Ignorance*, 251, argues that by these words Socrates, as opposed to Critias, indicates his awareness of his own ignorance and limitations, and that he also takes the issue as an important one.

sōphrosunē, that is, from their submission to their social limitations. He thinks that the artisans should serve him as a god with their products and services.

Throughout the dialogue, Plato emphasizes the need to take into account both the internal and the external aspects of human conduct. It is not surprising, therefore, that we find in Socrates' conversation with Critias two groups of words that represent the two aspects. In his first argument, Critias distinguishes between words that seemingly concern only the external and practical aspect (*prattein, ergazesthai, poiein*), as well as between their products.[210] He thereby distinguishes between two social classes, the aristocrats, who are concerned only with their own interests, and the artisans, who work and "make" things for them. Critias then adds that each person must be *sōphrōn*, that is, he must know his place in the social hierarchy. During the examination of Critias' view of social hierarchy, Socrates introduces into the conversation words seemingly relating only to the mental, theoretical activity (*gignōskein, epistēmē, eidenai, anepistēmosunē*). The use of these words changes the phrasing of Critias' proposal. Although new variations of his proposal keep emerging, Critias' view that *sōphrosunē* has to do with social hierarchy does not change. Socrates encourages Critias to examine his view and its practicality, by comparing *sōphrosunē* to knowledge of an art. Critias, however, assumes that practices are characteristic of only one class, of the artisans, and eventually separates the knowledge he associates with *sōphrosunē* entirely from practices. Critias is unable to examine critically his own soul and his beliefs.

Some scholars consider the phrase "knowledge of knowledge" (*epistēmē epistēmēs*) as the key philosophical issue in the dialogue, and they attempt to analyze the arguments about it as an end in itself.[211] However, this discussion

---

210. Also used in the dialogue is the word *draō* (161e1, 172b8), which refers to acting and doing in general. But it is not addressed by the characters directly as are its other synonyms.

211. Tuckey, *Plato's Charmides*, 36–37, 42–49, understands Plato as asking whether knowledge is knowable. Schmid, *Plato's Charmides*, 48, although referring to the dramatic context of this argument, claims that Critias refers to a master knowledge of a superior man, and concludes that Critias and Socrates present two different epistemological models (107–108). Tsouna, "Subject of Plato's *Charmides*," 54, argues that Critias sees self-knowledge as "a higher-order *epistēmē*." Moore and Raymond, *Charmides*, 84, argue similarly that Critias thinks of *sōphrosunē* as a "master knowledge." Morris, "Knowledge of Knowledge," suggests that the meaning of *epistēmē epistēmēs* is "a body of propositions about how to conduct refutations" and finding contradictions. He draws this conclusion with the help of Socrates' indication that he refutes Critias, as well as himself, because he fears that he would think he knows something that he does not know (166c–d). See also Tuozzo, *Plato's Charmides*, 209–44, and Kosman, *Virtues of Thought*, 227–45. Brann, *Music of the Republic*, 71, suggests that the dialogue consists of a change of subject: "the *Charmides* declares itself to be about soundmindedness and slithers off into theory of knowledge, knowing about knowing."

is not conducted strictly logically, but contaminated by Critias' obscured view that *sōphrosunē* concerns social hierarchy, and by Socrates' informal method to encourage Critias to examine the practicality of this view and to realize where he errs.[212] By the phrase "knowledge of itself" Critias means one's recognition of his social class, and by the phrase "knowledge of other kinds of knowledge" he means one's recognition of others' social class.[213] Socrates' strange process of questioning indicates that Critias consequently strips *sōphrosunē* itself of practicality. Later on, in the section "Discerning the Morally Good," another aspect of Critias' aristocratic view will be exposed, that the aristocratic *sōphrōn* should naturally rule over the artisans who are in turn *sōphrones* in accepting this.[214] Why does Critias mask his views with verbal acrobatics? Clearly, he knows that they would anger the masses, but perhaps he is also unable to speak more clearly, as he refuses to direct his mind to the connection between the internal thought and the external conduct. My analysis shows the danger in getting caught up in the discussion of "knowledge of knowledge" at the expense of losing sight of Plato's larger point. By this discussion, Plato intends to reveal the problematic nature of the aristocratic exploitative values, and the marginalization of artisans and their crafts.

212. Other scholars observe that the discussion between Socrates and Critias proceeds not strictly logically. See especially Notomi, "Origin of Plato's Political Philosophy," 246, who sees Critias' "definitions not as logically consequent, but as implying and revealing an underlying ideology," which is oligarchic. Levine, *Profound Ignorance*, 217, argues that Critias' proposals indicate that his concern is for only his own good, and his misunderstanding of *sōphrosunē* results from his ignorance about the good. See also Lampert, *How Philosophy Became Socratic*, 206, who indicates that Socrates implies that knowledge is indeed reflexive, but similar to the sense in which opinion is reflexive and enables one to form an opinion about an opinion.

213. Cf. Annas, "Self-Knowledge in Early Plato," 122. Although our interpretations differ from each other, I agree with her general observation that "self-knowledge is knowledge of oneself in relation to others." I contend that Critias intends to indicate by his proposal the kind of knowledge that one has concerning one's social position in relation to others.

214. Many scholars suggest that Critias indicates by his proposal an intention to rule over the artisans, as evident by my n. 238 below. For example, Brown, "Plato's *Charmides*," 320, who claims that Critias' definition reflects his wish to control others. Joosse, "*Sōphrosunē* and the Poets," 586, argues that Critias' aristocratic view is developed as he claims that *sōphrosunē* is "a master science that controls the expertises of workers in the city." Lampert, *How Philosophy Became Socratic*, 198, argues that Critias' proposal suggests his right to rule over others. Tuozzo, *Plato's Charmides*, 199–200, claims that part of Critias' intentions in this formulation of knowledge of other kinds of knowledge is to indicate the aristocratic management of the city. I argue that at the current stage of the dialogue Critias uses his proposal only to indicate that each person needs to know his social position in relation to others. Later on other aspects of his view are exposed, including his assumption that the aristocrats should rule over the artisans. See more below n. 238.

Socrates' third examination ends up with the *aporia* that he predicted. Socrates tells his silent listener that Critias saw his *aporia* and was forced and caught by it as well, just as happens when someone yawning affects those around (169c3–6). We may recall that previously Critias said that he would not be ashamed to admit that things he said were incorrect (164c9–d2). Now, however, Socrates specifically says that Critias, who is usually a man of good reputation, was embarrassed in front of the others present (*ēschuneto tous parontas*, 169c7).[215] Critias, therefore, refuses to agree with Socrates' claims, talks unclearly, and hides his *aporia* (169c5–6). Thus, his ignorance concerning the meaning of *sōphrosunē* is exposed.

The Expert as Speaker of Truth

The description of the *aporia* marks the middle of the conversation between Socrates and Critias, as three examinations precede it and three follow. Although Socrates claims that he experiences *aporia*, he is able to continue examining the flaws in Critias' soul and views. In this fourth examination (169d2–171c10) Socrates agrees to assume that knowledge (*epistēmē*) of knowledge (*epistēmē*) exists "in order that the discussion will progress" (169d2–4). He asks in various ways what then would be the benefit of *sōphrosunē*. Critias is unable to point out an answer. It turns out that Critias' aristocratic view implies that the *sōphrōn* would not be able to examine whether one is an expert or an impersonator, and would not be able to speak about the truth. Likewise, we learn that Critias' literary arguments are worthless for discussing the truth.

Socrates deliberately asks Critias a complex question – namely, what more can the *sōphrōn* know (*eidenai*) by the knowing of which he would know the things that he knows and the things that he does not know (169d5–7); and whether this is what Critias claims is the meaning of "to recognize (*gignōskein*) oneself" and "to be *sōphrōn*" (d7–8). Once again, we face three different proposals concerning the meaning of *sōphrosunē*: (1) knowledge of knowledge (*epistēmē epistēmēs*); (2) knowing (*eidenai*) the things that one knows and the things that one does not know; and (3) to recognize (*gignōskein*) oneself. The challenge that Socrates presents is to identify what the benefit would be in knowing the things that one knows and the things that one does not know. This is despite the fact that already in the previous examination Critias

215. Raymond, "*Aidōs* in Plato's *Charmides*," 38–39, compares Critias' shame with Charmides' *aidōs*. Raymond indicates rightly that Critias' shame is a result of his desire to receive respect from others, while Charmides' shame is a result of deference to authority. For other interpretations of the *aporia* that Socrates and Critias experience see e.g.: Politis, "Place of *Aporia*," "*Aporia* in the *Charmides*," and "*Aporia* and Searching."

approves that his opinion is that the knowledge of the *sōphrōn* does not apply to something that can be learned (168a6–10).

Critias does not answer Socrates' complex question. Instead, he says that if there is knowledge (*epistēmē*) that recognizes (*gignōskein*) itself, the person who has it would be like what he has (169d9–e2). He gives several examples. If one has quickness he is quick, if one has beauty he is beautiful, and if one has recognition (*gnōsis*) he recognizes (*gignōskōn*). He thus sums that when a person has recognition (*gnōsis*) of himself, he will recognize (*gignōskōn*) himself. Critias moves too easily from the formulation "knowledge of itself" back to the formulations "knowledge of oneself" and "to recognize oneself."

Socrates then says that he does not argue with this claim, but with another. He wonders whether it is necessary for a person to know the things that he knows and the things that he does not know. In Critias answering that what Socrates suggests is the same thing as what he claimed (170a1), we are to understand that Critias suggests that "recognizing yourself" is equivalent to "knowing what you know and what you do not know." However, we have already seen in the previous examination that Critias is unable to indicate what self-knowledge truly means. He does not examine critically his aristocratic interpretation of self-knowledge as recognizing your place in social hierarchy. Socrates wonders how these two formulations can be the same (170a2–4).

Socrates asks what could knowledge of knowledge (*epistēmē epistēmēs*) distinguish (*diairein*) other than that one thing is knowledge (*epistēmē*) and another is not knowledge (*ouk epistēmē*, 170a6–8). Critias answers that it would distinguish only this. Soon enough we see that knowing only this would have no value to the *sōphrōn* person. Critias agrees that the knowledge he associates with *sōphrosunē* would allow the *sōphrōn* only to distinguish that one has knowledge, but not what exactly are the things that one knows. He distinguishes the knowledge (*epistēmē*) he associates with *sōphrosunē* from the knowledge (and ignorance, *anepistēmosunē*) of arts such as medicine and politics, which apply to the healthy and the just (170a10–b11). Clearly, Critias does not want to associate *sōphrosunē* with the practices of the arts.

Next, Socrates uses the three words, *gignōskein*, *epistēmē*, and *eidenai*, in one short question:

> But that he recognizes (*gignōskei*) by means of this knowledge (*epistēmē*), how will he know (*eisetai*)?[216] (170b12)

Socrates intends to encourage Critias to think about the object to which each of the three related words applies. He also intends to make him realize that without addressing the things that a certain field of knowledge applies to, it is

216. Ὅτι δὲ γιγνώσκει, ταύτῃ τῇ ἐπιστήμῃ πῶς εἴσεται; (170b12).

not possible to confirm whether one has knowledge. For example, it is possible to know that one is an expert in medicine only by examining what he knows regarding the issues that medicine applies to, as health and disease. Socrates explains that a person will recognize (*gignōskei*) the healthy by knowledge of medicine; the harmonious by music; the building by house-building, but he will not know these things by means of the knowledge that Critias associates with *sōphrosunē* (170c1–4).

Socrates repeats his question but with slight, though significant, changes:

> Then if *sōphrosunē* is really knowledge (*epistēmē*) of other kinds of knowledge (*epistēmōn*), how will he know (*eisetai*) by means of it that he recognizes (*gignōskei*) the healthy thing or the building?[217] (170c6–7)

Socrates indicates that according to Critias' proposal *sōphrosunē* does not entail knowing (*eidenai*) the things that one knows and the things that one does not know. The *sōphrōn* does not know anything about the objects and issues that the arts apply to, that is, he does not understand the practices of the arts. Socrates thus concludes that *sōphrosunē* would merely allow the *sōphrōn* to know that one knows and the other does not know (170c9–d4). Absurdly, it will not allow him to examine what someone knows or understands (*epistatai*, 170d5–10). If this is the meaning of *sōphrosunē*, it does not seem to be something beneficial. This nonetheless fits Critias' view that *sōphrosunē* is merely one's recognition of one's place in the social hierarchy, and that it does not concern the practices of the arts or anything practical at all.

After denying the *sōphrōn* the ability to know things that relate to the practices of the arts, Critias then denies the artisans knowledge (*epistēmē*). He agrees that the doctor will know the distinction between health and disease, but that he will not know medicine itself, because medicine is knowledge (*epistēmē*), a domain that belongs to the *sōphrōn* alone (170e1–171a2). Critias splits the two aspects of human conduct, knowledge (*epistēmē*) and practice, between the *sōphrōn* (whether he is an aristocrat or an artisan) and the artisan. However, Socrates implies that this does not lead to splitting the benefit of the arts as well. The *sōphrōn* would not have any beneficial ability, while the artisan could practice his art, and would also be able to examine others and distinguish those who pretend or think that they know something from those who are true experts (170e1–3, 171c4–9).[218] We may infer that the *sōphrōn*

217. Σωφροσύνη δέ, εἴπερ μόνον ἐστὶν ἐπιστημῶν ἐπιστήμη, πῶς εἴσεται ὅτι τὸ ὑγιεινὸν γιγνώσκει ἢ ὅτι τὸ οἰκοδομικόν; (170c6–7).

218. Schofield, "Socrates Conversing with Doctors," suggests correcting the text by removing the word *ou* in 170e6, and deleting the lines 170e12–171a2, as he thinks that with those components the argument is "barely intelligible." See also discussion by Schmid,

aristocrat will not have any beneficial ability so long he does not engage in practical arts, while the *sōphrōn* artisan will have a beneficial ability.

Critias' aristocratic *sōphrosunē* is useless. Without practicing some kind of an art Critias would not be able to examine, or speak about, matters that the arts address. Critias agrees that in order to examine whether a doctor is truly an expert one needs to examine what he says and whether it is true, whether he practices what he preaches, and whether he does things correctly (171b7–10). Critias also agrees that without the knowledge of medicine it is impossible to examine the doctor in this way (171b11–13). They conclude that only the doctor would be able to examine other doctors (171c1–3), and an expert would be able to examine only those in his field of knowledge (171c4–9).[219] Socrates thus denies Critias' *sōphrōn* aristocrat any useful literary skills that would allow him to speak about the truth. Only experts can examine whether one says the truth and knows something. Critias, who cares for the literary field and for *sōphrosunē,* should now realize that he would not be able to excel in either of these, unless his knowledge would be directed to something other than itself, and unless it would be practical. Critias could have argued in defense that the *sōphrōn* person does not need to be an expert in every art, but can rather follow the connection between the theoretical knowledge and its practicality, as well as whether one practices what one preaches, but he lacks the presence of mind to suggest that.

Plato's Socrates, 114–20, who offers his alternative interpretation that the argument is intended to invoke the Socratic ideal of knowing what one knows and does not know.

219. Some scholars have addressed the problem indicated here, that in order to examine whether one is an expert in a certain field of knowledge the examiner needs to be an expert in the same field. Schmid, "Socratic Moderation and Self-Knowledge," 346, argues that Socrates' "*elenchic* process" leads to moderation in the sense of philosophical humility and that "one comes to know what one knows and does not know about good and evil, not what one knows and does not know about technical subjects." I will discuss Critias' proposal that *sōphrosunē* is "knowledge of good and bad" later in the section "Discerning the Morally Good." LaBarge, "Socrates and the Recognition of Experts," suggests that Plato's other dialogues "suggest ways in which someone might know that someone else is an expert even though he does not share that expertise." He claims that Plato gives various indications for what an expert is, such as the ability to teach, and acknowledged professional success. In addition, LaBarge suggests that common knowledge allows one to recognize an expert despite not being an expert in that field. While LaBarge searches for a solution for the problem in other dialogues and outside the dialogue, I argue that this problem needs to be resolved within the dramatic context of Critias' aristocratic views. LaBarge partially follows the work of Woodruff, "Plato's Early Theory of Knowledge," who argues that in Plato's early dialogues Socrates implies the concept of non-expert knowledge of a sort of common knowledge. Woodruff, 73, says that this is in addition to the knowledge of the arts, which have to be essentially "expert knowledge of the good." See also Gentzler, "How to Discriminate between Experts and Frauds."

Critias does not distinguish three types of objects of knowledge: people, things, and practices. Instead, he suggests that the knowledge of the *sōphrōn* applies only to knowledge. According to this, *sōphrosunē* would be useless. It would not allow the *sōphrōn* to examine whether one is an expert or an impersonator, and it would not allow him to speak about the truth. All these wonderful abilities, however, would be given to the artisans. We may gather that Critias, who does not want to practice any art and separates *sōphrosunē* from its practicality, cannot be an expert in any field, including the literary. Since Socrates is able to examine and reveal to us whether Charmides and Critias have *sōphrosunē*, should we conclude that he is an expert concerning *sōphrosunē*?

The Skills of a Well-Managed Person

Socrates' fifth examination includes two lengthy speeches in the format of questions (171d1–173a6). Each speech presents new proposals for the benefit that *sōphrosunē* produces. Socrates once again implies that *sōphrosunē* applies to activities, but now he suggests that it applies to the activity of management. The formulation of each speech as a question gives Critias a chance to examine Socrates' descriptions of the benefit of *sōphrosunē*, to learn, and to correct his own proposals. Critias does not take these opportunities, and we gradually get another glimpse into his soul: he is unable to manage himself, and as a result is unable to manage his family, and his *polis*.

The first question that Socrates asks (171d1–172a5) concerns the benefit of *sōphrosunē*, assuming, contrary to the conclusion of the previous examination, that the *sōphrōn* could know the things that one knows and the things that one does not know. Socrates clarified this proposal:

> . . . the *sōphrōn* would know the things that he knows and the things that he does not know, that some things he knows and that some things he does not know.[220] (171d3–4).

As we see, Socrates suggests that *sōphrosunē* would allow the *sōphrōn* to make distinctions between what he knows and what he does not know (171d4–5). However, Critias, and the reader, should question the feasibility of knowing things that you do not know, and even of knowing that some things you do not know. How could one know the things that one does not know? In the section "An Unreasonable Search" we will see that Socrates indeed intends Critias to consider this issue. In fact, the previous examinations already implied that

220. ᾔδει ὁ σώφρων ἅ τε ᾔδει καὶ ἃ μὴ ᾔδει, τὰ μὲν ὅτι οἶδεν, τὰ δ' ὅτι οὐκ οἶδεν (171d3–4).

the kind of knowledge proposed to be *sōphrosunē* does not apply to physical objects or data but to practices: not knowledge that, but knowledge how. It would be more reasonable to argue that one can recognize that one does not know how to do something. For example, when someone who is not a doctor feels sick, she may recognize that she does not know how to cure herself.[221] Socrates' following explanation suggests exactly that.

Socrates says that having this ability to distinguish what one knows and what one does not know, and to examine others likewise, would be very beneficial (171d5–6). It would allow those who have *sōphrosunē* and those ruled by them to lead their lives without mistakes (171d6–8). Thus, those who are *sōphrones* would not only benefit themselves but would also benefit those over whom they rule. Socrates' formulation is in the first person plural, and gives the impression that he and Critias are *sōphrones*. He then replaces the verb *eidenai* with the verb *epistamai* (171e1) that may be translated as "to know" or "to understand." He says that those who are *sōphrones* would not attempt to do what they do not understand, but will find those who do and hand the work over to them (171d8–e2). These *sōphrones* rulers would not allow anyone to do anything except what they can do correctly (e3–4). Socrates' suggestion is that the knowledge proposed to be *sōphrosunē* does not apply to physical objects but to practices and activities, even though these activities involve knowing things and may eventually lead to producing things, products. Socrates even says that by means of *sōphrosunē* a house, a city and every other thing will be well-managed (171e5–7). Thus, he once again emphasizes that *sōphrosunē* applies to activities, for now it is the activity of management. The connection made here between the virtue *sōphrosunē* and the political sphere is natural, since the Greeks interpreted *sōphrosunē* also as a political virtue.[222]

Socrates describes an imperfect world where some people are *sōphrones* and some are not. Nonetheless, the *sōphrones* are rulers, and they would benefit not only themselves but also those who are not *sōphrones*. While those *sōphrones* would rule others, they would also rule themselves, since each *sōphrōn* would prevent also himself from doing what he does not understand. This account implies that in an ideal world where everyone would have *sōphrosunē* there would be no need for ruling over others because each person would rule over oneself.

---

221. People still might assume they can do some things and later find out that they cannot, or they might assume they can learn how to do something while doing it, but might realize their mistake while attempting it.

222. North, *Sōphrosynē*, 15, indicates that class tension led to a new conception of *sōphrosunē* as a political virtue (*aretē politikē*), first used by the aristocratic, oligarchic faction, and later by the democrats.

Socrates' description seems to contradict Critias' first three proposals for what *sōphrosunē* is. Firstly, his description suggests that the *sōphrōn* person would benefit not only himself but also others. In contrast, Critias' first proposal "to do your own things" suggests that the *sōphrōn* aristocrat benefits only himself. Secondly, Socrates' description suggests that the *sōphrōn* person would be engaged in activities, either in the practices of the arts or in some kind of management. However, Critias' second proposal, "to recognize oneself," suggests that the aristocrat does not engage in practices, but enjoys the artisans' products and services similarly to the god Apollo. Thirdly, Socrates' description suggests that the *sōphrōn* person would rule over himself and over others by means of his knowledge. However, the examination of Critias' third proposal "knowledge (*epistēmē*) of itself and of other kinds of knowledge (*epistēmai*)," suggests that the knowledge of the *sōphrōn* would allow him only to know his and others' place in the social hierarchy.[223] How could the *sōphrōn* rule over himself or others? He would not understand by means of his knowledge anything that the arts apply to, and thus would not enjoy the benefit in having art expertise.

Socrates' description indicates that even managing a house or a city requires practical knowledge, and such managements should aim to benefit all the members of the house or the city. However, Critias is not engaged in servicing his city. As opposed to Socrates, he did not participate in the army expedition near Potidaea. He also does not manage well his house matters, as he does not fulfil his duty as Charmides' guardian to care for his health (headache) and for his well-being (*sōphrosunē*), but competes with him.

Socrates concludes that when error is removed and correctness leads the way, people do well (*eu prattein*) and beautifully (*kalōs*) every action/practice (*praxis*), and those who succeed (*eu prattontas*) are happy (171e7–172a3).[224] The phrase "to do well and beautifully" recalls Socrates' first question in the dialogue, whether anyone excels in wisdom or in beauty or in both. It also recalls Critias' description of Charmides as "beautiful and good" (*kalos kai agathos*), and Socrates' description of the family to which Critias and Charmides belong, as excelling both in beauty and in virtue and in all the things which are considered to constitute happiness. We now see, however, that

223. See North, "Period of Opposition," 13, on the view that *sōphrosunē* as "an unnatural restraint upon the strong" turns the strong person to a slave, and her references to the dialogues *Gorgias* (492c) and *Republic* (557b, 560D).

224. Tuozzo, "What's Wrong with These Cities," 334, rightly indicates that the description of a city without error should be understood in context of Socrates' opening fictitious story about the Thracian doctor. Zalmoxis says that the mistake of many is that they attempt to treat the patient (or to perform any craft) without addressing the matter of *sōphrosunē*. It seems that *sōphrosunē* is required for performing any craft beneficially.

Critias' knowledge and literary arguments do not apply to anything practical. He does not manage well either himself, his house, or his city. We should thus doubt that he could enjoy a successful life and become happy.

Finally, Socrates asks Critias whether what he had just explained is what they had previously said about *sōphrosunē*. Critias agrees (172a3–6), although, as we have seen, Socrates' description contradicts Critias' previous proposals. This confirms that Critias is unperceptive. Socrates concludes that they did not find in their previous examinations any kind of knowledge (*epistēmē*) as this one. Critias agrees again (172a7–9), although it does not seem that they had even tried to find what Socrates just proposed. In order to argue that this beneficial knowledge is possible, Critias would have to admit that something in his previous proposals is incorrect, and that the *sōphrōn* should be able to know something about practices. But he does not want to associate himself with practices.

Next, Socrates presents his second lengthy speech as a question. This speech is shorter than the previous one (172b1–c2), but raises considerations just as novel. Socrates asks whether the good thing that they discovered to be *sōphrosunē* is knowing/understanding (*epistamai*) knowledge (*epistēmē*) and ignorance (*anepistēmosunē*). He then elaborates that this would allow the *sōphrōn* person to learn more easily, and that everything would seem clearer to him since, in addition to everything he would learn, he would also have in mind this knowledge (*epistēmē*) that they propose as *sōphrosunē* (172b3–6). We may suspect that Critias, in showing that he does not learn and progress during the conversation, lacks *sōphrosunē*.

Socrates adds that the *sōphrōn* person would therefore be able to examine others more beautifully about what he had already learned, and those examining without it would do it poorly and inefficiently (172b6–8). Is Socrates an example of one who can examine others about what he learned concerning *sōphrosunē*? Critias, who does not have *sōphrosunē* not only examines poorly, but does not even attempt to examine his own social view or Socrates' social view. At the beginning of the conversation, Critias gives two long speeches concerning what *sōphrosunē* is, and Socrates examines each of them (see the above sections "The Producers and the Recipients of Goods" and "Know Your Place"). Now towards the end of the conversation, Socrates gives two speeches, and he presents each of them as a long-winded question, but Critias does not examine them. Not only does Critias not pick up on distinctions between his own proposals and Socrates', he does not even attempt to examine the relations between the two, because he is unwilling to admit in any way that his own proposals might be deficient.

In closing, Socrates asks Critias whether what he had just said is the benefit that they claim they would enjoy by having *sōphrosunē*, and whether this makes *sōphrosunē* a greater thing than it truly is. Critias answers that perhaps this is the case (172b8–c3). Socrates' questions suggest that the *sōphrōn* person would have various abilities, but Critias denies it. We gradually learn that Critias himself lacks the abilities he denies to *sōphrosunē*. The *sōphrōn* would be a well-managed person who is able to make distinctions between what he understands and what he does not. He would be able to learn easily, and to examine others easily about the things that he knows. The *sōphrōn* would therefore not only be a well-managed person, but would also be able to lead a well-managed house and city. How would he come to have these skills? Throughout the dialogue, the reader is encouraged to infer that he would acquire these skills as a result of his attention to the relations between the internal and the external aspects of human conduct. Critias, however, has shown that he lacks all these skills.

Socrates suggests that maybe they were looking for something completely useless (172c4–5). Their assumptions seem strange to him (172c5–6), for they assumed the possibility of so many things just in order to examine whether this kind of knowledge would benefit them (172c7–d2). However, they agreed incorrectly that *sōphrosunē* is a great, good thing, and would lead the management of the household and the *polis* (172d3–5). Critias is surprised, and requests that Socrates explain himself (172d6–173a5). Socrates thus turns to his sixth and final examination.

Discerning the Morally Good

The sixth and final examination continues to explore the benefit of *sōphrosunē* (172e6–175b2). Critias continues to disparage the artisans and the practice of the arts, denying them entirely the knowledge of good and bad. However, we may gradually appreciate that Critias, who lacks virtue, is the one who does not understand good and bad, and that he is an untrustworthy person.

Socrates says that if *sōphrosunē* is what they have so far assumed it to be, it is not clear that it would produce (*apergazetai*) for them something good (*agathon*, 172e6–173a1). Critias is surprised and expects Socrates to explain why. Socrates is about to indicate that *sōphrosunē*, thus construed, would not produce good things, or things at all. But before that, he begins describing a dream he has, which implies that *sōphrosunē* is something good that causes people to be good. Socrates indicates that it is yet to be determined whether his dream holds some truth (173a7–d3).[225] The dream is that if *sōphrosunē* ruled over us (*archō*, 173a8), everything would be done according to knowledge (*epistēmē*), and no one would deceive us by pretending to know what he does not know.

Socrates' dream involves various questions. Socrates mentions three artisans: the ship-captain, the doctor, and the general (173a8–b4). He asks whether the result of having *sōphrosunē* would be that our bodies would be healthier, and that we would be saved when in danger in the sea or in war. Socrates' examples are odd. The aim of the doctor is treating those who are sick rather than those who are healthy, and the aims of the ship-captain and the general are not merely saving people from death, but leading a ship to a certain destination, and leading a military operation. Socrates also asks whether equipment, clothing, footwear, and all other useful things would be produced skillfully if we used true artisans (*dēmiourgoi*, 173b7–c2).

Socrates' dream suggests that benefit is the result of practicing the arts together with having *sōphrosunē*, regardless of whether these arts lead to producing physical products as clothes and shoes, or whether they provide services as do the doctor, the ship-captain, and the general. Furthermore, using true artisans (*dia to alēthinois dēmiourgois chrēsthai*, 173c2) produces useful things (*chrēmata*, 173c1). This notion contradicts Critias' view that the artisans do not need to know whether they have done something beneficially; and that benefit is not determined by the way the artisans perform their work but by the recipients of their products (discussed in section above, "The Producers and the Recipients of Goods").

Socrates continues with the example of the practice of divination, that is, the knowledge (*epistēmē*) of the future (173c3–7). He suggests that when *sōphrosunē* is in charge of this art, imposters would be turned away and honest diviners would be appointed as diviners of the future.[226] Does this example imply that Socrates is an honest diviner of the truth? After all, his examinations reveal that Critias only pretends to know what *sōphrosunē* is, and earlier

---

225. See Moore and Raymond, *Charmides*, 31 n. 88, who indicate that by telling Critias to listen to his dream "whether it has come through horn or through ivory" Socrates paraphrases the words of Penelope in Homer's *Odyssey*, 19.563–67, that deceiving dreams "come through gates of ivory," while true dreams come through gates of horn. Socrates' formulation presents his dream as a yet to be examined proposal. Burger, "Socrates' Odyssean Return," 227–32, interprets Socrates' dream in the light of Penelope's dream about the return of her husband Odysseus to the palace (19.547, 535–81). Lampert, *How Philosophy Became Socratic*, 216–17, makes further comparisons between the *Charmides* and the *Odyssey* throughout his analysis. See also Brann, *Music of the Republic*, 84.

226. On divination in ancient Greece, see Flower, *The Seer in Ancient Greece*.

he even said that he "divines" (*manteuomai*) that *sōphrosunē* is something good (169b4–5).

Socrates deliberately refrains from explaining adequately over what *sōphrosunē* presides.[227] While at the beginning of his dream he says that *sōphrosunē* would rule (*archō*, 173a8) over people, as he continues he suggests that it would be in charge over (*epistateō*, 173c5) the art of divinity itself. The root of the word *epistateō* is *epista-*, which means "to stand on." This is also the root of the word *epistēmē*, which means "knowledge" or "understanding." Socrates uses this wordplay in order to indicate a connection between the knowledge of the *sōphrōn* and the control manifested by expertise of an artisan. However, Socrates' dream suggests that *sōphrosunē* somehow prevents people from doing what they do not know how to do, and from deceiving others by pretending to know what they do not know. The question regarding what *sōphrosunē* presides over will therefore return later on in this examination.

In the closing of his dream, Socrates says that when the human race would be equipped with *sōphrosunē*, people would act (*prattein*) and live knowledgeably/understandingly (*epistēmonōs*) because *sōphrosunē* would guard them from ignorance (173c7–173d3). How does *sōphrosunē* guard from ignorance? These lines continue to emphasize some kind of a connection between *sōphrosunē* and the arts, as they suggest that *sōphrosunē* would help conducting oneself knowledgeably including in arts. However, what this connection is may be explained only when the meaning of *sōphrosunē* is uncovered. In the concluding chapter I will address this issue.

The description of *sōphrosunē* in Socrates' dream suspiciously insinuates that Critias is not a *sōphrōn* person. We have seen that Critias pretends to know what he does not know, and is ignorant concerning the meaning of *sōphrosunē* (in the section above "The Practicality of *Sōphrosunē*").[228] Furthermore, at the opening of the dialogue, Critias tells Charmides that Socrates is a doctor for his headache. He compels Socrates to collaborate with his lie by suggesting that nothing prevents Socrates from pretending to be a doctor who knows the cure for Charmides' headache (155b1–6, in the section above "The Whole and Its Parts"). Socrates' dream suggests the contrary; the *sōphrōn* person detects

---

227. Schmid, *Plato's Charmides*, 135–36, also indicates this point, and suggests that Socrates' description of his dream is directed to refute Critias' interpretation of *sōphrosunē* as something that allows Critias to rule over people.

228. Levine, "Tyranny of Scholarship," 72, argues that Socrates gradually exposes Critias' ignorance. Schmid, *Plato's Charmides*, 141, argues similarly that Critias is unwilling to admit his limitations, but Socrates' method of refutation is intended to lead him to self-knowledge. See also above n. 199, for scholars who argue that the issue of ignorance is central to understanding the meaning of *sōphrosunē* in this dialogue.

deceivers and imposters and appoints only true experts.[229] Nothing seems to prevent Critias from pretending to know something that he does not know, or to compel others to do so.

Despite his utopian dream, Socrates says that they cannot yet learn how by acting knowledgeably/understandingly they would succeed and be happy (173d3–5). Here is Critias' response:

> But surely, he said, you will not easily find any other purpose than to succeed, even if you would disdain acting knowledgeably.[230] (173d6–7)

Critias claims that the purpose of acting knowledgeably is success. Socrates then asks him concerning what would the *sōphrōn* person act knowledgeably (173d8–9). This question is relevant, because as we have seen, Socrates' dream suggests that *sōphrosunē* has some kind of connection with the arts, but it does not indicate adequately what *sōphrosunē* is and over what it presides. Socrates asks Critias several times whether the knowledge ascribed to *sōphrosunē* concerns certain works associated with artisans: cutting shoe leather, bronze work, wool, and woodwork. Critias rejects all these examples (173d9–e5). Socrates therefore claims that Critias denies that the artisans who act knowledgeably and practice successfully their arts would be happy (173e6–10). We have already seen that Critias degrades the artisans because they work for others, and that he denies that they recognize whether they do something beneficial (see the section above "The Producers and the Recipients of Goods"). Now Critias also deprives the artisans of happiness. Nonetheless, Critias thinks that the artisans are *sōphrones* in working for others while performing their arts knowledgeably.

Socrates then urges Critias to explain who he thinks is a happy man, and what knowledge he would have. We already know that according to Critias the happy man has *sōphrosunē*, but it is not the same *sōphrosunē* that the artisans have. Socrates does not wait for Critias' answer and continues to ask whether Critias thinks that the happy man is the diviner who knows the future (173e10–174a2). Critias agrees, but does not explain why. He adds that he refers to another person as well (174a3), although he does not reveal who this person is. Socrates therefore attempts to extract the answer from him.

---

229. McKim, "Socratic Self-Knowledge," 73, argues that Socrates' dream rejects the possibility that "knowledge of knowledge" would allow the *sōphrōn* to know what one knows and what one does not know. Even if it would allow it, this would not ensure that the artisan would practice his art beneficially.

230. Ἀλλὰ μέντοι, ἦ δ' ὅς, οὐ ῥᾳδίως εὑρήσεις ἄλλο τι τέλος τοῦ εὖ πράττειν, ἐὰν τὸ ἐπιστημόνως ἀτιμάσῃς (173d6–7). Compare my translation to Schmid's, *Plato's Charmides*, 137, as opposed to that of Raymond and Moore, *Charmides*, 32.

He asks whether Critias thinks of a person that knows more than the diviner does, that is, not only the future (the things that will happen) but also the past (the things that happened), the present (contemporary things) and is ignorant of nothing (174a4–7). Assuming that such a person exists, Socrates says that Critias would probably agree that there is no one who would live more knowledgeably, and Critias agrees (174a6–9).

Socrates' description of a omniscient diviner who knows everything is peculiar. Does knowing data and facts *per se* make a person happy? For example, if one knows historical facts, would this make one happier? Socrates' conversation with Charmides already indicated that *sōphrosunē* does not imply doing everything by and for oneself (in the section above "Thinking for Yourself"). We should assume that *sōphrosunē* also does not mean knowing everything. We may suspect that Socrates subscribes to the importance of communal life.[231] As opposed to plain data, Socrates' dream indicated that practicing an art together with *sōphrosunē* has a direct influence on our lives.[232] The ship-captain, the doctor, the general (173a8–b4), and all artisans (173b7–c2), do and produce things skillfully.

Socrates says that he desires to know whether according to Critias all the kinds of knowledge (*epistēmai*) are equal, or whether only one of them can make a person happy (174a10–13). Critias answers that the kinds of knowledge are not equal to each other. Socrates then asks whether Critias thinks that the knowledge that makes one happy is that by which one would know the checkers game (*to petteutikon*), the calculated (*to logistikon*), or the healthy (*to hugieinon*, 174b1–8). His examples intentionally refer to things and not to activities. He begins with a kind of knowledge that applies to a game and Critias, annoyed by this example, rules it out entirely. Socrates ends his list with the knowledge that applies to the healthy, a much more serious matter. Critias thinks that the person that would know the healthy would be happier than those who have the knowledge of the game or the calculated (174b8). Why would the doctor be happier than those who have knowledge of the other mentioned things? Critias probably thinks that the doctor stands

231. I believe that Socrates implies here that the virtues of wisdom and *sōphrosunē* are not a result of knowing or memorizing data, but of some kind of deeper understanding of human action. A similar discussion concerning the knowledge of the virtue courage as opposed to the knowledge of the diviner appears in Plato's *Laches*, e.g., 196d. See also discussion by Santas, "Socrates at Work on Virtue," 450. In this context, see Lewis, *Solon the Thinker*, 32–35, who discusses the Greeks' concern with knowing what is beyond their immediate sight. He indicates Solon's impressive ability to see deeper into the consequences of situations. This partially explains Solon's reputation as a wise man.

232. Schmid, *Plato's Charmides*, 137, stresses a different but significant point, that Critias' view of wisdom does not include knowledge of what one knows as opposed to what one does not know, but assumes the possibility of knowing everything.

in a higher social position in society and by practicing his knowledge he earns more money that would benefit him.

Finally, Critias says that the knowledge that makes one happy is the knowledge (*epistēmē*) by which one would know the good thing (*to agathon*) and the bad thing (*to kakon*, 174b10).[233] Socrates' response is important for understanding the whole conversation with Critias. He says:

> You rogue, I said, for a long time you are dragging me around in a circle, hiding that it is not living knowledgeably that makes one succeed and be happy, and not all the other kinds of knowledge, but only this one which concerns the good and the bad.[234] (174b11–c3)

Socrates accuses Critias of dragging him around in a circle. To what circle does he refer?; and where did it begin? In order to answer these questions we must see that throughout the conversation Critias does not progress. Socrates does not intend to claim that there is a logical circularity in Critias' argument. There is no sense in which his argument assumes the very conclusion that he strives for. Instead, Socrates' remark is meant to indicate Critias' lack of progress. Once again Critias does not learn that good and bad can be traits of the artisans' souls, and of the way they perform their activities. He assumes

---

233. Some scholars suggest that Plato intended to convey that *sōphrosunē* is "knowledge of good and bad." See for example Irwin, *Plato's Moral Theory*, 88, and Schmid's criticism of Irwin's arguments, *Plato's Charmides*, 141–44. McKim, "Socratic Self-Knowledge," 74–75, argues that Socrates believes that *sōphrosunē* is knowledge of good and bad, but he will not conclude it so long as Critias does not admit his ignorance and that *sōphrosunē* is not "knowledge of knowledge." Press, "*Elenchos* in the *Charmides*," 265, argues that Plato does not present his doctrine about *sōphrosunē* explicitly, but "it is suggested that the kind of knowledge that *would* satisfy the beneficiality criterion is knowledge of good and evil." Kahn, "*Charmides* and the Proleptic Reading," 542, argues that the proposals "to do your own things" and "knowledge of good and bad" are presented as "the source of a happy life," and intended to be read proleptically, that is, in reference to the *Republic*, where Plato presents his doctrines on these issues. Kahn, 548–49, also suggests that the end of the *Charmides* raises a criticism over the ironical Socratic ignorance presented in the *Apology*. Kahn argues that the *Charmides* implies that the Socratic *elenchus* succeeds because Socrates had the knowledge of good and bad, but that this issue is addressed in depth only in the *Republic*. Lampert, *How Philosophy Became Socratic*, 233, claims similarly, that the "*Charmides* is an introduction to the *Republic*." I contend that if *sōphrosunē* were nothing other than knowledge of good and bad, it would not differ from any other virtue. Even if we hold the unity of virtues, it would not be clear how *sōphrosunē* differs from courage for example. This is actually suggested by Socrates in Plato's *Laches*, 199e.

234. ῏Ω μιαρέ, ἔφην ἐγώ, πάλαι με περιέλκεις κύκλῳ, ἀποκρυπτόμενος ὅτι οὐ τὸ ἐπιστημόνως ἦν ζῆν τὸ εὖ πράττειν τε καὶ εὐδαιμονεῖν ποιοῦν, οὐδὲ συμπασῶν τῶν ἄλλων ἐπιστημῶν, ἀλλὰ μιᾶς οὔσης ταύτης μόνον τῆς περὶ τὸ ἀγαθόν τε καὶ κακόν (174b11–c3).

that good and bad are in the artisans' products, depending on the aristocratic use of these products for their own benefit.

In the section "The Producers and the Recipients of Goods" we have seen that Critias presents an interpretation of "to do your own things" that distinguishes two kinds of *sōphrosunē* for the two social classes. The aristocrats are *sōphrones* in doing everything only for their own benefit, while the artisans are *sōphrones* although they work and make things for others as well. Socrates summarizes Critias' argument by using the word "good," and thus elucidates that Critias is concerned with the artisans' products. This leads Critias to argue that those who make (*poiein*) good things and not bad are *sōphrones*, and that the doing (*praxis*) of good is *sōphrosunē* (163e8–11). Socrates then gradually introduces into the conversation the words "recognize" (*gignōskein*), "knowledge" (*epistēmē*), and "know" (*eidenai*). He uncovers Critias' view that the artisans do not need to know whether their products end up being good or bad, beneficial or harmful. Critias denies that the good and bad can be traits of souls, and that the artisans' mental and practical activities may be conducted well or badly, beneficially or harmfully. According to him, only when the recipients themselves benefit by these products can the products be called good and beneficial.

In the final stage of their conversation, Socrates asks Critias about the knowledge that would make one happy, and what product/thing one would know by it. This leads Critias to his final proposal that *sōphrosunē* is knowledge of the good and the bad. Critias does not intend the morally good and bad. He continues to focus on the products that the artisans produce, and he supposes that he, as an aristocrat, knows better than the artisans do which of their products are good and which are not. Thus, Socrates expresses his exasperation by accusing Critias of dragging him in a circle.[235]

---

235. Levine, *Profound Ignorance*, 285–87, argues that the circularity is caused by Critias' selfish interest in his own good. Levine also observes that Critias suggests that benefit is extrinsic to the arts and requires a special kind of master knowledge. I understand the circularity slightly differently as resulting from Critias' linguistic focus on products, although I would grant Levine that we would not reach this circularity without Critias' selfishness. Scholars raise many other interpretations of the circularity. For example, Tuckey, *Plato's Charmides*, 77, argues that the circularity began with Critias' first proposal "doing good things." Socrates is ironical in blaming Critias of hiding this proposal from him, because he was the one who led Critias to it. Tuckey, 91, concludes that Plato wished to convey that *sōphrosunē* is a combination of the two proposals, "doing what is good with the knowledge that it is good." Brown, "Plato's *Charmides*," 315, says that "It is not clear what Socrates means by saying that Critias has been dragging him about in a circle." McKim, "Socratic Self-Knowledge," 73–74, argues that Socrates is the one who led Critias in a circle and hid from him the proposal "knowledge of good and bad."

We have seen that Critias' verbal gymnastics obscures his view of social hierarchy, but Socrates now indicates flat out what is the view that Critias keeps hiding or is simply unable to articulate clearly. This view is absurd: living knowledgeably, as the artisans do, does not entail knowing good and bad. Socrates' next question proves once again that Critias denies that the artisans' need to be good or to conduct their art in a good way in order to benefit others:

> Tell me, Critias, if you wanted to take this knowledge (*epistēmē*) out of the other kinds of knowledge (*epistēmai*), would medicine cure any less, or the shoe-making put shoes, weaving provide cloth or seamanship prevent dying at sea and generalship in battle [any less]?[236] (174c3–8)

Critias answers that removing completely the knowledge of good and bad from the arts would not make the arts any less beneficial (174c8). While in the first examination Critias argued that the artisan does not need to recognize whether he does something beneficial, now he claims that the artisan does not need to know the good and the bad at all.[237] Critias believes that knowing good and bad is not necessary for practicing any given art, because he assumes that goodness is external to the artisans and their activities. He focuses on the artisans' products, but assumes that only the recipients determine whether these products are good or bad. His move from "doing good and not bad" to "knowledge of good and bad" does not imply progress. He does not learn that there is a direct connection between being virtuous, being active outwardly, and benefiting oneself and others.

Socrates concludes that *sōphrosunē* would not benefit us, because according to Critias' previous arguments *sōphrosunē* is not knowledge of good and bad, but knowledge (*epistēmē*) of knowledge and other kinds of knowledge

236. ἐπεί, ὦ Κριτία, εἰ 'θέλεις ἐξελεῖν ταύτην τὴν ἐπιστήμην ἐκ τῶν ἄλλων ἐπιστημῶν, ἧττόν τι ἡ μὲν ἰατρικὴ ὑγιαίνειν ποιήσει, ἡ δὲ σκυτικὴ ὑποδεδέσθαι, ἡ δὲ ὑφαντικὴ ἠμφιέσθαι, ἡ δὲ κυβερνητικὴ κωλύσει ἐν τῇ θαλάττῃ ἀποθνῄσκειν καὶ ἡ στρατηγικὴ ἐν πολέμῳ; Οὐδὲν ἧττον, ἔφη (174c3–8).

237. Tuozzo, "What's Wrong with These Cities," 340–41, observes the strangeness in Socrates' indication that "knowledge of what one knows" and "knowledge of good" would not be beneficial. He also claims that the connection Socrates makes between the knowledge allowing craftsmen to make conditional goods and the "knowledge of good" is unclear. Tuozzo, 334, argues that the dialogue nonetheless implies that "knowledge of the good" is an unconditional good and is thus the meaning of *sōphrosunē*, and that it is socially directed towards the benefit of everyone. However, as I argued above, in n. 233, assuming that *sōphrosunē* is nothing other than knowledge of good and bad would not explain how it differs from any other virtue. For even if we hold the unity of virtues, we would have to clarify the domain in which *sōphrosunē* manifests and thefore how it differs from the way courage manifests, for example.

(*epistēmai*) and kinds of ignorance (*anepistēmosunai*). Critias is surprised. He is unwilling to admit that his previous proposal, that *sōphrosunē* is "knowledge of knowledge," is wrong. He suggests, therefore, that if *sōphrosunē* is knowledge (*epistēmē*) of other kinds of knowledge (*epistēmai*) it would be in charge over (*epistatai*) all kinds of knowledge and thus would also rule (*an archousa*) the knowledge of the good. Critias clearly uses words that Socrates used earlier to describe *sōphrosunē*, "rule" and "be in charge"/"supervise" (*archō*, 173a8; *epistateō*, 173c5). He therefore concludes that in this way *sōphrosunē* would benefit us (174d8–e2). Critias now exposes another aspect of his aristocratic view. He suggests that the *sōphrōn* man would not only know other kinds of knowledge, but would rule over them as well as over the knowledge of good and bad. He intends that the *sōphrones* aristocrats would rule over the artisans who have other kinds of knowledge, but he nonetheless assumes that those artisans do not themselves have the knowledge of good and bad.[238]

Critias does not seem to remember the course of the conversation and its conclusions. Socrates reminds him that they previously agreed that "knowledge of knowledge" and of "ignorance" is not beneficial, because it does not allow the *sōphrōn* to know the things that each kind of art (*technē*) applies to (174e3–8). For example, medicine, and not *sōphrosunē*, would be the artisan (*dēmiourgos*) producing the healthy (174e9–175a1). Socrates deliberately anthropomorphizes the art of medicine by describing it as a artisan/crafter . This allows him to emphasize that medicine is a productive art practiced by people. Socrates finally asks: how would *sōphrosunē* be beneficial if it is an artisan of no benefit? Critias answers that it would not be (175a6–8). Critias is unwilling to admit that his previous proposals are wrong, as he does not want to associate the aristocratic *sōphrosunē* with practicing the arts. He therefore answers that *sōphrosunē* would not be beneficial. Critias' conclusion is outrageous, but he is not alarmed.

238. Other scholars have observed that Critias thinks that as an aristocrat he should rule the artisans. Notomi, "Origin of Plato's Political Philosophy," 247, indicates that Critias explains his proposal that *sōphrosunē* is knowledge (*epistēmē*) of other kinds of knowledge, by the terms "rule" and "supervise" that appear in 173c and 174d–e. Notomi claims rightly that Critias presents his oligarchic views by distinguishing rulers from technicians who do not know their own good and obey the rulers. Press, "*Elenchos* in the *Charmides*," 263–64, argues that Critias assumes that his class is the one that knows how to rule. Press also rightly indicates that the end of the dialogue is merely directed at refuting Critias' "aristocratic-epistemic elitism." Schmid, *Plato's Charmides*, 129, argues that Critias sees himself as a "technocratic ruler" and that the "knowledge" associated with *sōphrosunē* "does not have self-critical moral function." Schmid, 135–36, also indicates that the description of Socrates' dream is directed at refuting Critias' view. Levine, *Profound Ignorance*, 286–87, argues that Critias intends that a few would rule the many, but because they have a master knowledge that allows them to oversee and rule the benefit of other kinds of knowledge. For other scholars who observe this issue, see above n. 214.

We have seen that Critias does not think about the morally good and bad, but about the instrumental use of products and services provided by artisans. That he does not distinguish the morally good from the bad is manifested throughout the dialogue. Socrates uncovers Critias' aspiration to become as a god who is worshiped by artisans, and to rule the artisans only for his own selfish interests. From the opening of the dialogue we learn that he is an untrustworthy man. He manipulates Charmides into the conversation by lying that Socrates is a doctor for his headache (155a7–b6). He thus attempts to compel Socrates to pretend that he is a doctor. Later on he lies that Charmides did not hear from him the answer "to do your own things" (161c2, 162c4–6). When Charmides renounces his hold over the conversation, Socrates says that for a long time during the conversation Critias wanted to compete and receive respect from Charmides and everyone present (162c1–3). Focused on himself, Critias does not fulfil his duty as Charmides' guardian.

Where does Critias err? Critias neglects to take into account the internal and the external aspects of human conduct together. He focuses on his literary arguments and avoids practices. He degrades the working class of artisans and the practices of the arts. He thus consistently avoids associating the aristocratic *sōphrosunē* with practices. This is the reason for Critias' lack of various abilities that throughout the conversation Socrates associates with *sōphrosunē*. Critias' self-knowledge does not derive from self-examination (section "Know Your Place"). He is unable to examine himself or Socrates with regard to whether their arguments (the internal) are possible and practical (the external), and as a result he is ignorant concerning the true meaning of *sōphrosunē* (section "The Practicality of *Sōphrosunē*"). He is not an expert in any practical field. He is not even an expert in the literary field, which he cares for, because speaking about the truth requires practical expertise on the discussed topic (see section above "The Expert as Speaker of Truth"). He is not a well-managed person and is unable to lead a well-managed house or city (see section above "The Skills of a Well-Managed Person"). Finally, we learn that Critias does not distinguish the morally good from the bad. Is he beyond saving?

An Unreasonable Search

In the final stage of the conversation between Socrates and Critias, Plato motivates us to think of what went wrong in their conversation. Socrates summarizes the flaws that led them to the awful, outrageous conclusion that *sōphrosunē* is useless (175a11–176d5). His summary involves many peculiarities intended to expose publicly Critias' immoral and ignorant soul.

Socrates blames himself in looking for something that apparently turns out to be worthless (175a9–11). He says that *sōphrosunē*, which they agreed to be the most beautiful of all things, would not have turned out to be worthless if he had been a better help in searching (175b1–2). As we have seen, however, it is Critias' aristocratic views about social hierarchy that led to depriving *sōphrosunē* of the ability to produce something beneficial. Despite his self-proclaimed responsibility, Socrates then uses the first person plural formulation in order to indicate that Critias and he together were defeated in every possible way (*nun de pantachē gar ēttōmetha*, 175b2–3).

Socrates does not accept the results of the conversation. He says that they did not find what "the lawgiver" ascribed to the word *sōphrosunē*, although they agreed to accept many things that do not follow reason (*logos*, 175b5). Does he have in mind a specific lawgiver? I will suggest in the concluding chapter that he does. Socrates then elaborates concerning the things that they agreed on, but the reader may notice that he is deliberately inaccurate.

Socrates says that they agreed that *sōphrosunē* is "knowledge of knowledge" (*epistēmē epistēmēs*) although reason (*logos*) did not permit it and denied it (*ouk eontos tou logou oude phaskontos einai*, 175b6–7). We may recall that during the conversation Critias insists that "knowledge of knowledge" is possible (section "The Practicality of *Sōphrosunē*"). Socrates agrees to accept this proposal only in order that the conversation will progress, and in order to reveal that Critias' views imply that *sōphrosunē* is not something beneficial (section "The Expert as Speaker of Truth").

Socrates also says that they agreed that "knowledge of knowledge" would allow us to know the things to which the other kinds of knowledge (*epistēmai*) apply, so that the *sōphrōn* would understand that he knows the things that he knows and that he does not know the things that he does not know (175b7–c3). We may recall, however, that Critias suggested that "knowledge of knowledge" would not apply to know-how, to the things and practices to which the arts apply (section "The Expert as Speaker of Truth"). This is because Critias avoids practices, as he associates practices with the artisans.

Socrates further says that they generously agreed without examination that it is possible for someone to know the things that he does not know. We can now confirm that Socrates, who fears lest he think he knows something that he does not know (166c7–d2), intended to reveal that Critias does not question the feasibility of one knowing the things that one does not know (171d4–5, section "The Skills of a Well-Managed Person").[239] Critias does not

---

239. Schmid, *Plato's Charmides*, 148, suggests a different interpretation to these lines. He claims that Socrates indicates that the hypothesis that knowledge of ignorance is possible is yet to be proved.

realize that, on the contrary, it is possible to know that you do not understand how to perform a certain practice.

Socrates anthropomorphizes the "reason" (*ho logos*) and the "search" (*hē zētēsis*). He thereby separates the interlocutors from their reason and their responsibility for the progress of the search. Nonetheless, he allows his listeners, and the reader, to gather that the "reason" (*ho logos*) represents Socrates himself, while the "search" (*hē zētēsis*) represents Critias.[240]

Socrates says that the reason (*ho logos*) did not permit what they accepted (175b7, 175c1). However, the search (*hē zētēsis*), being easy (*euēthikōn*) and not hard (*sklērōn*) on them, could not find out the truth (175c8–d2). It mocked the truth and proclaimed quite insolently (*panu ubristikōs*) that what they agreed to be *sōphrosunē* is worthless (175d2–5). Socrates, like the "reason," denies that Critias' proposals are possible. Clearly, the anthropomorphized "search" represents Critias. Critias is indiscriminately permissive. He does not attempt to correct his proposals or reject the changes that Socrates applies to them. This leads him to an *aporia*, and he cannot find out the truth. Critias prefers mocking the truth over admitting his own ignorance and his proposals being wrong. He thus insolently accepts that *sōphrosunē* is worthless. Clearly, his proposals fail to satisfy because he is incapable of correct reasoning and therefore incapable of investigating the matter.

Socrates' use of the concept *hubris* to describe Critias is deliberate. The Greeks considered *hubris* and *sōphrosunē* as opposites.[241] Aristotle identifies *hubris* as one of the causes for social strife, and says that it involves striving for superiority in honor and economic advantage.[242] This fits Critias' views and behavior in the dialogue. He focuses on self-benefit that he could gain from the service of the artisans, and he clearly competes with Charmides and strives to receive honor from him and the others present. It should be noted that the concept *hubris* came to be associated with tyrannical vice,[243] which fits Critias

240. Schmid, *Plato's Charmides*, 148–49, argues differently, that Socrates personifies the *logos* in order to emphasize that the argument was false and to make the reader reconsider it and the hypothesis that knowledge of ignorance is possible. Tuozzo, *Plato's Charmides*, 287, 291, argues that Socrates' summary of his conversation with Critias supplies the reader with indications concerning how to "continue the investigation."

241. On the contrast between *sōphrosunē* and *hubris* according to ancient writers, see North, *Sōphrosynē*, 11, 16, 18, 19–27, 50–51. On *hubris* as a crime in Attic law see Cohen, *Law, Violence, and Community*.

242. Aristotle, *Politics*, 5, 1302b1, and *Rhetoric*, 2.2, 1378b14–15, 1378b23–32. See discussions by Cohen, *Law, Violence, and Community*, 31, and Cairns, "Aristotle on *Hybris* and Injustice."

243. See North, *Sōphrosynē*, 16.

as he goes on to become a cruel tyrant. Critias masks his views of social hierarchy under his acrobatic verbal arguments, but Socrates reveals them.

In addition to separating the interlocutors from their reason and responsibility over the inquiry, Socrates on the one hand advises both his interlocutors, Charmides and Critias, to focus on the argument, and on the other hand he examines their souls. During the dialogue, Socrates says twice that he examines the proposals and not the person who suggests them. On the first occasion, Critias denies that Charmides heard from him the proposal "to do your own things." Socrates agrees with Charmides that it does not matter from whom he heard this answer, because, he says, they should examine not who said it but whether it is true (161c3–6). However, at the opening of the dialogue, Socrates suggested undressing Charmides' soul, and he continues to examine Charmides' soul even through his understanding of this proposal.

On the second occasion, Critias accuses Socrates of trying to refute him (*elenchein*, 166c4–6). Socrates says that if he does so, it is only in order to examine also himself, because he fears he would think he knows what he does not know (166c7–d2). Socrates then tells Critias to let go of whether the thing under refutation belongs to Critias or to Socrates, but to direct his mind to examining the argument itself while it is being refuted (166d9–e3). However, Socrates continues to examine Critias' soul and reveals his ignorance concerning the meaning of *sōphrosunē* and his reluctance to admit this ignorance.

Why does Socrates tell his interlocutors to focus on the argument? Socrates' interlocutors are concerned with their reputation. They strive for honor and avoid public shame. In order for the conversation to progress, and in order for his interlocutors to be able to progress by learning from the conversation, Socrates encourages them to put aside their concerns and to concentrate on examining what the truth is.[244]

Plato the dramatist clearly insinuates a connection between the flaws of Critias' soul in the dialogue and the historical Critias' awful role in history. Critias the babbler demonstrates his view that *sōphrosunē* is class-related, but Socrates' examination of his soul reveals that he is an ignorant and immoral man. Through the dramatized conversation, Plato conveys that *sōphrosunē* is a moral virtue that manifests itself in both mental activities (represented in the dialogue by wisdom) and outward practices (represented by beauty). A good and moral person is able to act skillfully and beneficially, and is active outwardly. Critias, however, focuses on his literary, sophistic skills and this may mistakenly seem to himself and the crowd as wisdom, but in fact his arguments demonstrate ignorance as they are obscure, fallacious, and impractical. This leads us to the ending of the dialogue.

244. Cf. Levine, *Profound Ignorance*, 211.

4

A Forceful Ending

Then with force, I said, and you will not give me a preliminary hearing?
Using force, he said, because this one here commands.

—PLATO, *CHARMIDES*, 176C7–8

The Force Opposing *Sōphrosunē*

PLATO USES SOCRATES' CONVERSATION with the disengaged Charmides to convey that being mentally active is an essential aspect of *sōphrosunē*. He uses Socrates' conversation with the self-centered babbler Critias to convey that this mental activity has to be directed outwardly. Paying attention to the connection between the internal and the external of human conduct is essential for both performing arts skillfully and acting morally. Plato uses the end of the dialogue to show the violent tendencies of Charmides and Critias. These tendencies prove that the cousins do not come any closer to learning what *sōphrosunē* is throughout their discussions with Socrates.

Since the conversation ended with the conclusion that *sōphrosunē* is something worthless, Socrates turns to Charmides and says that he is irritated (*aganaktō*) by two things. First, Charmides would not be benefited from *sōphrosunē*, if he is *sōphrōn* with regard to both his looks and to his soul (175d5–e2). Socrates' description of Charmides emphasizes once again the two aspects of *sōphrosunē*, one related to external appearance and the other to the internal soul. The second thing about which Socrates is irritated is the Thracian charm that he learned with seriousness, if it concerns something worthless (175e2–5). However, Socrates states, he does not think that *sōphrosunē* truly is something worthless, but that he is a bad (*phaulos*) inquirer (175e5–6). As we see, this is the second time that Socrates blames himself for the disheartening results of the conversation.

If *sōphrosunē* is a great good thing, and if Charmides has it, Socrates says, then Charmides is a blessed and happy person. Nonetheless, Socrates advises him to examine whether he has *sōphrosunē*, and to consider Socrates as a silly person who is unable to search with reason for what it is (175e6–176a4). Charmides, however assumes that Critias is no better than Socrates. He answers that he does not know if he has *sōphrosunē*, for how could he if they, Socrates and Critias, could not find what it is. Charmides says that he is not convinced that Socrates does not know what *sōphrosunē* is, and claims that he needs the charm (176b1–3). We may suspect that Charmides avoids declaring that he does not need *sōphrosunē* simply because he cares for the opinion of the crowd about him. He does not want to appear to them as an arrogant and annoying youth who disrespects the authority of the older Socrates (discussed in section "An Unengaged Beauty").

Charmides says that nothing prevents Socrates from using the charm over him until it would suffice (176b3–4). Clearly, he did not pay attention to Socrates' conversation with him and with Critias. He still does not realize that he must be active, not passive, with regard to Socrates' charm. Furthermore, during the conversation with Critias, Socrates suggested that *sōphrosunē* would prevent one from pretending to know how to do something (discussed in section "Discerning the Morally Good"). Does Socrates, who failed in motivating Charmides to be mentally active, know how to cure Charmides' soul?

Critias then responds by saying that if Charmides continues conversing with Socrates this will prove that he has *sōphrosunē* (176b5–8). Critias has failed to learn that being engaged in conversation is not enough to procure *sōphrosunē*. He thus motivates Charmides to continue speaking with Socrates, although he knows that Charmides is not whole-heartedly interested in such conversations. Charmides then proves that he knows his place as Critias' ward, and answers that it would be awful not to obey his guardian's command (*mē peithoimēn. . . ha keleueis*, 176b9–c3). Critias, in response, says that he does command Charmides to do so. Critias the aristocrat thinks that *sōphrosunē* means knowing your social place. While he commands both Charmides and Socrates to continue conversing with each other, he does not intend to participate actively in this plan to educate Charmides. He demonstrates his aristocratic view of *sōphrosunē* as knowledge that supervises other kinds of knowledge, but is not present in practices: he demonstrates supposed control over others without participating in the practice of teaching.

We may gather that Charmides and Critias have been talking for a moment only to each other, because Socrates asks the two cousins about what they are consulting. Their answer is that they have already consulted, and they thus exclude Socrates from the decision that Charmides will continue to converse with him. Socrates asks if they are going to use force or give him a "preliminary hearing" (*anakrisis*). By his choice of a word that refers to a legal proceeding, Plato perhaps intends to remind his reader of the role of Critias and Charmides in the suspension of these proceedings during the rule of the Thirty Tyrants as they executed people without a trial.[245] Charmides replies to Socrates that they will use force because Critias commands (176c7–8). This scene exposes the violent tendencies of the cousins.[246] Critias commands and uses force, but Charmides is not innocent either. He obeys Critias, after manipulating him to command him to have future conversations with Socrates, as Charmides is concerned with public opinion about him. It certainly does not mean that Charmides will become more actively engaged in future conversations. We may recall that at the opening of the dialogue Socrates asks Charmides whether he will take the charm from him by persuasion or without it (156a1–3). We may now suspect that taking it without Socrates' permission implies using force. Thus, Socrates suspected Charmides' forceful tendencies all along.[247] Charmides says that now Socrates needs to deliberate about what he wants to do (176c7–8). Socrates answers that there is no room for deliberation, because when one uses force over someone else, it does not allow resistance. Charmides then tells him not to resist (176d1–5).

Nothing prevents Critias and Charmides from forcing others into doing for them whatever they desire. Nothing prevents Charmides from obeying the authority of his awful guardian. Although Charmides and Critias force Socrates to continue conversing with them in the future, they do not possess true control over him. Throughout the dialogue, we have seen, Socrates

245. On the legal term *anakrisis*, and on the Thirty's executions without trials see for example: Moore and Raymond, *Charmides*, 36 n. 95; Dušanić, "Critias in the *Charmides*," 59–60; Krentz, *Thirty at Athens*, 64–65.

246. Tuozzo, *Plato's Charmides*, 301–2, argues against the common interpretation that Plato here alludes to the violence of the historical cousins as tyrants. Tuozzo, 300, argues that this exchange between Charmides and Socrates is merely "playful," and that Charmides "playfully threaten force" because he appreciates the benefit that he would receive from conversing with Socrates. Lampert, *How Philosophy Became Socratic*, 233, also describes Charmides' violent response as a "playful threat."

247. See also Vielkind, "Philosophy, Finitude, and Wholeness," 32–34, on the contrast between the description of Charmides' beauty in the dialogue and his historical figure as a tyrant.

obeys only the authority of his reason (*logos*) and of *sōphrosunē*. This recalls Plato's *Apology*, 32c, according to which Socrates opposed orders of the tyrants, such as the order to arrest a figure named Leon the Salamis whom the tyrants planned to dispossess and execute.[248] Socrates' beautiful discussions (*kaloi logoi*) do not succeed in curing the immoral souls of Charmides and Critias. They become cruel tyrants and die violently shortly thereafter. Plato, however, is interested in the souls of his readers, who have the opportunity to learn more than Charmides and Critias do in the palaestra and more than they did in their whole lives.

To Be or Not to Be in *Aporia*

The conversation with Critias ends with the conclusion that *sōphrosunē* is not something beneficial, but Socrates doubts this result. It appears, therefore, that the dialogue ends with an *aporia*, a lack of means to answer what *sōphrosunē* is. Before this final *aporia*, we encounter many other *aporiai*, supposedly experienced by Socrates (156b2; 167b6–9; 155c5; 169c3–6; 175b1–2), Charmides (162b8–9; 176a6–b1) and Critias (169c3–6, 175b1–4). We gradually learn, however, that neither of the characters experiences a genuine *aporia*, but for different reasons. Furthermore, I contend that Socrates, who doubts the conclusion that *sōphrosunē* is not something beneficial, has at least some sense of what *sōphrosunē* is, but does not intend to reveal it to his interlocutors unless they make an effort to learn and change.

At the beginning of the dialogue Socrates tells his silent listener that when Charmides sat next to him he experienced an *aporia*, and had difficulty conversing with him (155c5). We have seen that this description is merely intended to draw the attention of his silent listener, because the rest of his description suggests otherwise (see section above "The Whole and Its Parts"). Once Socrates finds out that Charmides is familiar with who he is and his name (156a4–8), he admits to Charmides that a moment ago he experienced an *aporia* about how he would explain to him the cure for his headache (156b2). A connection seems to be made here between Charmides' awareness of who Socrates is and Socrates' recovery from his *aporia*. We may infer that Socrates' earlier description of Charmides' appearance as the cause for his *aporia* is merely intended for his silent listener. Charmides' beauty is not the genuine cause for Socrates' *aporia*, but Critias' lie is. Socrates recovers from his *aporia* because he is relieved that he does not need to pretend to be a doctor.

---

248. See discussion by Brann, *Music of the Republic*, 86–87.

Charmides is disengaged from the conversation because he does not want to participate in it (above, Chapter 2). After giving two attempts at answering what *sōphrosunē* is, he raises the proposal "to do your own things," which he heard previously from Critias. Socrates encourages Charmides to examine this proposal as well, but Charmides does not make a true effort and finally admits that he does not know what it means, and that probably even the owner of this proposal does not know what he himself meant (162b8–10). Charmides is simply interested in handing over the conversation to Critias (161b3–7, 162c1–6). His self-proclaimed lack of knowledge does not reflect a genuine *aporia*, however, because it does not result from a genuine attempt to examine the matter. Charmides is a study in evasion, not engagement.

Socrates then turns to examine Critias' soul. After two examinations with him, at the beginning of their third, he tells Critias that he experiences an *aporia* and that he will show him concerning what (167b6–9). Socrates then goes on to examine Critias' soul and views, and the examination ends up with his predicted *aporia* (169c3–6). As opposed to Socrates and Charmides, Critias does not admit his lack of knowledge in any stage of the dialogue, but hides his *aporia*. Socrates tells his silent listener that when Critias saw him in his *aporetic* situation, he was caught by it as well (169c3–6). He also says that Critias was embarrassed and did not want to admit it (169c3–d1). Critias competes with Charmides and does not want to admit that he is not better than him. However, we may doubt whether he experiences a genuine *aporia* either, since he continues to insist that his proposals are correct despite the fact that they turn out to be impossible and impractical.

Socrates' *aporia*, however, does not imply that he himself lacks a sense of what *sōphrosunē* is, but that Critias' proposal is flawed and that Critias' stubborn insistence on it is perplexing. The *aporia* that Socrates claims he experiences, and Critias denies having, occurs in the middle of the conversation, preceded by three examinations and followed by three. Does the fact that Socrates is able to show that his interlocutors' proposals do not satisfy indicates that he has a better sense of what *sōphrosunē* is?

At the end of the dialogue Socrates, Charmides, and Critias, experience a kind of communal *aporia*. Socrates declares that they were defeated in every way and could not find what *sōphrosunē* is (175b1–4). He thus suggests that Critias experiences an *aporia* as well, although Critias does not admit it. Despite the awful result of the conversation, Socrates claims that he thinks that *sōphrosunē* is something useful (175e2–176a2). This, once again, should make us speculate whether Socrates does not experience a genuine *aporia*. After all, they were defeated simply because Critias did not back down from his flawed proposals which reflect his contorted, aristocratic views about social hierarchy.

Socrates then advises Charmides to examine whether he has *sōphrosunē* or whether he needs the Thracian charm (175e2–176a2). Charmides does not turn to examine himself, but immediately answers that he does not know whether he has *sōphrosunē*, and asks how he could know what it is if Socrates and Critias themselves cannot find out what it is (176a6–b1). We may suspect that Charmides publicly doubts his ability to know what *sōphrosunē* is because he cares for the opinion of the crowd about him. He does not want to appear as a youth who does not know his place and thinks that he knows better than his guardian and the well-known Socrates. Thus, Charmides, once again, does not experience a genuine *aporia*. His self-proclaimed lack of knowledge is not a result of a genuine effort to inquire into the matter and himself, but of his concern for public opinion about him.[249] Furthermore, Charmides also indicates that Critias does not know what *sōphrosunē* is, and thus implies that Critias experiences *aporia*. Even then, however, Critias does not admit it publicly.

Socrates, Charmides, and Critias are consistent dramatic characters. They do not experience a genuine *aporia*, although for different reasons.[250] Charmides does not make a genuine effort to examine himself with regard to the matter at hand. Critias refuses to acknowledge that his proposals are incorrect and that he does not know what *sōphrosunē* is. Socrates, we may suppose, has at least some sense of what *sōphrosunē* is, as he encourages his interlocutors to form an opinion about it by taking into account both the internal and the external aspects of human conduct. Socrates is also confident that *sōphrosunē* is good for its possessor, but does not intend to reveal to his interlocutors his own opinion concerning what *sōphrosunē* is so long as they do not make an effort to learn and change. In a dialogue where the characters are consistent and do not change, it is no wonder that the ending is *aporetic*. How does this *aporetic* dialogue serve Plato in conveying his opinions concerning what *sōphrosunē* is? The answer will be revealed in the next, concluding chapter.

249. That Charmides does not experience a genuine *aporia* is also argued by Schmid, *Plato's Charmides*, 150–51.

250. For other interpretations of Plato's method of questioning and the *aporiai* in the dialogue *Charmides* see for example Schmid, *Plato's Charmides*, 86, 64–78, who argues that the Socratic *elenchus* is intended to lead his interlocutors to self-knowledge, to cure Charmides of his "weakness of thought," and Critias of his arrogance and unawareness of his limitations. Tuozzo, *Plato's Charmides*, 6–51, suggests that the Socratic *elenchus* is a positive practice, and that Socrates somewhat succeeds in educating Charmides and Critias. See also: Tarrant, "Naming Socratic Interrogation in the *Charmides*"; Politis, "Place of *Aporia*," "*Aporia* in the *Charmides*," and "*Aporia* and Searching."

5

Conclusion: What Is *Sōphrosunē*?

"...I divine that *sōphrosunē* is something beneficial and good."

—SOCRATES, IN PLATO, *CHARMIDES*, 169B4–5

Well-Ordered and Disordered Lives

WE MAY NOW CONCLUDE the analysis of the philosophical content that Plato wished to convey through his dialogue concerning the virtue *sōphrosunē*, which he thinks has to do with an orderly relation between the internal and the external aspects of human conduct. In his philosophical drama Plato presents four characters. We gradually learn why Charmides appears beautiful, Critias appears wise, Chaerephon appears crazy, and why Socrates is a *sōphrōn* character.[251]

251. Press, "*Elenchos* in the *Charmides*," 265, argues that the dialogue is "an enactment of *sōphrosynē*," and that "Rather than a propositional definition of *sōphrosynē*, we come to a clearer vision of what it is and what it is not to be *sōphrōn*. And rather than acquire a definition by means of a purely logical proof that might obtain our rational assent, we acquire a vision by means of arguments complemented by the imaginative and emotional attractiveness of Socrates' and repulsiveness of Charmides' and Critias' characters and comportment." I agree only with some aspects of Press' claims, that the dialogue is an enactment of what it means to be and not to be *sōphrōn*, and that Plato does not provide a formal argument for what *sōphrosunē* is. The drama certainly gives the reader a vision of *sōphrosunē*. However, contrary to Press, I contend that this is because of the dialectic nature of the dialogue. Plato encourages the reader to compare the characters, what they

At the opening of the dialogue we learn that Charmides is considered to be exceptionally beautiful. We gradually learn that his beauty is not merely a hereditary trait. He nurtures his physical appearance by coming regularly to the palaestra. In addition, he displays his aristocratic manners, as evidenced by his consideration for the upper-class opinion about him, and by his consequent two proposals, which are based on others' opinions concerning the expected behavior of an aristocratic youth, that *sōphrosunē* means (1) doing everything calmly and (2) shame. Charmides' beautiful appearance, therefore, is a manifestation of an orderly arrangement of his physical features,[252] and of an orderly behavior that accords with quiet traits expected of an aristocratic youth. The crowd perceives his attractive beauty through the sense of sight. Charmides, however, neglects his soul. While focusing on the opinion of his fellow aristocrats about his appearance, he consequently fails to think for himself about the meaning of *sōphrosunē*. His reluctance to think for himself is eventually dramatized through raising a proposal that he heard from his cousin Critias for what *sōphrosunē* is. He thus renounces his hold of the conversation and motivates Critias to take over. His soul is deficient and therefore not beautiful, and consequently we are led to conclude that his appearance and behavior also should not be considered beautiful.

Plato presents Critias as a foil to Charmides. As opposed to Charmides, Critias is considered by some as wise, because he pays attention to his soul by nurturing his literary, sophistic skills. The crowd perceives his orderly verbal expression by listening to him. However, Critias' verbal arguments do not apply to anything practical, because in his mind it is the role of only one social class—the peripheral social class, the artisans—to engage in productive practices. All his proposals for what *sōphrosunē* is, including the famous ancient phrase "recognize yourself" and the contemporary, much-discussed phrase "knowledge of knowledge," are utilized by Critias merely to represent aspects of his view of social hierarchy. While Critias focuses on his literary skills, he avoids engaging in productive practices, and therefore is an expert in nothing and not truly wise.

Although Chaerephon might seem a marginal figure in the dialogue, his character is significant for understanding Plato's full conception of *sōphrosunē*. Chaerephon appears to be neither beautiful nor wise, and thus represents a completely disordered character. This is why at the opening of the dialogue Socrates describes him as crazy (153b2). Chaerephon is oblivious to both his

---

say, and what they do. He thus allows the reader to conclude a very basic definition for what *sōphrosunē* is. See also Levine, *Profound Ignorance*, 13–14.

252. On beauty as orderly arrangement of the parts, see Aristotle's *Poetics*, 1450b34, and *Metaphysics* 1078a36.

external appearance (beauty) and his verbal expression (wisdom). His be-havior is disordered and impulsive, because he jumps from the middle of the crowd, oblivious of the way he appears to others, and runs towards Socrates. His behavior is contrasted with that of others in the palaestra, who calmly greet Socrates only from afar. Chaerephon's verbal expression is also disor-dered. He asks Socrates two questions, but in reverse logical order; first he asks how Socrates was saved from the battle (153b4), and only then whether he was at the battle at all (153c3).

What about Socrates? The crowd may think that he is a disordered person but for reasons other than those for which Chaerephon is considered crazy. Socrates is not young and beautiful as Charmides, which explains why his entrance to the palaestra does not provoke the enthusiasm that Charmi-des' entrance does. Socrates also does not show the absolute confidence in his knowledge that Critias does. Socrates claims that they would need a great man to show whether there exists something the power of which is directed towards itself, and whether this thing is knowledge. However, he claims that he does not trust himself to do this task (169a). Furthermore, at the end of the dialogue he takes the blame for the poor results of their investigation concern-ing *sōphrosunē* (175a9–11, 175b1–2, 175e5–6). Socrates therefore appears to be neither beautiful nor wise.

Despite his apparent disorder, we gradually learn that Socrates has at least some sense of what *sōphrosunē* is. This is manifested through his con-cern for the relation between the internal and the external aspects of human conduct. Plato opens the dialogue with a description of Socrates' return on an indefinite evening from his military service near Potidaea. On the following morning, Socrates immediately goes to the palaestra of Taureas and there he asks people about the situation inside Athens. Clearly, Socrates is concerned with both the external and the internal affairs of Athens, and demonstrates his civic-mindedness. Socrates also attempts to encourage his interlocutors in the palaestra to take into account both the internal and the external aspects of their conduct. However, Charmides consistently abstains from thinking for himself while focusing on upper-class opinions concerning his appearance, and Critias consistently ignores the practicality of his arguments, as he focuses on the aristocratic conception of social hierarchy.

Socrates also narrates the details of his conversation in the palaestra to a silent listener. This listener is even worse than Chaerephon, Charmides, and Critias, because he is opaquely inactive, which explains why he never responds to Socrates. We may conclude that Socrates' narration is intended to encourage his listener to become a more active participant in life, by tell-ing him his story about three characters, each demonstrating some kind of passivity towards either the internal or external aspects of human conduct, or even both.

Through his philosophical drama, Plato allows his reader to learn that the virtue *sōphrosunē* is manifested in an orderly relation between the internal and the external aspects of one's human conduct. He demonstrates that leading an orderly life is essential for attaining personal happiness, as well as for the stability of the community as a whole. Actually, Charmides' first proposal suggests that *sōphrosunē* is doing everything orderly (*kosmiōs*), in addition to calmly (159b3). Socrates, however, conspicuously ignores the component of orderliness in his proposal, and brings it back only at the end of his examination and thus refutes it (160c7).[253] The fact that Charmides does not object to Socrates' peculiar move, and his following behavior and proposals, suggest that he does not understand what kind of order *sōphrosunē* concerns, and clearly lacks this order himself. We may now wrap up the interpretation that Plato wished to convey for the meaning of *sōphrosunē*:

> **Sōphrosunē is: to do (everything) in an orderly way**
> **(*to kosmiōs dran*)[254]**

Having a good order with regard to the relation between the internal and the external aspects of human conduct would manifest in three main ways: (1) being outwardly active; (2) self-management; and (3) civic-mindedness (benefiting both oneself and others).[255]

Being Outwardly Active

The presence of *sōphrosunē* leads to being outwardly active. This is reflected in Socrates' character by him actively narrating to a silent listener the details of a conversation he previously had in the palaestra of Taureas. His silent listener, on the contrary, is completely inactive and never responds. Socrates addresses him in the vocative "o nobleman" (155d3), which may indicate that he is an aristocrat. By his narration, Socrates intends to cause his silent listener

253. See discussion in Chapter 2, section "The Opinion of the Many," and n. 106.

254. On the appearance of the word *draō* in the dialogue, see above n. 210.

255. Cf. Ludlam's claim, *Plato's Republic*, 250, that "the truly prudent is an active, consistently beneficial, person." Other scholars reached different conclusions concerning the dialogue. Tuckey, *Plato's Charmides*, 80–91, concludes that *sōphrosunē* is "doing what is good with the knowledge that it is good." Schmid, *Plato's Charmides*, 144–46, suggests that Socratic *sōphrosunē* concerns self-knowledge with regard to what you know and what you do not know. Levine, *Profound Ignorance*, 327–30, suggests that *sōphrosunē* is self-knowledge and knowledge of ignorance. Tuozzo, *Plato's Charmides*, 304, suggests that *sōphrosunē* is knowledge of good and bad.

to become more engaged in life. Socrates tells him about other aristocrats who demonstrate passive tendencies in a way that would allow him to uncover where they err.

Thus, even in the palaestra Socrates is outwardly active. He returns on an indefinite evening from his military duty outside Athens, and on the following morning, he immediately goes to the palaestra and asks those he meets there about the situation inside Athens. Clearly, he is concerned with both the external and the internal affairs of his *polis*. The people in the palaestra, by contrast, are engaged in aristocratic leisure. They clearly did not take part in the military activities of the *polis*. Socrates, nonetheless, encourages them to become outwardly active.

Chaerephon demonstrates his energetic enthusiasm towards Socrates' entrance and Charmides' beauty. However, he is described as crazy, because of his passivity concerning himself. He is oblivious to his own external appearance and verbal expression. While those present at the palaestra behave calmly when Socrates enters, they become as enthusiastic as Chaerephon once the young, beautiful Charmides enters, but thereafter they become silent listeners while Socrates turns to examine the souls of the aristocratic cousins Charmides and Critias.

Socrates' examinations reveal that Charmides actively nurtures his physical appearance, but is passive with regard to his soul. While he focuses on upper-class opinions concerning his external appearance, he never thinks for himself. Critias, on the other hand, is verbally active, but passive with regard to practices. Thus, his literary arguments are useless because they do not apply to anything practical.

While the silent listener is completely inactive, Chaerephon, Charmides, and Critias demonstrate different types of activeness. Their activeness, however, is not a result of taking into account both the internal and the external aspects of human conduct. We therefore learn that they are not orderly and outwardly active, and that this indicates their lack of *sōphrosunē*.

Self-Management

The presence of *sōphrosunē* leads to self-management. This is why traits like discipline and self-control are commonly associated with *sōphrosunē*.[256] Chaerephon, Charmides, and Critias manifest in different ways their control over other people, but not over their own lives.

256. See above n. 2.

Chaerephon's crazy behavior indicates lack of self-management, but it leads to a certain control over Socrates. He impulsively jumps from the crowd, grabs Socrates' hand, leads him towards Critias, and literally makes him sit there (*me kathizei*, 153c6).

Charmides, although a young man who must obey authority, has control over others through his attractive appearance and manipulative tendencies. Socrates emphasizes that Charmides' beauty is powerful through a line from a poem by Cydias, advising one to be careful not to go like a fawn in front of a lion and to be taken as meat (discussed in the section "The Whole and Its Parts"). Through his attractive beauty, Charmides controls the adults and supposedly even Socrates, who says that he seemed to himself to be taken by this kind of creature (155e1–2). Charmides also controls Critias, his guardian, by means of his manipulative tendencies. He motivates Critias to replace him in the conversation, as he raises a proposal for what *sōphrosunē* is, which he previously heard from him, and provokes Critias by suggesting that he might not know what he meant by his own proposal. However, Charmides abstains from thinking for himself about what *sōphrosunē* is, and cannot cure his headache. He clearly lacks self-management.

Critias controls Charmides as he manipulates him to join the conversation by the false assertion that he found a doctor for his headache. He controls Socrates by compelling him to pretend to be that doctor. Critias also aspires to control the artisans in order to benefit himself with their services and products. He forces stipulative, sophistic distinctions between words, and forces his own negative conception of the artisans on Hesiod (section "The Producers and the Recipients of Goods"). At the end of the dialogue, Critias forces Socrates to continue conversing with Charmides. Socrates' examinations, however, reveal that Critias' arguments do not apply to anything practical. We should therefore doubt that he has self-management. Socrates further indicates that Critias does not understand the practices of the arts, and therefore cannot control the artisan's benefit or manage well a city (discussed in sections "The Skills of a Well-Managed Person" and "Discerning the Morally Good"). Clearly, Critias is also unable to manage well his house, as he does not fulfill his duty as Charmides' guardian; instead of caring for Charmides' health and education, Critias competes with him.

On the face of it, Chaerephon, Charmides, and Critias manifest some kind of control over Socrates. However, Socrates' reactions indicate that he is not truly controlled by them, and he thus manifests his self-management. Chaerephon forces Socrates to sit next to Critias, but Socrates exploits this situation to raise a discussion about the youth and philosophy. Critias lies that Socrates is a doctor for Charmides' headache but Socrates overcomes it by crafting a fictitious story about a medicine that concerns *sōphrosunē*. Charmides' beauty is powerful, but Socrates quickly overcomes the alleged power it has over him. Despite the fact that Charmides and Critias force him to continue associating with them, Socrates continues to obey the fictitious Thracian authority. He does not agree with Critias that *sōphrosunē* is something worthless, and he will not give to the beautiful, noble Charmides the medicine for his headache so long as Charmides does not whole-heartedly hand his soul over to treatment.

Civic-Mindedness

Socrates emphasizes throughout the dialogue that *sōphrosunē* is something good and beneficial for the individual and the community, as it causes people to be good and beneficial. However, we gradually learn that Chaerephon, Charmides, and Critias assume that benefit comes from something external to the soul and they focus only on their own selfish interests.

Chaerephon is attracted to Socrates' information about the camp in Potidaea. He makes Socrates sit next to him and Critias in order to hear more about it. He is also attracted to Charmides' beauty. He gazes at Charmides and waits to see him getting undressed. While he remains a silent listener during the conversation, we may infer that he also enjoys listening to it. This crazy character clearly focuses on the immediate satisfaction coming from sense perceptions. Charmides uses people like Charephon who are attracted to immediate sensual satisfaction. Charmides is aware of the crowd's attraction to his external appearance and his well-mannered behavior. Socrates implies that Charmides uses his beauty to persuade others into giving him what he wants. Charmides, however, does not realize that he would truly benefit himself only by focusing on his own mental activity and by thinking for himself. Critias also understands benefit as coming from something external to the soul. He assumes that benefit is a result of the instrumental use of products. He does not realize that benefit is a direct result of mental and practical activities such as those engaged in by the artisans. He therefore exploits the artisans in order to satisfy his desire for products, and this in itself is a manifestation of his oligarchic nature.[257]

Plato does not have any of his characters propose that *sōphrosunē* concerns restraining desires. Only through the drama may we learn that this is because Chaerephon, Charmides, and Critias are not interested in restraining their desires. Plato implies that this is one important indication for their lack of *sōphrosunē*. They misunderstand the moral meaning of benefit. Socrates'

257. See Ludlam, *Plato's Republic*, 77–86, on temperance and the nature of the oligarch according to the *Republic*.

examinations indicate that taking into account the relation between the internal and the external aspects of human conduct would lead to understanding the moral meaning of benefit, and therefore also to restraining unnecessary and harmful desires. People who are *sōphrones* are engaged in life rather than exploiting others for their self-interests. They learn more easily how to perform artistic activities. They do only what they understand, and refrain from pretending to know what they do not understand. Thus, everything they do is conducted beneficially as far as possible, and hence benefits both themselves and others.

As opposed to Chaerephon, Charmides, and Critias, Socrates is civic-minded. He is concerned with the external and the internal aspects of his own conduct, of Athens' affairs, and of his fellow citizens.

〜

The dialogue *Charmides* suggests that we cannot truly call a person "good and beautiful" unless he possesses a certain order and harmony with regard to his soul and body that makes him a moral human being. This order leads to being active outwardly, self-managing, and benefitting both oneself and others. We may now observe that this implies the unity of the virtues. The manifestation of orderly behavior in certain circumstances relating to one's body and soul may be interpreted as *sōphrosunē*, but without such an order, it seems unlikely that one could be called also wise, just, or courageous.[258]

My analysis indicates that the virtue *sōphrosunē* is manifested by a consistent consideration of the relation between the internal and the external of human conduct. This means that it can be exemplified by learning or performing well a *technē*, and by awareness of an inability to learn or to perform well any kind of activity and refraining from doing what one does not know. We may conclude that acquiring a good order with regard to the relation between the internal and the external aspects of human conduct is an ongoing process. No one can self-proclaim to always succeed in it, and thus to possess *sōphrosunē* unerringly. This may very well be why Socrates consistently professes his ignorance. However, some considerations may be given in future research to the reasons that Plato uses the virtue *sōphrosunē* in analogy to crafts and arts (*technē*).[259] The characters in the philosophical drama do not clarify whether

---

258. Ludlam, *Plato's Republic*, 15, 250–51, claims similarly that "The cardinal virtues are aspects of the one virtue, and as aspects, they are actually one thing seen in different ways, and not different parts of one entity." Ludlam specifies that being *sōphrōn* is differentiated as "to one's body and soul."

259. On other interpretations for the connection Plato makes between *sōphrosunē* and

Plato thought that virtue is a kind of *technē*, or merely needs to accompany the performance of any *technē*. Still needing to be explored is whether *sōphrosunē* as "doing everything orderly" and the resulting restraint from unnecessary and harmful desires for physical beauty or material products can be understood as a *technē*. Moreover, the fact that Plato has Socrates conversing with the youth Charmides, who unfortunately was educated by a distorted aristocratic world-view, suggests that Plato saw education at an early age as significant in developing *sōphrosunē*. We may therefore speculate over the method of such an ideal education, and whether it includes merely Socratic conversations or also practical experiences.

∽

Why Plato wrote a dialogue and not a treatise may now be finally concluded. Charmides and Critias propose various suggestions as to what *sōphrosunē* is. Their proposals are not completely nonsensical, as we would assume that a virtuous life would involve a state of calmness and recognizing your own limitations, for example. However, Charmides and Critias misinterpret these proposals because of their vices. Plato's philosophical drama demonstrates that ideas do not create history by themselves. It is people with virtues or vices who influence the course of events as they act upon their opinions and interpretations. Plato, therefore, dramatizes a philosophical conversation. He illustrates two attractive characters that live disordered lives because they lack *sōphrosunē*, and two unattractive characters, of whom one is crazily disordered, but the other is a *sōphrōn* man who lives an orderly life. The traits of these four characters are summarized in Table 3 below.

	Charmides	Critias	Chaerephon	Socrates
Characterization	The physically attractive	The eloquent	The crazy	The civic-minded
Apparent trait	Beauty	Wisdom	Neither beauty nor wisdom	Neither beauty nor wisdom
Focuses on	The external	The internal	Neither the external nor the internal	Both the external and the internal
Sōphrosunē	Not *sōphrōn*	Not *sōphrōn*	Not *sōphrōn*	The *sōphrōn*
Order	Physical order	Verbal order	Disordered physically and verbally	Well-ordered, Internally and externally

technē, see above n. 189.

	Charmides	Critias	Chaerephon	Socrates
Being out-wardly active	Active concerning his external, physical appearance, but mentally inactive	Active mentally/verbally, but inactive outwardly	Actively reacts to sensual pleasures, oblivious of his physical appearance and verbal expression	Active outwardly
Self-manage-ment	Lacks self-management, controls others through his beauty and manipulations	Lacks self-management, controls others with force	Controls others due to complete lack of self-control	Self-managed
Civic-minded-ness	Benefits himself by exploiting others' attraction to his external appearance	Benefits himself by instrumental use of products made by the lower class	Benefits himself through sensual pleasures	Benefits himself and others

Table 3: The Full Characterization

The Status of Being Wise and Beautiful

Plato, as we have seen, was very skillful in dramatic writing, and he exploited this for conveying his philosophical ideas concerning *sōphrosunē*. He surely assumed that what he conveys is in some sense timeless and universal, but he also worked within the context of background, existing knowledge, and events in Athens and the area at his time. Plato wrote the dialogue *Charmides* during the first half of the fourth century BCE,[260] but he sets this fictional drama in the fifth century BCE, after the famous battle of Potidaea (432 BCE), around one to five years before his own birth. The battle was a catalyst for the long Peloponnesian War (431–404 BCE) which resulted with the defeat of Athens by Sparta and the installation of the pro-Spartan oligarchy of the Thirty Tyrants to govern it (404 BCE). Plato uses historical figures as his characters, two of whom will have taken a significant role in the notorious regime of the Thirty. Critias was one of the leading tyrants, and Charmides, his cousin and

---

260. For speculations on the date of the dialogue, see above n. 1, and below n. 297.

ward, was appointed as one of ten to rule over the port of Athens, Piraeus.[261] In the dialogue, Plato portrays the cousins still young, attractive in the eyes of others, politically uninvolved, and twenty-eight years before their role in the notorious regime of the Thirty. However, even as young men, Plato portrays them as morally flawed and indicates that their flaws were rooted in their ancestral aristocratic world-view. Plato has Socrates go even further back into history to the beginning of the sixth century BCE, through the description of the ancestors of the cousins as enjoying the supposedly hereditary aristocratic traits beauty and virtue. Why does Plato go deeper into history?

Plato's broad intention is to warn his contemporary readers from the recurrence of history. By going deeper into history, he implies that the moral flaws of the oligarchic cousins uncovered in the dialogue are rooted in the Athenian tradition and in the continuing Athenian social class tension.[262] The Athenian class tension reached a climax at the beginning of the sixth century BCE, as well as at the end of the fifth century BCE leading to the rule of the Thirty Tyrants, a tension that continued to thrive when Plato wrote his dialogue, and throughout the fourth century BCE.[263]

Plato alludes to the cousins' noble birth and uncovers their dangerous aristocratic views in various ways. The first question that he has Socrates ask in the dialogue is whether, during his recent military absence, anyone of the youth has come to excel in wisdom or in beauty or in both (153d1–5). Why of all traits he focuses on "wisdom" and "beauty" would have been easy for Plato's contemporary reader to instantly grasp; for the twenty-first-century reader, it requires filling certain gaps concerning basic historical background of Greek Athenian traditions. By means of their interest in wisdom and beauty Plato deliberately alludes to the cousins' noble birth, as the two traits call to mind the socially charged aristocratic epithet "beautiful and good" (*kalos kagathos*).[264]

261. On the battle of Potidaea, the Peloponnesian War, and the historical role that Charmides and Critias took in the regime of the Thirty, see discussion in Chapter one, section "Four Answers in Four Characters."

262. On the debate between the supporters of democracy and the supporters of oligarchy in the sixth and fifth centuries BCE, see: Krentz, *Thirty at Athens*, 18–27; Andrewes, *Greek Tyrants*, 7–19, 78–91.

263. On this Greek social debate, see Kagan, *Fall of the Athenian Empire*, 106–8, and Donlan, *Aristocratic Ideal*. See also Ober, *Mass and Elite*, 17–19, on the Athenian class tension and its danger to the stability of the *polis*, and 289–92 on the continuation of the aristocratic ethos during the fourth century BCE. See also Carter, *Quiet Athenian*, 26.

264. See my discussion on the epithet *kalos kagathos* in Chapter 1, section "Does It All Stay in the Family?" See also Tuozzo, *Plato's Charmides*, 305–10, who in his concluding chapter also indicates that a connection is made in the dialogue between the term *kalos kagathos*, the traits beautiful/noble and good, and *sōphrosunē*. However, he does not see a connection between these aspects and Socrates' opening question in the dialogue.

Greek aristocrats used this epithet to claim their inherent superiority over the lower classes, leading to their exclusive economic and political competence.[265] Even the oligarchic groups and the Thirty Tyrants, to which Charmides and Critias belonged, used this epithet, as well as the virtue *sōphrosunē*,[266] to refer to themselves, despite the evils that they perpetrated.[267] It is no wonder, therefore, that in the dialogue Critias says that Charmides is quite beautiful and good (*kalos kai agathos*, 154e3, discussed in section "Does It All Stay in the Family?").

Plato further alludes to the noble birth of the cousins through Socrates' description of the traits of the families from which they descend. When Critias praises Charmides as exceptional in looks and *sōphrosunē* among those of his age (157c7–d4), Socrates says that it is appropriate that Charmides will excel in such things because he is a descendant of two excellent families. Socrates thus implies that the cousins' good traits are considered inherited. When he praises Charmides with respect to his family (157d9–158b4), he begins with the paternal side from which Critias also descends, and thus, as if incidentally though deliberately, praises Critias as well.

Socrates strangely mentions members of this family who lived several generations earlier, in the seventh and sixth centuries BCE. He mentions an earlier figure named Critias II the son of Dropides II,[268] whose name our Critias IV (ca. 460–403 BCE) clearly inherited. This older Critias II, Socrates says, was praised by many poets for his excellence in beauty and virtue (*aretē*, 158a1). This sole appearance of the word "virtue" in the dialogue, despite the dialogue's focus on *sōphrosunē*, one of the cardinal virtues, is intended to draw attention to the context in which it is raised. Socrates' praise of the cousins as descendants of a family that excels in both beauty and virtue, and his insinuation that these traits are considered inherited, call to mind once again the socially charged aristocratic epithet *kalos kagathos*. Plato does not call out explicitly Charmides' and Critias' aristocratic origin, because this would have been unneeded for his contemporary readers. His readers knew that as aristocrats the historical cousins used the epithet *kalos kagathos* to re-

---

Moreover, his overall analysis differs greatly from mine.

265. See above n. 75.

266. The oligarchs ascribed the virtue *sōphrosunē* to themselves despite their evil deeds, as indicated by e.g.: Gomme, "Interpretation of *Kaloi Kagathoi*," 68; Rademaker, *Sōphrosynē and Rhetoric*, 216–18, 269; Donlan, *Aristocratic Ideal*, 171. That the historical Critias wrote about Spartan *sōphrosunē*, see above n. 32.

267. See above n. 76. That the oligarchs used pejoratives against the lower classes see above n. 72.

268. See discussion in Chapter 1, section "Does It All Stay in the Family?," and Plato's stemma in Nails, *People of Plato*, 244.

fer to themselves, and they were familiar with the ongoing Athenian social debate between the haves and have-nots which continued to thrive through the fourth century BCE.[269]

Socrates' opening question suggests the possibility of excelling in both wisdom and beauty. The idea that the two traits should appear together in an ideal person clearly does not surprise the cousins, because as aristocrats they associate these traits with the epithet *kalos kagathos*. However, throughout the dialogue each of the cousins is portrayed as obstinately concerned about excelling in only one of these two traits: Charmides nurtures his external appearance, and Critias nurtures his poetic skills. Plato thus allows his reader to gather that the cousins do not satisfy their contemporary noble ideal. However, Plato is not interested in questioning their noble birth, but in revealing that they misunderstand the morally "beautiful and good."

Plato has Socrates change his focus from the distinction between "wisdom" and "beauty" to the virtue *sōphrosunē*, and thus attempt to direct his interlocutors from focusing on either beauty or wisdom, to focusing on two equally important aspects of human conduct. However, the virtue *sōphrosunē* is not introduced instead of or in addition to the virtue "wisdom." We gradually learn that *sōphrosunē* manifests in two aspects, the internal and the external, of human conduct. Plato has Socrates use the traits "beauty" and "wisdom"—as well as "beauty" and "virtue," the duality of body and soul, and the medical leaf and charm—merely to represent these two aspects (discussed in the section "The Whole and Its Parts"). Charmides and Critias each focuses on only one of these two aspects, and this in itself demonstrates that they are deficient in *sōphrosunē*.

Plato presents Charmides and Critias as foils against each other. Charmides focuses on upper-class opinions concerning his external appearance, and neglects his soul. Externally, he looks like a beautiful and well-mannered youth, as his proposals for what *sōphrosunē* is and his behavior, both correspond with the aristocratic world-view of inculcating quiet traits in the youth. Socrates' examinations, however, reveal that because of his deference to authority and quiet traits Charmides is disengaged from the discussion, and never thinks for himself. Critias, on the other hand, is an aristocratic adult who does focus on his mental, intellectual activity. He seems to himself and to others to be wise (161b8–c1, 162b1–3) because of his literary and poetic experience (162d7–e2). However, Socrates' examinations reveal that Critias assumes that it is the role of only one social class, the artisans, to engage in practical activities. We therefore gradually learn that Critias' theoretical arguments are useless, as they do not apply to anything practical.

269. See above n. 263.

Traditionally the section of the dialogue that has attracted most scholarly attention is Socrates' discussion with Critias about the puzzles involving the "knowledge of knowledge." However, while reading the dialogue as a dramatic encounter among historical characters within their natural cultural context, we see that the discussion of "knowledge of knowledge" is not intended by Plato to serve an end in itself, but to serve a broader purpose. The discussion serves Plato in revealing the problematic nature of aristocratic exploitative values. The "knowledge of knowledge" represents Critias' devaluation and marginalization of the artisans and their crafts. However, Plato indicates that the role of essential workers in a well-functioning society is central.

When Plato's criticism over the cousins' traditional aristocratic views and education is uncovered, the peculiar context in which Solon the great lawgiver is mentioned in the dialogue becomes conspicuous. Critias claims that Charmides is considered by others and by Charmides himself as philosophical and poetic. Socrates then replies that these characteristics come to both of them, Charmides and Critias, from their kinship (*sungeneia*) to Solon (154e8–155a4). As a matter of historical fact, the relation of the cousins' family to Solon is not completely clear. As far as the evidence shows, Solon was a contemporary and probably merely a friend of Dropides II, an ancestor of the two cousins,[270] who was probably an archon immediately succeeding Solon.[271] Even if we assume that Solon was an ancestor of the cousins, Plato's contemporaries must have been sensitive to the absurdity in linking the tyrannical cousins with Solon's democratic philosophy and poetics.[272]

At the beginning of the sixth century BCE, when Athens suffered a severe social and economic crisis resulting from class tension, Solon was authorized as sole archon to mediate between the arrogant, rich aristocrats and the exploited poor. Solon's constitutional reforms mark the beginning of the gradual democratization of Athens.[273] From the end of the fifth century through the fourth century BCE Solon came to be considered as the founder of the Athenian democracy, and his name was often mentioned in the political

---

270. See above n. 78.

271. Philostratus, *Lives of the Sophists* 1.16.

272. I agree with Lewis, *Solon the Thinker*, 72–73, that Plato's mention of Solon here with respect to his poetic and philosophical traits indicates the great intellectual heritage of Solon. I additionally argue that Plato thus intends to imply to the vast contrast between Solon and the tyrannical cousins.

273. Solon was appointed probably around 594 BCE, as indicated by Lewis, *Solon the Thinker*, 1, n.1, 11. On the Athenian class tension and Solon's political role, see Ober, *Mass and Elite*, 60–65. See in addition Noussia-Fantuzzi, *Solon, Poetic Fragments*, 6–7, on the problem of dating Solon's archonship and legislations, and 19–44 on Solon's legislations and reforms.

arena.[274] Although Solon, as far as the evidence shows, does not use the word *sōphrosunē* in the remains of his poems, the orators of the fourth century BCE consider him as one of the most *sōphrōn* lawgivers.[275] In the remains of his poetry, he clearly conveys his practical wisdom,[276] including criticizing the arrogance and greed of the aristocrats, while acknowledging the centrality of essential workers in society.[277]

Vastly different from Solon, Critias and Charmides advocated an aristocratic ethos. They attempted to bring an end to the democracy, they constituted an oligarchy, and took down Solonian legislations.[278] In the dialogue it is suggested that they lack *sōphrosunē* and their practical wisdom is undermined; Charmides is inactive mentally and disengaged from the conversation, and Critias devalues productive practices while marginalizing essential workers. Clearly, Plato's contemporaries' jaws would have dropped at the connection that he has Socrates make between the oligarchic cousins and Solon's poetic and philosophical traits.

Socrates mentions Solon once again during his praise of the family of Charmides and Critias. He says that Solon is one of the poets who praised Critias II, the son of Dropides II, in beauty and virtue. Thus, Solon's poetic skills are emphasized again. However, since the evidence is insufficient, we may only speculate as to how Plato's contemporary readers reacted to this notion, and on whether Solon really did praise this older Critias and why.

As we see, Socrates mentions Solon twice, but not for his historical political role. However, I contend that Solon's heritage is implicitly present in other places in the dialogue. One allusion to Solon's heritage is made by Socrates' question to Critias, who he considers a happy man (173e6–174a1). Although it is true that the Greeks often were concerned with questions about happiness, the context in which Socrates raises his question seems to recall the famous legend about the encounter of Solon with Croesus, the King of

---

274. Solon came to be considered the founder of the democracy and his name was frequently mentioned by political orators during the fourth century BCE. See: Noussia-Fantuzzi, *Solon, Poetic Fragments*, 20 n. 5; Ober, *Mass and Elite*, 106–7; Lewis, "Slavery and Lawlessness," 38–39.

275. See discussion and a quote from Aeschines below. See also North, *Sōphrosynē*, 16–17, on the Solonian *sōphrosunē*.

276. Solon is mentioned as one of the seven sages, all of whom exemplified common traits of eloquence, poetics, and practical wisdom. See discussion by Noussia-Fantuzzi, *Solon, Poetic Fragments*, 9–10.

277. See for example Gerber, *Greek Elegiac Poetry*, 112–23, frr. 4–6, and below n. 289.

278. The Thirty Tyrants revised the democratic laws, and took down what they argued were ambiguous laws legislated by Solon. See discussion by Krentz, *Thirty at Athens*, 61–62, 64.

Lydia in Sardis.[279] The gist of the legend is as follows. Solon, who has traveled in the world and met many people, is invited to Croesus' palace. After Croesus shows him his wealth and treasures, he asks Solon whether he has seen a man who is the happiest, in other words, whether he had seen anyone happier than him. Solon is not impressed by Croesus' power and wealth. He explains whom he considers a happy man. He says that Tellus of Athens is the happiest man he had seen. When Croesus angrily asks who then he considers to be the second happiest man, Solon answers that these are the brothers Cleobis and Biton. Solon mentions three simple men who, although not wealthy, lived moderately, performed good deeds and died well. He indicates that one's fortune may change up until the very last day of his life, and that therefore only after death it is truly possible to evaluate one's happiness.[280] Croesus tragically learns later on in his life that his fortune can change too, but more important for our discussion is the fact that Solon is not impressed by Croesus' great wealth and power. He tells Croesus that "he who is very rich is not more blest than he who has but enough for the day" (Herodotus' *Histories*, 1.31.24–5).[281]

Socrates' question, who is a happy man, may be understood as an intertextual reference to this legend. It allows the reader to liken Critias to Croesus. Critias, as Croesus, focuses on commodities, and considers status and wealth as the criteria for happiness. He therefore claims that the artisans are not happy, although they live knowledgeably by practicing their arts. Critias appreciates the doctor more than the checkers player (174a10–b10) and the shoe maker (163b7–8), because of his higher social status and wealth. However, he considers the wealthy, unproductive aristocrat as the happiest man, because he has access to goods without needing to work for others.[282]

279. The legend appears in different versions in various sources. The earliest source seems to be Herodotus, *Histories* 1.29–33. Plutarch, *Lives: Solon* 27–28, already indicated that this legend is probably fictitious because of chronological inconsistencies, but that it is very famous and conforms with Solon's wisdom. Diogenes Laertius, *Vitae Philosophorum* 1.2.50, also mentions that the legend is famous and that it is therefore unneeded to elaborate about its content. On Aristotle's references to this legend see next n. 280. For discussions on this legend see for example: Noussia-Fantuzzi, *Solon, Poetic Fragments,* 11–17; Brown, "Solon and Croesus"; Lloyd, "Cleobis and Biton"; Lewis, *Solon the Thinker,* 33 n. 26; North, *Sōphrosynē,* 33.

280. Aristotle, *Nicomachean Ethics* 1100a10–b, interprets Solon's intentions by the claim that evaluating one's happiness requires looking also at the end of one's life. Aristotle, 1179a10–15, mentions Solon's good account that those who are happy are moderately (*metriōs*) equipped with external goods, have practiced good deeds, and as he thought, lived in a *sōphrōn* way.

281. I here follow the translation by Godley, Herodotus, *Persian Wars.*

282. In addition, we may speculate whether Critias' death measures up to Solon's standard of dying well. There seems to have been an ancient debate on whether Critias died nobly, as indicated by Philostratus, *Lives of the Sophists* 1.16, Diels and Kranz, *Die*

Another allusion to the Solonian heritage may be understood by Socrates' conclusion at the end of the dialogue that they did not find to what the lawgiver (*ho nomothetēs*, 175b4) ascribed the word *sōphrosunē*.[283] The lawgiver mentioned here could be a wise authority like Solon. That Solon was one of Athens' great lawgivers who paid special attention to *sōphrosunē* is emphasized, for example, by Plato's near contemporary Aeschines:

> Look, o Athenians, with how much intention concerning *sōphrosunē*, did that Solon, the old lawgiver (*nomothetēs*), as well as Draco and those lawgivers of that time. First they legislated concerning the *sōphrosunē* of our children, and explicitly demonstrated what the free child should practice (*epitēdeuein*), and how he should be brought up; then, second, concerning the youths, and third in order concerning the other age groups, not only concerning common men, but also concerning the public orators.[284] *Against Timarchus* 6.6–7.6

Furthermore, in light of Plato's criticism of Critias' aristocratic views, and the continuous Athenian debate between the aristocrats and the commoners, Critias' arguments in the dialogue can be viewed as part of criticism of the Solonian tradition. Critias devalues the artisans. He uses Hesiod to argue that the work of artisans is disgraceful (ironically, a thoroughly un-Hesiodic view), and that the artisans are ignorant of the good and the bad. Plato also has Critias argue that the person who inscribed on the temple of Apollo the sayings "nothing in excess" (*mēden agan*) and "a pledge and ruin is near" (*enguē para d' atē*) misunderstood the meaning of *sōphrosunē* as well as of the saying "recognize yourself" (discussed in the section "Know Your Place"). The historical Critias says in one of the fragments of his poems that the originator of the saying "nothing in excess" is Chilon of Sparta, one of the seven sages.[285] In light of his pro-Spartan attitude and praise of Spartan moderation in drinking in other fragments of his poems,[286] we should doubt that the Critias of Plato's dialogue criticizes Chilon of Sparta. It is plausible, however, that he criticizes the Solonian interpretation associated with this saying. Diogenes Laertius, for

---

Fragmente der Vorsokratiker, 88 A 13.

283. Moore and Raymond, *Charmides*, 34 n. 90, point to the dialogue *Cratylus* (388d–389a) where the word *nomothetēs* simply refers to a coiner of words.

284. My translation slightly differs from others' such as by Adams, *Aeschines. Speeches*.

285. Freeman, *Pre-Socratic Philosophers*, 155, Critias, fr. 7; Diels and Kranz, *Die Fragmente der Vorsokratiker*, fr. 88 B 7; Diogenes Laertius, *Vitae Philosophorum* 1.41.1. See discussions by: Carter, *Quiet Athenian*, 62–63; Tuckey, *Plato's Charmides*, 15–16. On the seven sages, see for example Lewis, *Solon the Thinker*, 12 n. 2.

286. See above n. 32.

example, associates the saying "nothing in excess" with Solon,[287] and Plato, in the dialogue *Protagoras* (343a–b), associates this saying, and the saying "recognize oneself," with the seven sages including Solon, while referring to Spartan wisdom.[288]

In the remains of his poems, Solon warns the aristocrats of unrestrained excess. He claims that excessive dominance of wealth and power as well as arrogance (*hubris*), lead to social disorder,[289] as was viewed also by many later thinkers including Aristotle.[290] Solon, therefore, advocated good order (*kosmos, eukosmia, eunomia*) in the soul, in speech, and in the *polis*.[291] In contrast, Critias, in the dialogue, focuses on the instrumental use of the artisans' goods. He assumes that as an aristocrat he is entitled by birth to be served by the artisans, and towards the end of the dialogue Socrates indicates his *hubris*.[292]

As for the saying "a pledge and ruin is near" (*enguē para d' atē*), it is a warning from obliging contracts especially concerning money. This saying can also be understood in context of the Solonian tradition, as advice directed to the lower classes, following Solon's reforms for abolishing debts and

---

287. Diogenes Laertius, *Vitae Philosophorum* 1.63. Whether Solon is its originator is uncertain; see discussion in Noussia-Fantuzzi, *Solon, Poetic Fragments*, 10–11.

288. Plato's description may very well be a distortion adopted for literary purposes, as scholars doubt the possibility that the seven sages actually met and conceived these inscriptions together. See also: Babbitt, *Moralia II*, Plutarch's *The Dinner of the Seven Wise Men*, 346–7; See also Diogenes Laertius, *Vitae Philosophorum* 1.40–42; Morgan, "Philosophy at Delphi," 554; Noussia-Fantuzzi, *Solon, Poetic Fragments*, 9–11. The seven sages were associated with various sayings relating to *sōphrosunē* by the mid-fifth century, as indicated above in n. 179.

289. Lewis, "Slavery and Lawlessness," 22 n. 7, provides adequate translations of Solon's relevant fragments. Fr. 6: "For excess (*koros*) breeds *hybris*, whenever great wealth follows a man whose disposition (*noos*) is flawed." Fr. 4.5–8: "But the citizens themselves by their foolishness are willing to destroy the great city, persuaded by material goods, and the disposition (*noos*) of the people's leaders is unjust; they are about to suffer many pains from great *hybris*." See also Lewis, 21, 26, and 37–38, on Solon's poem 4, which identifies *hybris* as leading to the slavery of the poor and to disorder in the *polis*. See also Lewis, *Solon the Thinker*, 108–30. On the use of the content of Solon's fr. 6 in the *Theognidea*, 149–54, see Noussia-Fantuzzi, *Solon, Poetic Fragments*, 45, 55–63.

290. See Noussia-Fantuzzi, *Solon, Poetic Fragments*, 36 n. 90; and above n. 242.

291. See Lewis, *Solon the Thinker*, 11–22, on Solon's thought regarding the *polis* as a *kosmos*; 23–41 on psychic qualities leading to order in the *polis*; and 60–73 on order in speech.

292. According to North, *Sōphrosunē*, 11, "good order" (*eunomia*) was opposed to *hubris* from Homer, and, 97, 110–11, "order" (*kosmiotēs*) was associated with *sōphrosunē* by writers of the fifth century BCE, including Gorgias and his pupils. For other ancient figures that connected *sōphrosunē* with orderly conduct, see for example discussion by Rademaker, *Sōphrosynē and Rhetoric*, 236–7, on Isocrates and Aeschines.

debt bondage of the poor to the aristocrats.[293] We may conclude that taken together, "nothing in excess" as advice to the upper class and "a pledge and ruin is near" as advice to the lower class would attend to the class tension by educating society as a whole and leading to *sōphrosunē* in both classes and to a well-ordered *polis*.[294]

Throughout the dialogue Plato has Socrates reveal the contorted views of the tyrannical cousins Charmides and Critias. However, he does not imply that the democratic faction satisfies its ideal either. Chaerephon, who was a supporter of the democrats, is portrayed in the dialogue unfavorably as crazy. Moreover, Plato, through the content of this dialogue, implies that even the democrats failed to take into account the two aspects, the internal and the external, of human conduct together. The Athenian democratic empire demonstrated unrestrained excess in its external affairs. According to Thucydides it was the growth of Athens that provoked Sparta (*Histories* 1.23, 75), and Athenian allies revolted against Athens because of the difficulty in paying tribute (1.99). During their long war, the democrats clearly neglected to attend to the internal affairs of their city and the education of the youth, which explains why Critias and Charmides would go on to become cruel tyrants.

Furthermore, it was under the reestablished democracy, several years after the fall of the regime of the Thirty, that Socrates was sentenced to death (399 BCE). Socrates was accused of corrupting the youth, probably including associating with Critias, who inflicted terrible evils on the city (Xenophon, *Memorabilia* 1.2.12–18; Aeschines, *Against Timarchus* 173).[295] The end of the dialogue *Charmides* supplies a response to this accusation. Despite Socrates' efforts to encourage his interlocutors to recover from their dangerous aristocratic views by taking into account the two aspects of *sōphrosunē* together,

293. On the saying "a pledge and ruin is near" (*enguē para d' atē*) see above n. 179. See also: Noussia-Fantuzzi, *Solon, Poetic Fragments*, 32–38, who discusses Solon's reforms for abolishing debts and debt bondage, and Lewis, "Slavery and Lawlessness."

294. It should be noted that according to Plutarch, *Lives: Solon* 1.1, and Diogenes Laertius, *Vitae Philosophorum* 1.53, Solon was a descendant of Kodros. Since the Palaestra of Taureus was located in front of the sanctuary of the kings Kodros and Neleus, and of Basile, one must wonder why Plato decided to mention only Basile. On the palaestra and the sanctuary, see above n. 9.

295. See above n. 41. According to Xenophon's *Memorabilia* 1.2.12–19, Socrates' teachings of Critias and others demonstrated his being *kalos kagathos* by speaking about virtue (2.17). Critias, on the other hand, remained *sōphrōn* only so long as he was in the company of Socrates (2.18). On this description see Pownall, "Critias in Xenophon," 11. See also Notomi, "Origin of Plato's Political Philosophy," 249, on the historical Critias' failing notion of *sōphrosunē*.

Charmides and Critias force Socrates to continue associating with them without the intention to change themselves.[296]

Through his dialogue, Plato warns his contemporary readers against the recurrence of history. He is aware of the danger to the stability of any society that would come from an exploitative external policy, as the revival of the fourth century democrats' imperialism;[297] and he was aware of the danger that would come from an exploitative internal policy, as the aristocratic elite of his *polis* employed against essential workers. Still today, Plato's warnings must be heard.

296. On the indication that Socrates did oppose the orders of the tyrants see discussion in Chapter 4, section "The Force Opposing *Sōphrosunē*," and above n. 248. Desjardins, "Why Dialogues," 123–24, suggests a different interpretation of Plato's Socrates, as reinterpreting traditional concepts without abandoning the Greek tradition.

297. Tuozzo, *Plato's Charmides,* 102 n. 3, suggests similarly, though for different reasons, that Plato may be warning his readers against the imperialistic policy.

Bibliography

Adams, Charles Darwin. *Aeschines. Speeches.* Loeb Classical Library 106. Cambridge: Harvard University Press, 1919.

Adkins, Arthur W. H. "*Polu pragmosyne* and 'Minding One's Own Business'. A Study in Greek Social and Political Values." *Classical Philology* 71 (1976) 301–27.

Altman, William. H. F. "*Laches* Before *Charmides*. Fictive Chronology And Platonic Pedagogy." *Plato: The Internet Journal of the International Plato Society* 10 (2010) 1–28.

Andrewes, Antony. *The Greek Tyrants.* Classical History and Literature. London: Hutchinson University Library, 1954.

Annas, Julia. "Self-Knowledge in Early Plato." In *Platonic Investigations: Studies in Philosophy and the History of Philosophy 13*, edited by Dominic J. O'Meara, 111–38. Washington, DC: The Catholic University of America Press, 1985.

Arieti, James. A. "How to Read a Platonic Dialogue." In *The Third Way: New Directions in Platonic Studies*, edited by Francisco J. Gonzalez, 119–32. Lanham: Rowman & Littlefield, 1995.

———. *Interpreting Plato: The Dialogues as Drama.* Savage, MD: Rowman & Littlefield, 1991.

Balaban, Oded. "The Meaning of 'Craft' (τέχνη) in Plato's Early Philosophy." *Archiv für Begriffsgeschichte* 49 (2007) 7–30.

Balme, Maurice. "Attitudes to Work and Leisure in Ancient Greece." *Greece & Rome* 31 (1984) 140–52.

Barker, Andrew. "Problems in the *Charmides*." *Prudentia* 27.2 (1995) 18–33.

Ben, N. van der. *The Charmides of Plato. Problems and Interpretations.* Amsterdam: Grüner, 1985.

Benson, Hugh. H. "A Note on Socratic Self-Knowledge in the *Charmides*." *Ancient Philosophy* 23 (2003) 31–47.

Bourriot, Félix. *Kalos Kagathos. Kalokagathia. D'un terme de propagande de sophistes à une notion sociale et philosophique. Étude d'histoire athénienne.* Hildesheim: Olms, 1995.

Brandwood, Leonard. *The Chronology of Plato's Dialogues.* Cambridge: Cambridge University Press, 1990.

Brann, Eva. *The Music of the Republic: Essays on Socrates' Conversations and Plato's Writings.* Philadelphia: Paul Dry Books, 2004.

Brennan, Tad. "The Implicit Refutation of Critias." *Phronesis* 57 (2012) 240–50.

Brown, Harold. "Plato's *Charmides*: *Sōphrosynē* and Philosophy." PhD diss., New School for Social Research, 1979.

Brown, Truesdell S. "Solon and Croesus." *Ancient History Bulletin* 3 (1989) 1–4.

Bruell, Christopher. "Socratic Politics and Self-Knowledge: An Interpretation of Plato's *Charmides*." *Interpretation: A Journal of Political Philosophy* 6.3 (1977) 141–203.

Brumbaugh, Robert. "Four Types of Plato Interpretation." In *Plato's Dialogues: New Studies and Interpretations*, edited by Gerald A. Press, 239–48. Lanham, MD: Rowman & Littlefield, 1993.

Buis, Emiliano J. "*Apragmosyne*." In *The Encyclopedia of Greek Comedy*. Vol. 1, edited by Alan H. Sommerstein, 68–69. 3 vols. Hoboken, NJ: Wiley Blackwell, 2019.

———. "*Polypragmosyne*." In *The Encyclopedia of Greek Comedy*. Vol. 3, edited by Alan H. Sommerstein, 741–42. 3 vols. Hoboken, NJ: Wiley Blackwell, 2019.

Burger, Ronna. *The Phaedo: A Platonic Labyrinth*. New Haven: Yale University Press, 1984.

———. "Socrates' Odyssean Return: On Plato's *Charmides*." In *Socratic Philosophy and Its Others*, edited by, Christopher Dustin and Denise Schaeffer, 217–35. Lanham, MD: Lexington, 2013.

Burkert, Walter. *Greek Religion: Archaic and Classical*. Translated by John Raffan. Oxford: Blackwell, 1985.

Byrd, Miriam. "The Summoner Approach: A New Method of Plato Interpretation." *Journal of the History of Philosophy* 45 (2007) 365–81.

Cain, Rebecca Bensen. *The Socratic Method: Plato's Use of Philosophical Drama*. Continuum Studies in Ancient Philosophy. London: Continuum, 2007.

Cairns, Douglas L. *Aidôs: The Psychology and Ethics of Honour and Shame in Ancient Greek Literature*. Oxford: Clarendon, 1993.

———. "Aristotle on *Hybris* and Injustice." In *Les philosophes face au vice, de Socrate à Augustin*, edited by Christelle Veillard et al., 147–74. Philosophia Antiqua 154. Leiden: Brill, 2020.

———. "*Kalokagathia*." Review of *Kalos Kagathos. Kalokagathia*: D'un terme de propagande de sophistes à une notion sociale et philosophique: Étude d'histoire athénienne, by F. Bourriot. *Classical Review* 47 (1997) 74–76.

Campbell, David A. *Greek Lyric*. Vol. 2: *Anacreon, Anacreontea, Choral Lyric from Olympus to Alcman*. Loeb Classical Library 143. Cambridge: Harvard University Press, 1988.

Carter, L. B. *The Quiet Athenian*. Oxford: Clarendon, 1986.

Clay, Diskin. "The Origins of the Socratic Dialogue." In *The Socratic Movement*, edited by Paul A. Vander Waerdt, 23–47. Ithaca: Cornell University Press, 1994.

Cohen, David. *Law, Violence, and Community in Calssical Athens*. Key Themes in Ancient History. Cambridge: Cambridge University Press, 1995.

Corlett, Angelo J. "Interpreting Plato's Dialogues." *Classical Quarterly* 47 (1997) 423–37.

———. *Interpreting Plato's Dialogues*. Las Vegas: Parmenides, 2005.

Crane, Gregory. "The Fear and Pursuit of Risk: Corinth on Athens, Sparta and the Peloponnesians (Thucydides 1.68–71, 120–121)." *Transactions of the American Philological Association* 122 (1992) 227–56.

Danzig, Gabriel. "The Use and Abuse of Critias: Conflicting Portraits in Plato and Xenophon." *Classical Quarterly* 64 (2014) 507–24.

Davies, Philip. "'*Kalos Kagathos*' and Scholarly Perceptions of Spartan Society." *Historia: Zeitschrift für Alte Geschichte* 62 (2013) 259–79.

Desjardins, Rosemary. "Why Dialogues? Plato's Serious Play." In *Platonic Writings, Platonic Readings*, edited by Charles L. Griswold Jr., 110–25, New York: Routledge, 1988.

Diels, Hermann. *Die Fragmente der Vorsokratiker*. Edited by Walther Kranz. Berlin: Weidmann, 1952.

Donlan, Walter. *The Aristocratic Ideal and Selected Papers*. Wauconda, IL: Bolchazy-Carducci, 1999.

———. "The Origin of *Kalos kagaqos*." *American Journal of Philology* 94 (1973) 365–74.

Donovan, Brian R. "The Do-It-Yourselfer in Plato's *Republic*." *American Journal of Philology* 124 (2003) 1–18.

Doran, Ryan P. "Moral Beauty, Inside and Out." *Australasian Journal of Philosophy* 99 (2020) 396–414.

Dover, Kenneth. J. *Greek Homosexuality*. Cambridge: Harvard University Press, 1978.

Dušanić, Slobodan. "Critias in the '*Charmides*.'" *Aevum* 74.1 (2000) 53–63.

Dyson, M. "Some Problems concerning Knowledge in Plato's '*Charmides*.'" *Phronesis* 19.2 (1974) 102–11.

Ehrenberg, Victor. "*Polypragmosyne*: A Study in Greek Politics." *Journal of Hellenic Studies* 67 (1947) 46–67.

Eisenstadt, Michael. "A Note on *Charmides* 168e9–169a1." *Hermes* 109.1 (1981) 126–28.

Eliade, Mircea. *Zalmoxis, the Vanishing God*. Translated by Willard R. Trask. Comparative Studies in the Religions and Folklore of Dacia and Eastern Europe. Chicago: University of Chicago Press, 1972.

Faraone, Christopher A. "A Socratic Leaf Charm for Headache (*Charmides* 155b–157c), Orphic Gold Leaves, and the Ancient Greek Tradition of Leaf Amulets." In *Myths, Martyrs, and Modernity: Studies in the History of Religions in Honour of Jan N. Bremmer*, edited by Jitse Dijkstra et al., 145–66. Studies in the History of Religions 127. Leiden: Brill, 2009.

Findlay, J. N. *Plato: The Written and Unwritten Doctrines*. New York: Humanities, 1974.

Fisher, Nick. "Athletics and Sexuality." In *A Companion to Greek and Roman Sexualities*, edited by Thomas K. Hubbard, 248–68. Blackwell Companions to the Ancient World. Malden, MA: Wiley Blackwell, 2014.

Flower, Michael Attyah. *The Seer in Ancient Greece*. Berkeley: University of California Press, 2008.

Ford, Andrew. "The Beginnings of Dialogue: Socratic Discourses and Fourth-Century Prose." In *The End of Dialogue in Antiquity*, edited by Simon Goldhill, 29–44. Cambridge: Cambridge University Press, 2008.

Freeman, Kathleen. *Ancilla to the Pre-Socratic Philosophers*. Cambridge, Massachusetts: Harvard University Press, 1983.

Gadamer, Hans-Georg. *The Relevance of the Beautiful and Other Essays*. Translated by Nicholas Walker, edited by Robert Bernasconi. Cambridge: Cambridge University Press, 1986.

Gentzler, Jyl. "How to Discriminate between Experts and Frauds: Some Problems for Socratic Peirastic." *History of Philosophy Quarterly* 12.3 (1995) 227–46.

Gerber, Douglas E. *Greek Elegiac Poetry: From the Seventh to the Fifth Centuries BC*. Loeb Classical Library 258. Cambridge: Harvard University Press, 1999.

Gocer, Asli. "*Hesuchia*, a Metaphysical Principle in Plato's Moral Psychology." *Apeiron: A Journal for Ancient Philosophy and Science* 32.4 (1999) 17–36.

Gomme, A.W. *A Historical Commentary on Thucydides*. Vol. 1. Toronto: Oxford University Press, 1945.

————. "The Interpretation of *ΚΑΛΟΙ ΚΑΓΑΘΟΙ* in Thucydides 4.40.2." *Classical Quarterly* 3.1–2 (1953) 65–68.

Gonzalez, Francisco J. *Dialectic and Dialogue. Plato's Practice of Philosophical Inquiry.* Evanston, IL: Northwestern University Press, 1998.

————, ed. *The Third Way: New Directions in Platonic Studies.* Lanham, MD: Rowman & Littlefield, 1995.

Graziosi, Barbara. "Hesiod in Classical Athens: Rhapsodes, Orators, and Platonic Discourse." In *Plato and Hesiod*, edited by G. R. Boys-Stones and J. H. Haubold, 111–32. Oxford: Oxford University Press, 2010.

Griswold, Charles L., Jr. "*E Pluribus Unum?* On the Platonic 'Corpus.'" *Ancient Philosophy* 19 (1999) 361–97.

Guthrie, W. K. C. *The Greeks and Their Gods.* London: Methuen, 1950.

Halper, Edward. "Is Knowledge of Knowledge Possible: *Charmides* 167a–169d." In *Plato: Euthydemus, Lysis, Charmides: Proceedings of the V Symposium Platonicum Selected Papers*, edited by Thomas M. Robinson and Luc Brisson, 309–16. Sankt Augustin: Academia, 2000.

Harris, Marjorie S. "Beauty and the Good." *ThePhilosophical Review* 39.5 (1930) 479–90.

Hazebroucq, Marie-France. *La Folie Humaine et ses Remèdes. Platon. Charmide ou de la modération.* Paris: Vrin, 1997.

Herodotus. *The Persian Wars.* Volume I: *Books 1–2.* Translated by Godley, A. D. Loeb Classical Library 117. Cambridge: Harvard University Press, 1920.

Howland, Jacob. "Re-Reading Plato: The Problem of Platonic Chronology." *Phoenix* 45.3 (1991) 189–214.

Humble, Noreen. "*Sōphrosunē* and the Spartans in Xenophon." In *Sparta: New Perspectives*, edited by Stephen Hodkinson and Anton Powell, 339–53. London: Duckworth, 1999.

Hyland, Drew A. *The Virtue of Philosophy: An Interpretation of Plato's Charmides.* Athens: Ohio University Press, 1981.

————. "Why Plato Wrote Dialogues." *Philosophy & Rhetoric* 1 (1968) 38–50.

Irwin, Terence. *Plato's Moral Theory: The Early and Middle Dialogues.* Oxford: Clarendon, 1977.

Irwin, Terence and Fine, Gail. *Aristotle. Introductory Readings.* Indianapolis: Hackett, 1996.

Joosse, Albert. "*Sōphrosunē* and the Poets: Rival Interpretations in Plato's *Charmides.*" *Mnemosyne* 71 (2018) 574–92.

Kagan, Donald. *The Fall of the Athenian Empire.* Ithaca: Cornell University Press, 1987

Kahn, Charles H. "Greek Religion and Philosophy in the Sisyphus Fragment." *Phronesis* 42.3 (1997) 247–62.

————. *Plato and the Socratic Dialogue.* Cambridge: Cambridge University Press, 1999.

————. "Plato's *Charmides* and the Proleptic Reading of Socratic Dialogues." *The Journal of Philosophy* 85.10 (1988) 541–49.

Kingsley, Peter. *A Story Waiting to Pierce You. Mongolia, Tibet and the Destiny of the Western World.* Point Reyes, CA: Golden Sufi Center, 2010.

Koning, Hugo H. *Hesiod, the Other Poet. Ancient Reception of a Cultural Icon.* Mnemosyne: Monographs on Greek and Latin Language and Literature 325. Leiden: Brill, 2010.

————. "Plato's Hesiod: Not Plato's Alone." In *Plato and Hesiod*, edited by G. R. Boys-Stones and J. H. Haubold, 89–110. Oxford: Oxford University Press, 2010.

Kosman, Aryeh. *Virtues of Thought: Essays on Plato and Aristotle.* Cambridge: Harvard University Press, 2014.

Krentz, Peter. *The Thirty at Athens.* Ithaca: Cornell University Press, 1982.

LaBarge, Scott. "Socrates and the Recognition of Experts." *A Journal for Ancient Philosophy and Science* 30.4 (1997) 51–62.

Lamb, W. R. M. *Plato with an English Translation.* Vol. VIII. Loeb Classical Library. London: Heinemann, 1955.

Lampert, Laurence. *How Philosophy Became Socratic: A Study of Plato's Protagoras, Charmides and Republic.* Chicago: University of Chicago Press, 2010.

Lawton, Carol L. *Attic Document Reliefs: Art and Politics in Ancient Athens.* Oxford: Clarendon, 1995.

Lear, Andrew. "Ancient Pederasty: An Introduction." In *A Companion to Greek and Roman Sexualities*, edited by Thomas K. Hubbard, 106–31. Malden, MA: Wiley Blackwell, 2014.

Lesses, Glenn. "Crafts and Craft-Knowledge in Plato's Early Dialogues." *Southwest Philosophical Studies* 13 (1982) 93–100.

Levine, David Lawrence. *Profound Ignorance: Plato's Charmides and the Saving of Wisdom.* Lanham, MD: Lexington, 2016.

———. "The Tyranny of Scholarship." *Ancient Philosophy* 4.1 (1984) 65–74.

Lewis, John. "Slavery and Lawlessness in Solonian Athens." *Dike* 7 (2004) 19–40.

———. *Solon the Thinker: Political Thought in Archaic Athens.* London: Duckworth, 2006.

Lloyd, Michael. "Cleobis and Biton (Herodotus 1,31)." *Hermes* 115.1 (1987) 22–28.

Luckhurst, K. W. "Note on Plato *Charmides* 153B." *Classical Review* 48.6 (1934) 207–8.

Ludlam, Ivor. "A Paradigm Shift in Reading Plato." In *Plato and His Legacy,* edited by Yosef Z. Liebersohn et al., 77–100. Newcastle, UK: Cambridge Scholars, 2021.

———. *Hippias Major: An Interpretation.* Stuttgart: Steiner, 1991.

———. "Plato on the Good: Hippias Minor and Hippias Major." In *For a Skeptical Peripatetic. Festschrift in Honour of John Glucker,* edited by Yosef Z. Liebersohn et al., 78–100. Sankt Augustin: Academia, 2017.

———. *Plato's Republic as a Philosophical Drama on Doing Well.* Lanham, MD: Lexington, 2015.

Luz, Menahem. "The Erlangen Papyrus 4 and Its Socratic Origins." *International Journal of the Platonic Tradition* 8 (2014) 161–91.

———. "Knowledge of Knowledge in Plato's *Charmides*." In *Greek Philosophy and Epistemology,* edited by Konstantine Boudouris, 100–110. Athens: Ionia, 2001.

McAvoy, Martin. "Carnal Knowledge in the *Charmides*." *Apeiron: A Journal for Ancient Philosophy and Science* 29.4 (1996) 63–103.

McCabe, Mary Margaret. "Looking Inside Charmides' Cloak: Seeing Others and Oneself in Plato's *Charmides*." In *Platonic Conversations,* 174–89. Oxford: Oxford University Press, 2015.

McCoy, Miriam B. "Philosophy, *Elenchus*, and Charmides' Definition of *Sōphrosunē*." *Arethusa* 38.2 (2005) 133–59.

McKim, Richard. "Socratic Self-Knowledge and 'Knowledge of Knowledge' in Plato's *Charmides*." *Transactions of the American Philological Association* 115 (1985) 59–77.

McPherran, Mark L. "Socrates and Zalmoxis on Drugs, Charms, and Purification." *Apeiron: A Journal for Ancient Philosophy and Science* 37.1 (2004) 11–33.

Miller, Mitchell H. *Plato's Parmenides: The Conversion of the Soul.* Princeton: Princeton University Press, 1986.

Moore, Christopher. "Chaerephon the Socratic." *Phoenix* 67.3–4 (2013) 284–300.

Moore, Christopher, and Raymond, Christopher. *Plato. Charmides: Translated, with Introduction, Notes, and Analysis.* Indianapolis: Hackett, 2019.

Morgan, K. A. "Philosophy at Delphi. Socrates, Sages, and the Circulation of Wisdom." In *Apolline Politics and Poetics*, edited by Lucia Athanassaki et al., 549–68. International Symposium. Athens: European Cultural Centre of Delphi, 2009.

Murphy, David J. "Doctors of Zalmoxis and Immortality in the *Charmides*." In *Plato. Euthydemus, Lysis, Charmides: Proceedings of the V Symposium Platonicum Selected Papers*, edited by Thomas M. Robinson and Luc Brisson, 287–95. Sankt Augustin: Academia Verlag, 2000.

———. "More Critical Notes on Plato's *Charmides.*" *Mnemosyne* 67 (2014) 999–1007.

Morris, F. T. "Knowledge of Knowledge and of Lack of Knowledge in the *Charmides.*" *International Studies in Philosophy* 21.1 (1989) 49–61.

Nails, Debra. "Mouthpiece Shmouthpiece." In *Who Speaks for Plato? Studies in Platonic Anonymity*, edited by Gerald A. Press, 15–26. Lanham, MD: Rowman & Littlefield, 2000.

———. *The People of Plato: A Prosopography of Plato and Other Socratics.* Minneapolis: Hackett, 2002.

Nikityuk, Elena. "*Kalokagathia*: to a Question on Formation of an Image of the Ideal Person in Antiquity and During Modern Time." *Studia Antiqua et Archaeologica* 25.2 (2019) 429–42.

North, Helen F. "A Period of Opposition to *Sōphrosynē* in Greek Thought." *Transactions and Proceedings of the American Philological Association* 78 (1947) 1–17.

———. *Sōphrosunē: Self-Knowledge and Self-Restraint in Greek Literature.* Ithaca: Cornell University Press, 1966. Reprint, Sophron Editor, 2019.

Notomi, Noburu. "Critias and the Origin of Plato's Political Philosophy." In *Plato. Euthydemus, Lysis, Charmides: Proceedings of the V Symposium Platonicum Selected Papers*, edited by Thomas M. Robinson and Luc Brisson, 237–50. Sankt Augustin: Academia, 2000.

Noussia-Fantuzzi, Maria. *Solon the Athenian, the Poetic Fragments.* Mnemosyne Supplements 326. Leiden: Brill, 2010.

Ober, Josiah. *Mass and Elite in Democratic Athens: Rhetoric, Ideology, and the Power of the People.* Princeton: Princeton University Press, 1989.

Ormand, Kirk. *Controlling Desires. Sexuality in Ancient Greece and Rome.* Austin: University of Texas Press, 2018.

O'Sullivan, Neil. *Alcidamas, Aristophanes and the Beginnings of Greek Stylistic Theory.* Hermes Einzelschriften, 60. Stuttgart: Steiner, 1992.

Page, Denys L., ed. *Poetae Melici Graeci.* Oxford: Oxford University Press, 1962.

Parke, W. H. and Wormell, W. E. D. *The Delphic Oracle, Vol. I.* Oxford: Blackwell, 1956.

Percy, William Armstrong, III. *Pederasty and Pedagogy in Archaic Greece.* Urbana: University of Illinois Press, 1996.

———."Reconsiderations About Greek Homosexualities." *Journal of Homosexuality* 49.3–4 (2005) 13–61.

Planeaux, Christopher. "Socrates, Alcibiades, and Plato's τα Ποτειδεατικα. Does the *Charmides* Have an Historical Setting?" *Mnemosyne* 52 (1999) 72–77.

Plutarch. *Moralia, Volume II. The Dinner of the Seven Wise Men.* Translated by Frank Cole Babbitt. Loeb Classical Library 222. Cambridge: Harvard University Press, 1928.

Politis, Vasilis. "*Aporia* and Searching in Early Plato." In *Remembering Socrates: Philosophical Essays*, edited by Lindsay Judson and Vassilis Karasmanis, 88–109. Oxford: Clarendon, 2006.

———. "The *Aporia* in the *Charmides* about Reflexive Knowledge and the Contribution to Its Solution in the Sun Analogy of the Republic." In *Pursuing the Good: Ethics and Metaphysics in Plato's Republic*, edited by Douglas Cairns and Fritz-Gregor Herrmann, 231–50. Edinburgh: Edinburgh University Press, 2007.

———. "The Place of *Aporia* in Plato's *Charmides*." *Phronesis* 53.1 (2008) 1–34.

Pownall, Frances. "Critias in Xenophon's *Hellenica*." *Scripta Classica Israelica* 31 (2012) 1–17.

Press, Gerald A. "*Charmides*." In *The Bloomsbury Companion to Plato*, edited by Gerald A. Press, 41–43. Bloomsbury Companions. London: Bloomsbury, 2012.

———. "The *Elenchos* in the *Charmides*, 162–175." In *Does Socrates Have a Method?: Rethinking the Elenchus in Plato's Dialogues and Beyond*, edited by Scott, Gary Alan, 252–65. University Park: Pennsylvania State University Press, 2002.

———. "The Logic of Attributing Characters' Views to Plato." In *Who Speaks for Plato? Studies in Platonic Anonymity*, edited by Gerald A. Press, 27–38, Lanham, MD: Rowman & Littlefield, 2000.

———. "Plato's Dialogues as Enactments." In *The Third Way: New Directions in Platonic Studies*, edited by Francisco J. Gonzalez, 133–52. Lanham, MD: Rowman & Littlefield, 1995.

———. *Plato's Dialogues: New Studies and Interpretations*. Lanham, MD: Rowman & Littlefield, 1993.

———, ed. *Who Speaks for Plato? Studies in Platonic Anonymity.* Lanham, MD: Rowman & Littlefield, 2000.

Rademaker, Adriaan. *Sōphrosynē and the Rhetoric of Self-Restraint: Polysemy & Persuasive Use of an Ancient Greek Value Term.* Mnemosyne, Bibliotheca Classica Batava Supplementum 259. Leiden: Brill, 2005.

Raubitschek, E. A. "Ein neues Pittakeion." *Wiener Studien* 71 (1958) 170–72.

Raymond, Christopher C. "Αἰδώς in Plato's *Charmides*." *Ancient Philosophy* 38 (2018) 23–46.

Reece, Andrew. "Drama, Narrative, and Socratic *Erōs* in Plato's *Charmides*." *Interpretation: A Journal of Political Philosophy* 26.1 (1998) 65–76.

Robinson, Thomas M. and Brisson, Luc, eds. *Plato. Euthydemus, Lysis, Charmides. Proceedings of the V Symposium Platonicum Selected Papers.* Sankt Augustin: Academia, 2000.

Rutherford, Richard B. *The Art of Plato.* London: Duckworth, 1995.

Santas, Gerasimos. "Socrates at Work on Virtue and Knowledge in Plato's *Laches*." *Review of Metaphysics* 22 (1969) 433–60.

Schmid, W. Thomas. *Plato's Charmides and the Socratic Ideal of Rationality.* SUNY Series in Ancient Greek Philosophy. Albany: State University of New York Press, 1998.

———. "Socratic Moderation and Self-Knowledge." *Journal of the History of Philosophy* 21 (1983) 339–48.

Schofield, M. "Socrates on Conversing with Doctors." *Classical Review* 23.2 (1973) 121–3.

Schultz, Anne-Marie. *Plato's Socrates as Narrator: A Philosophical Muse.* Lanham, MD: Lexington, 2013.

Shapiro, A. H. "The Attic Deity Basile." *Zeitschrift für Papyrologie und Epigraphik* 63 (1986) 134–36.

Shorey, Paul. "Emendation of Plato *Charmides* 168b." *Classical Philology* 2.3 (1907) 340.

Skinner, Marilyn B. *Sexuality in Greek and Roman Culture*. Malden, MA: Wiley Blackwell, 2006.

Stalley, R. F. "*Sōphrosunē* in the *Charmides*." In *Plato. Euthydemus, Lysis, Charmides. Proceedings of the V Symposium Platonicum Selected Papers*, edited by Thomas M. Robinson and Luc Brisson, 265–77. Sankt Augustin: Academia, 2000.

Tarrant, Harold. "Naming Socratic Interrogation in the *Charmides*." In *Plato. Euthydemus, Lysis, Charmides. Proceedings of the V Symposium Platonicum Selected Papers*, edited by Thomas M. Robinson and Luc Brisson, 251–58. Sankt Augustin: Academia, 2000.

———. "Where Plato Speaks: Reflections on an Ancient Debate." In *Who Speaks for Plato? Studies in Platonic Anonymity*, edited by Gerald A. Press, 67–80, Lanham, MD: Rowman & Littlefield, 2000.

Thesleff, Holger. "Looking for Clues: An Interpretation of Some Literary Aspects of Plato's 'Two-Level Model.'" In *Plato's Dialogues: New Studies and Interpretations*, edited by Gerald A. Press, 17–43. Lanham, MD: Rowman & Littlefield, 1993.

———. "The Philosopher Conducting Dialectic." In *Who Speaks for Plato? Studies in Platonic Anonymity*, edited by Gerald A. Press, 53–66, Lanham, MD: Rowman & Littlefield, 2000.

———. "Platonic Chronology." *Phronesis* 34.1 (1989) 1–26.

———. *Studies in Platonic Chronology*. Commentationes humanarum litterarum 70. Helsinki: Societas Scientiarum Fennica, 1982.

Tsouna, Voula. "Socrates' Attack on Intellectualism in the '*Charmides*.'" *Apeiron: A Journal for Ancient Philosophy and Science* 30.4 (1997) 63–78.

———. "What Is the Subject of Plato's *Charmides*?" In *For a Skeptical Peripatetic: Festschrift in Honour of John Glucker*, edited by Yosef Z. Liebersohn et al., 34–63. Sankt Augustin: Academia, 2017.

Tuckey, T. Godfrey. *Plato's Charmides*. Cambridge Classical Studies. 1951. Reprint, Amsterdam: Hakkert, 1968.

Tuozzo, Thomas M. "Greetings from Apollo: *Charmides* 164c–165b, Epistle III, and the Structure of the *Charmides*." In *Plato. Euthydemus, Lysis, Charmides: Proceedings of the V Symposium Platonicum Selected Papers*, edited by Thomas M. Robinson and Luc Brisson , 296–305. Sankt Augustin: Academia, 2000.

———. *Plato's Charmides: Positive Elenchus in a "Socratic" Dialogue*. New York: Cambridge University Press, 2011.

———. "What's Wrong with These Cities? The Social Dimension of *Sophrosune* in Plato's *Charmides*." *Journal of the History of Philosophy* 39 (2001) 321–50.

Vielkind, John N. "Philosophy, Finitude, and Wholeness: A Dialogue with Plato's *Charmides*." PhD diss., Duquesne University, 1974.

Vlastos, Gregory. *Socrates: Ironist and Moral Philosopher*. Cornell Studies in Classical Philology 50. Ithaca, NY: Cornell University Press, 1991.

———. *Socratic Studies*. Edited by Myles Burnyeat. Cambridge: Cambridge University Press, 1994.

Wankel, Hermann. "*Kalos kai Agathos*." PhD diss., University of Würzburg, 1961.

Wellman, Robert R. "The Question Posed at '*Charmides*' 165a–166c." *Phronesis* 9.2 (1964) 107–13.

Witte, Berndt. *Die Wissenschaft vom Guten und Bösen: Interpretationen zu Platons 'Charmides'*. Untersuchungen zur antiken Literatur und Geschichte 5. Berlin: de Gruyter, 1970.

Wolfsdorf, David. "Hesiod, Prodicus, and the Socratics on Work and Pleasure." *Oxford Studies in Ancient Philosophy* 35 (2008) 1–18.

Wolpert, Andrew. "The Violence of the Thirty Tyrants." In *Ancient Tyranny*, edited by Sian Lewis, 213–23. Edinburgh: Edinburgh University Press, 2006.

Woodruff, Paul. "Plato's Early Theory of Knowledge." In *Epistemology*, edited by Stephen Everson, 60–84. Cambridge: Cambridge University Press, 1990.

———. *Thucydides: On Justice, Power and Human Nature*. Indianapolis: Hackett, 1993.

Zuckert, Catherine. *Plato's Philosophers: The Coherence of the Dialogues*. Chicago: University of Chicago Press, 2009.

Index